MANAGING HUMANS

BITING AND HUMOROUS TALES OF A SOFTWARE ENGINEERING MANAGER

Michael Lopp

Apress·

Managing Humans: Biting and Humorous Tales of a Software Engineering Manager

ISBN-13 (pbk): 978-1-4302-4314-4

ISBN-13 (electronic): 978-1-4302-4315-1

Trademarked names, logos, and images may appear in this book. Rather than use a trademark symbol with every occurrence of a trademarked name, logo, or image we use the names, logos, and images only in an editorial fashion and to the benefit of the trademark owner, with no intention of infringement of the trademark.

President and Publisher: Paul Manning
Lead Editor: Jeff Olson
Editorial Board: Steve Anglin, Mark Beckner, Ewan Buckingham, Gary Cornell, Louise Corrigan, Morgan Ertel, Jonathan Gennick, Jonathan Hassell, Robert Hutchinson, , Michelle Lowman, James Markham, Matthew Moodie, Jeff Olson, Jeffrey Pepper, Douglas Pundick, Ben Renow-Clarke, Dominic Shakeshaft, Gwenan Spearing, Matt Wade, Tom Welsh
Coordinating Editor: Rita Fernando
Copy Editor: Damon Larson
Compositor: SPi Global
Indexer: SPi Global
Production Editor: Brigid Duffy
Cover Designer: Anna Ishchenko

Distributed to the book trade worldwide by Springer-Verlag New York, Inc., 233 Spring Street, 6th Floor, New York, NY 10013. Phone 1-800-SPRINGER, fax 201 348-4505, e-mail orders-ny@springer-sbm.com, or visit www.springeronline.com.

For information on translations, please contact us by e-mail at info@apress.com, or visit www.apress.com.

Apress and friends of ED books may be purchased in bulk for academic, corporate, or promotional use. eBook versions and licenses are also available for most titles. For more information, reference our Special Bulk Sales–eBook Licensing web page at www.apress.com/bulk-sales. To place an order, email your request to support@apress.com

To my family.
All of my family.

Contents

About the Author vii

Acknowledgments viii

Preface to the Second Edition ix

Part I   The Management Quiver

Chapter   1. Don't Be a Prick 3

Chapter   2. Managers Are Not Evil 7

Chapter   3. The Rands Test 17

Chapter   4. How to Run a Meeting 27

Chapter   5. The Twinge 33

Chapter   6. The Update, the Vent, and the Disaster 39

Chapter   7. The Monday Freakout 47

Chapter   8. Lost in Translation 51

Chapter   9. Agenda Detection 57

Chapter 10. Dissecting the Mandate 63

Chapter 11. Information Starvation 69

Chapter 12. Subtlety, Subterfuge, and Silence 75

Chapter 13. Managementese 81

Chapter 14. Fred Hates the Off-Site 85

Chapter 15. A Different Kind of DNA 93

Chapter 16. An Engineering Mindset 97

Chapter 17. Three Superpowers 103

Chapter 18. Saying No 109

Part II   The Process is the Product

Chapter 19. 1.0 117

Chapter 20. How to Start 127

Chapter 21. Taking Time to Think 133

Chapter 22. The Value of the Soak 139

Chapter 23. Managing Malcolm Events 143

Chapter 24. Capturing Context 149

Chapter 25. Trickle Theory 153

Chapter 26. When the Sky Falls 159

Chapter 27. Hacking Is Important 167

Part III   Versions of You

Chapter 28. Bored People Quit 173

Chapter 29. Bellwethers 179

Chapter 30. The Ninety-Day Interview 185

Chapter 31. Managing Nerds 189

Chapter 32. NADD 197

Chapter 33. A Nerd in a Cave 201

Chapter 34. Meeting Creatures 207

Chapter 35. Incrementalists and Completionists 213

Chapter 36. Organics and Mechanics 217

Chapter 37. Inwards, Outwards, and Holistics 223

Chapter 38. Free Electrons 227

Chapter 39. Rules for the Reorg 231

Chapter 40. An Unexpected Connection 237

Chapter 41. Avoiding the Fez 241

Chapter 42. A Glimpse and a Hook 249

Chapter 43. Nailing the Phone Screen 255

Chapter 44. Your Resignation Checklist 259

Glossary 265

Index 275

About the Author

Michael Lopp is a veteran engineering manager who has never managed to escape the Silicon Valley. In over 20 years of software development, Michael has worked at a variety of innovative companies including Apple, Netscape, Symantec, Borland, Palantir, and a startup that slowly faded into nothingness.

In addition to his day job, Michael writes a popular technology and management weblog under the nom de plume "Rands," where he discusses his management ideas, worries about staying relevant, and explains that while you might be handsomely rewarded for what you build, you will only be successful because of your people. His weblog can be found at www.randsinrepose. com.

Michael lives in the Redwoods of Northern California with his family. He surfs, plays hockey, and drinks red wine whenever he can because staying sane is more important than staying busy.

Acknowledgments

I'd like to acknowledge and thank:

- The readers of Rands in Repose who not only unwittingly guided the initial creation of this work by reading, commenting, and mailing, but whose continued interest allowed me to develop a far superior second edition.

- Melanie Baker, my editor, whose infinite patience and unique Canadianness keeps Rands sounding like Rands. She would never allow the word Canadianness into a proper book.

- Tom Paquin, who years ago took the time to guide me and shape my thinking regarding how to be a good manager.

- John Gruber, my dear friend, who inspires me with his writing and who I don't see enough.

- 42. You are the answer and I don't really care about the question.

I would also like to thank Steve Jobs for not firing me when he had the chance.

Preface to the Second Edition

This remains a work of semi-fiction.

A book on management is filled with insight, ideas, and opinions about how to manage people. All of this information is based on real life experience with actual people I still know. While I'd love to tell you that all my management experiences have been positive, they haven't. I've lost my shit a couple of times, and there were witnesses. These witnesses are the ones who helped me pull it together and gave me another page for this book.

All the names of people referred to in the chapters of this book are fake. I've taken everyone that I've known and mentally thrown them into a bag, shaken said bag, and pulled out Fez, Phil, and Frank. Using these constructed characters, I create a story, sometimes set in a familiar company I actually worked for—like Apple, Netscape, Palantir, or Borland—which allows me to explain whatever management insight I'm relaying. Like my characters, my stories are fake. My hope is that they still ring true in your head because while they are fantastic stories, they are based on real experiences.

The icing on this semi-fictional cake is Rands. This is a name I began using in the mid-1990s for my virtual presence. When I began weblogging about management, the name stuck. Think of Rands as your semi-fictional guide walking you through the fake stories of fake people that have had incredible relevant (yet fake) experiences.

Rands has a bit of attitude, but, then again, so do I.

The Management Quiver

For having shot a bow and arrow maybe ten times in my life, it's odd that I think of management skills as being arrows in quiver. But the metaphor works. Much of management is about solving problems, and what better way to solve a problem than to tape it to a target, step back, pull out the right arrow, and fire. Whether you hit the target or not, there's a gratifying plunk sound. That's the sound of progress.

We all have managers, and whether you're the director of engineering or an individual contributor, one of your jobs is to figure your manager out. What does he want? How does he deal with a crisis? How does he communicate? As you learn each of these lessons, you get an arrow. It's not only a reminder that you learned something, but it's a tool you throw in your quiver so that the next time you see a similar problem you grab the right arrow, carefully aim, and shoot.

Don't Be a Prick

The beauty of writing for the web is that there really is no plan. I have the luxury to mentally fumble about with any topic. Increasingly, those topics have focused on engineering management, and with the publication of each article, I increasingly received the email asking, "Where's the book?" Yeah so, I'd always wanted to publish a book, but there's a problem. What's the pitch? *Be a good manager? Zzzzzzzzz.* I needed a compelling truth that elegantly tied all of my repostings together.

Flash back to the middle of the dot-com implosion. We, the merry crew of a failing startup, are drinking . . . a lot. There are various bars around corporate headquarters, and each has a distinct purpose. There's the dive bar that's great for post-layoff parties. The booze is cheap, and if you're looking to blow off some I'm-really-not-worthless steam, you can pick a fight with the toothless sailor slung over the bar or the guy who just laid you off.

Down the street is the English pub. The beer is better, they have a selection of whiskey, and they have edible food. This is where we get philosophical about the current organizational seizure we're experiencing in our three-year slide toward irrelevancy.

We're there now. We're drinking heavily because the company has just been sold to a no-name public company who will quickly dismantle the one for which we've bled. Everyone knew we'd be here at some point, but no one expected to be the last one standing. And no one expected the CEO to show up.

This isn't the CEO that built the company. He's been gone for over a year. This is the guy the board of directors brought in to sell the startup. Sure, he tried to turn us around, but remember, we're in the middle of a financial nuclear winter here. Money is no longer free.

Those who got a glimpse of the CEO's resume before he arrived knew the gig was up. His last four jobs ended in the company being finely sliced into nothingness. It's called "maximizing shareholder value."

And here we are. Hammered on tequila, the last four of us from engineering, two guys from tech support . . . and the CEO. Even though we're dizzy with booze, we're fundamentally uncomfortable with the presence of our CEO because we consider him to be an unfeeling prick.

And that's it.

That's the basic truth behind my management book. It's also a great title.

Don't Be a Prick.

Right, so my editors will probably have an issue with the word "prick" in the title. So we'll call it a working title.

The CEO in question is actually not a prick. Good guy. Straight talker. Good financial sense. Many failing companies did a lot worse than ours, but that isn't the point. The reason we sat there drunk and uncomfortable was because we had absolutely no connection with this guy. He was the mechanical CEO.

My definition of a great manager is someone with whom you can make a connection no matter where you sit in the organization chart. What exactly I mean by *connection* varies wildly by who you are and what you want. And, yes, that means great managers have to work terribly hard to see the subtle differences in each of the people working for them.

See. See the people who work with you. They say repetition improves long-term memory, so let's say it once more. You must *see* the people who work with you.

If you don't have an inkling of what I'm talking about yet, it might be a good time to set this book down and head over to the programming section of the bookstore, because it's time to reconsider that pure engineering career track. Being a manager is a great job (I mean it), but it's your ability to construct an insightful opinion about a person in seconds that will help make you a phenomenal manager. Yes, in a technical management role, you need both the left and right sides of the brain, but just because you write great code doesn't mean you're going to have a clue about how to lay off 70 percent of your staff.

Every single person with whom you work has a vastly different set of needs. Fulfilling these needs is one way to make them content and productive. It is your full-time job to listen to these people and mentally document how they are built. This is your most important job. I know the senior VP of engineering is telling you that hitting the date for the project is job number one, but you are not going to write the code, test the product, or document the features. The team is going to do these things, and your job is managing the team.

Silicon Valley is full of wildly successful dictators. These are the leaders who are successful even though they are world-class pricks. This book is going to push you as far from prickdom as possible, and if that means I'm decreasing the chance you'll end up on the front page of the *Wall Street Journal* labeled a "corporate bulldog with vision," well, I've done my job.

You get to choose the type of manager you will be, and if you want to work with your team—if you want to learn from them, if you want them to trust you—well, I've got some advice for you. Lots of it. Keep reading.

Again, the CEO at the startup was not a prick. He just showed up at the company's wake and assumed that we'd be comfortable with his presence because *he was the CEO*. We knew he was CEO. More importantly, we knew he'd spent exactly zero time using our products. We'd never seen him there on the weekends. Come to think of it, he was never there on Fridays either, because he commuted from another state. We had no shared experience with him other than three strange meaningless all-hands meetings filled with slide projectors, spreadsheets, and monotony.

The CEO believed that these spreadsheet-laden, all-hands meetings was all the connection he needed to build a relationship and, for the duration of those meetings, he was right. We felt well informed after his meetings, but our needs were different a week later when rumors of layoffs started up. They were drastically different a month later when that layoff went down and the CEO was nowhere to be seen. *Prick.*

Organizations of people are constantly shifting around. They are incredibly messy. In this mess, judgments of you and your work will be constructed in moments—in the ten-second conversations you have in the hallway, and in the way you choose to describe who you are.

Meanwhile, you need to constantly assess your colleagues, determine what they need, and figure out what motivates them. You need to remember that what worked one day as a motivational technique will backfire in two months because human beings are confusing, erratic, and emotional. In order to manage human beings in the moment, you've got to be one.

And that's why a better title for this book is: *Managing Humans.*

Managers Are Not Evil

A trusted employee, who has been working in my group at the startup for years, asks, "What, exactly, do you do?"

Slack.

Jawed.

Amazement.

This guy always tells me the straight dope, so I knew he was asking because he honestly does not know.

Let's recap my day. I got to work just after 8 a.m. After my usual 30 minutes of scrubbing and answering e-mail, I did a quick check of tech news, taking a quick pulse of the planet, and then it's off to my first meeting. It's my boss's staff and it runs for almost two hours as usual. After that meeting, I spend 30 minutes digesting notes from that meeting into actual tasks for myself and the team while also tidying the corporate news I received for my own staff meeting.

Lunch. I ate with the web applications team today. It's 30-plus minutes and then I'm back for bug database scrubbing—a daily 30-minute task before a cross-functional meeting that turned ugly. I needed someone to do something and they are incapable of doing it and that means I'm screwed. After that 60-minute debacle, I've got an hour and a half of one-on-ones. It's during this time that I am asked the lamest question ever: "What, exactly, do you do?"

My first reaction to this question is the wrong one. I want to leap over the table, grab my friend by the shoulders, shake him, and yell, *"While you were uselessly staring at that one bug this morning, I was keeping this organization moving, pal."* My second reaction is to take a deep breath, so I do.

This basic what-do-you-do disconnect between employees and managers is at the heart of why folks don't trust their managers or even find them to be evil.

There Is Evil

My background: I've worked at six different companies in the past 20 years. In those years, I've had ten different jobs ranging from QA engineer to director of engineering. Similarly I've worked for a variety of managers, from first-line managers to CEOs. I've never worked outside of engineering, but, especially in the senior management roles, I've been exposed to the inner workings of the vastly different functional groups that make up a company.

I've seen a lot of varieties of organizational pride and panic. At both Borland and Netscape, I experienced the company vibe as it shifted from "We're the Microsoft killer!" to "We're screwed!" At the startup, I showed up as employee number 20 and watched it grow to 250 employees before the Internet bubble eroded the company to 50 folks wondering what to do with all the extra hardware.

These drastic shifts in organizational perceptions showed me managers who were great at the pride part, but turned into jerks when the panic started. Likewise, new leaders and lessons showed up during the panic—leaders who were quietly getting their work done during the pride.

In all of this, I can count the number of truly evil people I worked with on one hand. There are evil managers out there. So I apologize—I lied in the title of this chapter. These are genuinely evil and mean people who put themselves before their team, who lie, and who have absolutely no ability to lead There are fewer than you think, but they are out there and my only advice is, upon meeting them, to run away as quickly as possible.

Chances are, your manager is not evil, so you don't need to run. Still, you do need to understand how he's built.

Your Manager's Job

The first and most basic frustration folks have with the management is the easiest to explain. You are frustrated because you're busting your ass, but each time you walk by your boss's offices, he's got his feet kicked up on the table, coffee in one hand, the other hand jumping hither 'n' fro, and he's talking to some guy you don't know. How in the world could this be work?

Here's the deal: your manager's job is not your job.

Ever had a meeting with a completely different part of your company? Maybe you're in engineering and you're talking with facilities about getting additional space for your team. Your goal is clear, "I need more space," but once the meeting kicks off, you realize that you and facilities are speaking a different language. It's English, but the context is wildly different. Those facilities guys are rambling about lease agreements, safety codes, and scads of unfamiliar acronyms. In five minutes, it's clear that you have no idea what they really do.

Before that meeting, if I asked you what the role of facilities was in your company, you would've scrunched your face and mumbled something about cube construction. I trust that, like me, you're an optimist and you believe that everyone in your company is busily working on whatever they do. I also believe that because you don't understand what they do, you are automatically biased against them. You believe that because you understand your job intimately, it is more important than anyone else's.

In your head, you are king. It's clear what you do; it's clear what is expected of you. There is no person who rules you better than yourself because you know exactly what you're about. Anyone outside of your head is a mystery because they are not you. In a social situation, it's entertaining to figure out what another person is about, but in an employee/manager situation, there's more at stake. Who is this guy who decides whether or not I get a raise? What's he saying to my VP about me? Does he see me as a success or a failure? Who is that guy in his office anyway? *What does he do all day?*

I am not going to explain what your manager does all day. Sorry.

I am going to hand you seven critical questions that you need to answer in order to figure out if this guy is capable of looking out for number one—you. Ideally, you'd be able to get answers to these questions before you took a new job, but you didn't and now you're working for a manager who isn't speaking your language. These questions might give you insight into where he's coming from.

Where Does Your Manager Come From?

I'm going to start and finish here because the pedigree of your manager determines not only how you should communicate, but also what to expect when the shit hits the fan.

Ironically, the second most common complaint I've heard from frustrated employees is, "My manager has no idea what I do." It's good to know the problem goes both ways, no? There are a couple of possible causes for this situation. Your manager may not care what you are doing. It doesn't mean the work you are doing is good or bad, it's just not on his radar. Some folks find this arrangement of ignorance to be a cozy, warm blanket. It's a no-fuss job. *No awkward hallway conversation, just me and my code and . . . I'm what? I'm fired? Holy shit.* Well, that's the risk of having a covert job. No one knows your value, which puts you first in line when it's time to trim the workforce.

Another likely situation is that your manager doesn't actually understand what you're doing because he was never an engineer. I'm not talking about the prequalified disasters where some brainiac on senior staff decided it was a good idea to put the head of marketing in charge of engineering, I'm talking about the engineering managers who are hiding the fact they never really did much coding. Sure, they can talk the talk and they're buzzword-compliant, but what was their last programming assignment? What piece of code are they really proud of? Is their degree in computer science?

If you're getting vague answers full of words that sound right, my guess is you've got a faker on your hands. I'm talking about someone who has managed to wedge their way into a position of engineering leadership on their chutzpah and not their technical ability. You're not automatically screwed in this scenario. A person who can convince the organization they've got leadership ability and hide the fact they haven't a clue what a pointer is . . . has, well, moxie.

This person has spent their entire career wondering, "When are they going to figure me out?" This paranoia has given them solid information-detection skills, which can be useful to you and your organization. They know when the layoff is coming, they know how to talk to senior management, but they don't know how to talk to you because you're actively, passionately doing something they're clueless about and they believe they have to maintain the appearance they know what they're doing.

If this is your manager and you believe there is value in what they do, your job is to figure out how to speak their language. Maybe they snuck out of QA? OK, then speak QA. Maybe they just never got around to that computer science degree? OK, take the time to teach them about your work. I'm not talking teaching this guy Objective C, I'm talking 15 minutes at the whiteboard with flowcharts. This is *what I do* and this is *why it matters*.

Your manager is your face to the rest of the organization. Right this second, someone you don't know is saying something great about you because you took five minutes to pitch your boss on your work. Your manager did that. You gave him something to say.

How Is He Compensating for His Blind Spots?

Now we're going to pick on your favorite manager. Tell me about him. Probably a great communicator, funny guy; charismatic, you say? He probably inspired you. You can probably quote a few of his more infamous sayings, like "Better is the enemy of done." The question is, what are his blind spots?

Each manager, good or bad, is going to have a glaring deficiency. Maybe he did escape from QA and now he's the director of engineering. Perhaps he's a stunning technologist with absolutely no sense of humor. The question is, does he recognize he has a blind spot?

I ask the same question in every interview I have: "Where do you need help?" Whether it's an individual contributor, a manager, or my new boss, I'm always curious where people see their weaknesses. A flippant "I'm solid across the board" response is a terrifying red flag. I'm a fan of pride; I want you to sell yourself in a interview. But if you suggest that you're flawless, all I'm thinking is that your flaws are so big that you can't talk about them or you have no clue what they are.

A manager's job is to take what skills they have, the ones that got them promoted, and figure out how to make them scale. They do this by building a team that accentuates their strengths and, more importantly, reinforces where they are weak. Dry technologists need team members who are phenomenal communicators, folks who can tell a joke and socially glue the organization together. Those vision guys with zero technology chops need you, the strong technologist, to tell them what is technically possible.

A manager's job is to transform his glaring deficiency into a strength by finding the best person to fill it and trusting him to do the job.

Does Your Manager Speak the Language?

OK, so you're in a square room. There are two clear windows in this room, one on each side. In front of each window is a microphone which, when turned on, pipes whatever you say to whoever is on the other side of the window. Now, your manager is on the other side of one window and your best work friend is behind the other. It's Friday, and I want you to give your weekly status report to your friend. Something like: "Monday was a disaster. I got in late because I whooped it up on Sunday night. Took a stab at the spec, but left a little early because I was hung over. Tuesday and Wednesday were pretty good. Finished the spec, closed some bugs, went to the cross-functional review, got some good feedback. You should read the current version. Thursday was meeting hell. Got nothing done. Three useless hours. Friday, well, I had a beer at lunch and I'm leaving early."

Now, spin around and give your status to your boss.

"Finished the spec early in the week, good mid-week cross-functional review. Lots of meetings later in the week."

I do not care if you work for the world's best manager. I do not care if he was the best man in your wedding. You are going to give a vastly different sequence of events because you are not talking to a person when you talk with your manager; you are talking to the organization. You instinctively know that telling your boss that you had a beer at lunch is a bad idea, not because he'd know it, but because the organization would.

The language you are speaking when you talk to your manager is a flavor of managementese (see Chapter 13 for more on managementese). Yeah, the language that Scott Adams has made millions of dollars exploiting. It is a carefully constructed language that is designed to convey information across the organization.

Managementese allows managers from very different parts of the organization to communicate even though their respective jobs are chock-full of different acronyms and proper names. And yeah, managementese sounds funny.

An example: "Our key objective for this project is the schedule. We need to keep our teams focused on their respective goals, but also keep them cross-pollinating so they can error correct on their own."

When you hear that, you think, "Why can't he talk like a human?" He's not talking to you. He's talking to other managers and he's saying some very Rands-like things, like "Commitments matter!" and "The team is smarter than the individual!" It'd be great if managers could speak with a little more art, but the job at hand is to spread information across the organization as efficiently as possible. And a local dialect of managementese is the best way. Besides, they still need to talk to you, which leads us to ...

How Does Your Manager Talk to You?

My first piece of advice to all new managers is: "Schedule one-on-ones with direct reports, keep them on the same day and time, and never cancel them." With this in mind, some of the trickiest transitions for me during the day are when these one-on-ones show up. I'm deep in some problem, writing a specification, answering a critical e-mail, and this person walks in my office and they want to talk about I don't know what ... *I'm working in the zone here, people.* In the brief second I try to figure out some way to reschedule this meeting, I remind myself of a simple rule, "You will always learn something in your one-on-one."

When is your manager giving you a chance to tell him what's in your brain? I'm worried if your answer isn't "at a one-on-one," but I'm not panicking, yet. Maybe your manager is one of these organic types who likes to jump you in the hallway and gather relevant bits. Terrific. Does he do it consistently or when he needs something? The former is great; the latter is a problem waiting to happen.

What is a manager learning in a one-on-one? Much of what you're talking about in a one-on-one your manager already knows. You're concerned about the reorg, right? Well, everyone is and he's already talked to four other people about their concerns. You think the field engineers are a bunch of twits? So does he. A good manager has his finger on the pulse of their organization and the one-on-one usually echoes much of that pulse, so why is he carving out 30 minutes for every person on his team?

He wants to learn.

Whether it's a one-on-one or a random hallway conversation, your manager should always be in active information acquisition. He should love it when you stop him in the hallway and tell him, "I hate your favorite feature." See, the thing is, he's been losing sleep over that feature for the past three days and he can't figure out why. Your random hatred just shoved his thinking in another direction.

Managers who don't have a plan to talk to everyone on their team regularly are deluded. They believe they are going to learn what is going on in their group through some magical organizational osmosis and they won't. Ideas will not be discovered, talent will be ignored, and the team will slowly begin to believe what they think does not matter, and the team is the company.

How Much Action per Decision?

When the new VP showed up for his first day at the startup, he was wearing a Members Only jacket. Sky blue. I didn't know they still made these throw-backs to the 1980s. A jacket that lived under the tagline, "When you put it on, something happens." I'd given the VP a thumbs up during the button-up-and-tie phase of the interview, so I gave him the benefit of the doubt.

Three months in, we had a problem. Members Only was doing a phenomenal job of discussing and dissecting the problems facing engineering. We'd leave meetings fresh with new ideas and promises of improvements, but then nothing would happen. OK, so follow-up meeting. WOW! He gets it. I'm fired up again. Let's roll. Ummm, two more weeks and nothing is happening here.

Now, me being the director of engineering, you can argue that the onus of action was on me. Problem was, I was doing everything I signed up to do. The VP wasn't. He wasn't talking with the CEO about our new plans. He wasn't handling the other director who was totally checked out, sleeping on the job. When the third follow-up meeting was scheduled, the VP again demonstrated his solid problem-solving skills, but I wasn't listening anymore. I was waiting for when we got the next-steps portion of the conversation where I'd pull up the meeting notes from the previous two meetings and carefully point out these were the same next steps as *the last two meetings.*

The act of delegation is a slippery slope for managers. Yes, you want to figure out how not to be a bottleneck in your organization and, yes, you want to figure out how to scale, but you also want to continue to get your hands dirty. Members Only's problem was he believed his job was purely strategic. Think big thoughts; delegate the results of those thoughts to the minions. He was a pure delegator and he'd forgotten how to do real work.

Pure delegators are slowly becoming irrelevant to their organizations. The folks who work for pure delegators don't rely on them for their work because they know they can't depend on them for action. This slowly pushes your manager out of the loop and, consequently, his information about what is going on in his organization becomes stale. Then, the CEO walks into your boss's office and asks, "How's it going?" The third time your boss gives the same generic answer, the CEO goes to you and asks the same question. When you respond with, "Well, we're fucked," the CEO has an entire other conversation with your manager

Real work is visible action managers take to support their particular vision for their organization. The question you need to answer for your manager is simple: does he do what he says he's going to do? Does he make something happen?

Where Is Your Manager in the Political Food Chain?

Back at Netscape, Internet Explorer was threatening, but we were under the illusion the sky was not falling. We were merrily planning the next release of the browser under the assumption that Microsoft was going to somehow screw up their browser. Besides, it wasn't about the browser anymore; it was about owning the entire desktop. Yes, someone was actually suggesting the browser wasn't an application; it was an *operating system, people.* The perception of unlimited money makes people stunningly stupid, by the way. Anyhow, of course, everyone at Netscape wanted to be on the "next-generation browser" project. We were just waiting for the execs to crown a director to run the effort.

When the promotion came and it was some engineering manager from an acquired company we'd never heard of, heads were scratched. Until that time, the core engineering team at Netscape was a private club. We'd expected one of our long-time proven managers to the lead the effort. Nope, Mike the New Guy got it and, in a week, he went from no name to the hottest ticket on Middlefield Road.

What happened? Well, turns out the engineering managers were playing a lot of roller hockey and, while they played, Mike the New Guy was working it. He was chatting it up with the execs, getting to know the relevant *players, pawns, and free electrons* in the organization (see Chapter 9 for more about players and pawns, and Chapter 38 for more on free electrons). Mike the New Guy was hungry. He was driven, and after six months of incessantly demonstrating this hunger, the execs gave him the keys to the executive washroom. Mike the New Guy was a made guy.

Just like delegation, the act of navigating politics in an organization is slippery. The difference between a manager who knows what's going on in an organization and one who is a purely politically driven slimeball is thin. But I would take either of those over some passive manager who lets the organization happen to him. Politically active managers are informed managers. They know when change is afoot and they know what action to take to best represent their organization in that change.

Of all the questions in this chapter, understanding your manager's place in the political food chain is the trickiest because you're often not in the meetings where he is interacting with his superiors. Those are the situations where you understand what their view is of him and, therefore, his organization. The next best gauge of your manager's political clout is cross-functional meetings where his peers are present. How are they treating him? Is it a familiar conversation or are they getting to know him? Should they know him? If it's his meeting, is he driving it? If it's not his meeting, can he actively contribute?

The organization's view of your manager is their view of you. I'm glad you're a C++ rock star, but the problem is, your manager is a passive non-communicator who doesn't take the time to grok the political intrigue that is created by any large group of people. I see him as a non-factor and you're living in the shadow of a non-factor.

Sorry.

What Happens When They Lose Their Shit?

Pride and panic. The two delicious ends of the management spectrum. Pride is when it's going swimmingly. Great product release, selling well. Hired that phenomenal guy from the other group who is going to totally write us another fabulous product. More requisitions in the pipeline. Golly, I can't imagine it going better, can you?

Getting to pride is usually the end result of a lot of work and a little luck. What you can learn from your manager in this phase is how they'll deal with that swelling head of theirs. Do they take care of those who got them there? Do they have a plan for what's next? All of these are interesting developments, but they don't show you half as much as panic and there is no bigger panic than a layoff.

Your manager is not a manager until he participated in a layoff. I mean it. I know he fired that one Fez and he hired a bunch of the team, but those are individual, isolated activities (see Chapter 41 for more about the Fez). He hasn't truly represented the company until he actively participates in the constructive deconstruction of an organization. There is no more pure a panic than a layoff, and you want to see who your manager will become because it's often the first time he sees the organization is bigger than the people.

A layoff is a multi-month affair. By the time it's been announced on the front page of CNET, it's been bouncing around the boardroom and your boss's staff meeting for a couple of weeks. This means your boss has been staring at you for the past couple of weeks in one-on-ones and ignoring everything you say because he's trying to figure out how to lay off half of his staff. You are very interested in who he becomes during this time because that is actually the person you've been working for these past few years.

Once you've got a confirmed layoff, you need to go back to each of the questions on this list and ask them again. How is he talking to you? How is he talking with the organization? What is he doing to make up for the fact that pretty much everything stops in a company when a layoff is leaked? Is he staying politically active? Or is he checking out? All of these observations teach you about your boss and, conveniently, give you insight into whether or not you should be looking for another gig.

Panic backs a person into a corner and their only means of getting out of that corner is relying on skills that have worked for them in the past. This is how a normally friendly manager can turn into a backstabbing asshole when it comes to a layoff. See, they were an asshole before; you just weren't there to see it. If you are lucky enough to see this behavior as well as make it through the layoff, well, you learned two things. First, this guy I work for degrades to jerk when the sky falls. Second, he values me enough to keep me around. The question remains: are you going to hang around waiting for him to be a jerk to you?

The Big Finish

When the first layoff hit Borland, I was two years into my QA stint. I don't remember wondering what a layoff was and I don't remember wondering if I was going to lose my job. What I remember is that the senior VP of applications walked around the building, gathered the product team up, and then told us the straight dope about the layoff . . . in the hallway. This is what the layoff is about, this is who is affected, and this is when it's happening. I'd never interacted with Rob, the VP, in my life and, come to think of it, I never really interacted with him again. Still, I think fondly of the guy because during a time of stress, he illuminated. He didn't obfuscate.

A successful organization is built of layers of people that are glued together with managers. Each layer is responsible for a broad task, be it engineering or QA or marketing. Between each layer is a manager whose job it is to translate from one layer to the next . . . in both directions. He knows what his employees want. He knows what his manager wants, and he's able to successfully navigate when those wants differ.

The way he navigates these waters is by knowing the answer to two questions. Question #1: Where did I come from? Being able to relate to those you manage comes from intimately understanding their job. It allows you to speak their language. Question #2: Where am I going? A plan for your manager's next big move is his incentive. It puts him in the uncomfortable position of trying to discern the murky political motivations of the major influencers of your company. It might not be a skill set he has, but he's never going to stop trying because he knows where he wants to go. He's got a map defined by his motivation.

Why do you care that your boss wants to be VP of software? You care because his success is your success. If he doesn't know that, he might be evil.

The Rands Test

It's hard to pick a single best work by Joel Spolsky, but if I were forced to, I'd pick "The Joel Test: 12 Steps to Better Code."[1] It's his own, highly irresponsible, sloppy test to rate the quality of software, and when anyone asks me what is wrong with their team, I usually start by pointing the questioner at the test. *Start here.*

It's a test with 12 points, and, as Joel says, "A score of 12 is perfect, 11 is tolerable, but a 10 or lower and you've got serious problems." More important than the points, his test clearly documents what I consider to be healthy aspects of an engineering team, but there are other points to be made. So it is completely an homage to Joel that I offer the Rands Test.

I was employee number 20 at the first start-up I worked at, and the first engineering lead. Over the course of two years, the team and the company exploded to close to 200 employees. This is when I discovered that growing rapidly teaches you one thing well: how communication continually finds new and interesting ways to break down. The core problem centers on the folks who've been around longer and who also tend to have more responsibility. As far as they're concerned, the ways they organically communicated before will remain as efficient and simple each time the group doubles in size.

They don't. A growing group needs to continually invest in new ways to figure out what it is collectively thinking so anyone anywhere can answer the question, "What the hell is going on?" This is the first question the Rands Test answers. As I'll explain shortly, the second question the Rands Test helps you answer is selfish. The second asks, "Where am I?"

---

[1] www.joelonsoftware.com/articles/fog0000000043.html

The Rands Test: 11 Possible Points

Let's start with bare-bones versions of the questions, and then I'll explain each one.

- Do you have a one-on-one?
- Do you have a team meeting?
- Do you have status reports?
- Can you say no to your boss?
- Can you explain the strategy of the company to a stranger?
- Can you explain the current state of business?
- Does the guy/gal in charge regularly stand up in front of everyone and tell you what he/she is thinking? Are you buying it?
- Do you know what you want to do next? Does your boss?
- Do you have time to be strategic?
- Are you actively killing the Grapevine?

Note While I'll explain each point from the perspective of a leader or manager, these questions and their explanations apply equally to individuals.

Do you have a consistent one-on-one where you talk about topics other than status? (+1)

I think you'd be hard-pressed to find anyone who would suggest one-on-ones are a bad idea, but the one-on-one is usually the first meeting that gets rescheduled when it hits the fan. I'm of the opinion that when it hits the fan, the last thing you want to do is reschedule one-on-one time with the folks who either are responsible for it hitting the fan or are the most qualified to figure out how to prevent future fan-hittage.

Furthermore, as I wrote about in Chapter 6, "The Update, the Vent, and the Disaster," conveyance of status is not the point of a one-on-one; the point is to have a conversation about something of substance. Status can be an introduction, status can frame the conversation, but status is not the point. A healthy one-on-one needs to be strategic, not a rehashing of tactics, status, and data that can easily be found elsewhere.

A one-on-one is a weekly investment in the individuals that make up your team. If you're irregularly doing one-on-ones or not making them valuable conversations, all you're doing is reinforcing the myth that managers are out of touch.

Do you have a consistent team meeting? (+1)

The team meeting has all the requirements of the one-on-one—consistency and a focus on topics of substance—but don't give yourself a point just yet.

Status does have a bigger role in a team meeting. As I'll talk about shortly, the Grapevine is a powerful beast, and a team meeting is a chance to kill messages it transmits. I have a standing agenda item for all team meetings that reads "gossip, rumors, and lies," and when we hit that agenda item, it's a chance for everyone on the team to figure out what is the truth and what is a lie.

After that's done, my next measure of a team meeting is, Did we make tangible progress on something? I don't know what you build, so I don't know what's broken on your team, but I do know that something is broken, and a team meeting is a great place to not only identify the brokenness, but also to start to discuss how to fix it.

If you're killing lies and fixing what's broken in a team meeting, give yourself a point.

Are handwritten status reports delivered weekly via e-mail? (−1)

If so, you lose a point. This checklist is partly about evaluating how information moves around the company, and this item is the second one that can actually remove points from your score. Why do I hate status so much? I don't hate status; I hate status reports.

My belief is that e-mail-based status reports are one of the clearest and best signs of managerial incompetence and laziness. There are always compelling reasons why you need to generate these weekly e-mails. *We're big enough that we need to cross-pollinate. It's just 15 minutes of your time.*

Bullshit. The presence of rigid, e-mail-based status reports comes down to control, a lack of imagination, and a lack of trust in the organization.

I want you to count the number of collaboration tools you use on a daily basis to do your job—not including e-mail. If you're a software engineer, I'm guessing it's a combination of version control, bug tracking, wikis, CRM, and/or project management software. All of these tools already automatically generate a significant amount of status regarding what has tactically gone down each week.

When someone—my boss or someone who outranks me—asks for a status report, my first thought is, "I'm already generating piles of status on these various tools; why not just look at those?"

Well, there's a lot of noise in those tools. So write a report that takes out the noise—collaboration tools are built around reporting. The status information is out there. In what managerial textbook does it say it's a good idea to distribute the task of figuring out what is going on to the people who are performing the work? That's, like, your job.

Well, what I really want is your high-level assessment of the week. Three things that are working, three things that aren't, and what we're going to do about it. OK, now we're talking. I can do a strategic assessment of the week, but why don't we just put that at the beginning of the one-on-one? That way when you have questions (and you will), we can have a big fat debate.

But I'd like to have a record I can review later. Super, feel free to write down anything we talk about.

Yes, status reports are a hot button for me. I've written hundreds of them and each time I've begun one, I start by thinking, "Why in the world do I feel like I'm performing an unnecessary act?" Status reports usually show up because a distant executive feels out of touch with part of his or her organization, and they believe getting everyone to efficiently document their week is going to help. It doesn't. E-mailed status reports say one thing to 90 percent of the people who write them: "You don't value my time." This leads me to my next point . . .

Are you comfortable saying no to your boss? (+1)

Perhaps a better way to phrase this point is, Do you feel your one-on-one with your boss is somehow different than every other meeting you have during the week? Part of healthy communication structure is when information moves easily around the team, organization, and company, and if you walk into a meeting with your boss always on your best behavior and unwilling to speak your mind, I say something is broken.

Yes, he is your boss, and that means he writes your annual review and can affect the trajectory of your career, but when he opens his mouth and says something truly and legitimately stupid, your contractual obligation as a shareholder of the company is to raise your hand and say, "That's stupid. Here's why . . ."

Easier said than done, Rands.

OK, don't say it's "stupid."

Here's the deal. I believe that leaders who think they're infallible slowly go insane with power created by the lie that being wrong is a sign of weakness. I screw up—likely regularly—and I've been doing various forms of this gig for 20 years. While it still stings when I stumble upon or others point out my screw-ups, I'd sooner I admit I fucked up, because then I can figure out what I really did wrong faster, and that starts with someone saying no.

Can you explain the strategy of your company to a stranger? (+1)

Moving away from communications, this point is about strategy and context. If I were to walk up to you in a bar and ask what your company did, could you easily and clearly explain the strategy?

This is the first point that demonstrates whether you have a clear map of the company in your head, and you might be underestimating the value of this map. If you're a leadership type, chances are you can draw this map easily. If you're an individual, you might think this map is someone else's responsibility, and you'd be partially correct: it is someone else's job to define the map, but it's entirely your responsibility to understand it so you can measure it.

As you'll see with the following questions, the Rands Test isn't just about understanding communications, it's about understanding context and strategy. How do you think the employees of HP and Netflix feel given the strategy flip-flops recently? Safe or suspicious? Let's keep going . . .

Can you tell me with some accuracy the state of the business? (Or could you go to someone somewhere and figure it out right now?) (+1)

It's a brutal exaggeration, but I think you should independently judge your company the same way that Wall Street does: your company is either growing or dying. Have you ever watched the stock price of a publicly traded company the day after they announce that they are going to miss their earnings numbers? More often than not, no matter what spin the executives have, the stock is hammered. It's irrational, but what I infer when I see this happen is that Wall Street believes the company has begun a death cycle. If the executives can't successfully predict the state of their business, something is wrong.

I realize this isn't fair, and there are myriad factors that contribute to the health of the business every single day, and I encourage you to research and understand as many of those as possible. But when you're done, I'd also like you to have a defensible opinion regarding the state of the business, or at least a set of others whose opinions you trust.

This is a picture that you are constantly building, and this is an easier task if you've given yourself a point on the prior question regarding company strategy. If you have a map of what the company intends to do, it's easier to understand whether or not it's doing it. This leads us to ...

Is there a regular meeting where the guy/gal in charge gets up in front of everyone and tells you what he/she is thinking? (+1) And are you buying it? (+1)

My previous point regarding context involves the person in charge. In rapidly growing teams and companies, there's a lot going on—every single day. When the team was small, the distribution of information was easy and low-cost because everyone was within shouting distance. At size, this communication becomes more costly at the edges. Directors, leads, and managers—these folks tend to stay close to current events because it's increasingly their job, but it's also their job to take steps to keep the information flowing, and it starts with the CEO.

On a regular basis, does your CEO stand up and give you his impressions of what the hell is going on? Whether it's 10 or 10,000 of you, this is an essential meeting that

- Gives everyone access to the CEO
- Allows him/her to explain their vision for the company
- Hopefully allows anyone to stand up and ask a question

If the value of this meeting isn't immediately obvious to you, I'd suggest that you are one of those lucky people who already has a good map of the company, as well as a sense of the state of the business. That's awesome—here's a bonus point for you: does the CEO's version of the truth match yours, or is he/she in a high Earth orbit with little clue what is actually going on? Give yourself a point if it's the former, and if it's the latter, what does that say about the state of the business? Growing or dying?

Can you explain your career trajectory? (+1)
Bonus: Can your boss? (+1)

Next, switching gears a bit, give yourself a point if you—right this very moment— can tell me your next move. You're already doing something, so explain what you're going to do next. It's a simple statement, not a grand plan. "One day, I'd like to lead a team."

Part of a healthy organization isn't just that information is freely moving around; it's what the folks receiving and retransmitting it are doing with it. You're going to mentally file and ignore a majority of this information, but every so often a piece of information will come up in a one-on-one, a meeting, or a random hallway conversation, and it will be immediately strategically useful for you to know what you want to do next.

- Angela got a promotion and her team is great, and I've always wanted to be a manager.

- Jan just opened a requisition, and his group is working on technology I need to learn.

- They fired Frank. That creates a very interesting power vacuum . . .

You can argue that even without a plan you'd make the same opportunistic leap, but I've found that having a map is usually a better way of getting to a destination.

There's a bonus point here as well. Does your boss know what you want to do next? She likely has even more access to the information moving around the company, and whether she likes it or not, she has equal responsibility to figure out how to get you from here to there.

Do you have well-defined and protected time to be strategic? (+1)

If you gave yourself two points on the prior question, congratulations; I think you're in better shape than most, but there's one more point. Are you making progress toward this goal? Can you point to time on your calendar or even just in your head where you are growing toward your goal?

I like being busy. Like really busy. Like getting in, grabbing a cup of coffee, and suddenly finding the coffee is cold, it's 6:00 p.m., and I forgot to eat busy. Busy feels great, but busy is usually tactical, not strategic. This is why I'm constantly maintaining my Trickle List[2]—it's my daily reminder of doing work that is larger than right now.

If you have time in which you're investing in yourself while at work, and your boss is cool with it—give yourself a point.

Are you actively killing the Grapevine? (+1)

When Grace walks in your office, you know she knows something by the look on her face. She moves to the corner of the office and starts with, "Did you hear . . . ?" and the story continues. It's a doozy, full of corporate and political intrigue, resulting in your inevitable response: "No. Way."

---

[2] www.randsinrepose.com/archives/2008/08/18/the_trickle_list.html

Being part of a secret feels powerful. In a moment, the organization reveals a previously hidden part of itself, and in that moment you feel you can see more of the game board. *So, that's why they fired him. I was wondering.* Grace finishes with the familiar, "Don't tell anyone," which is ironic since that's precisely what was asked of her 15 minutes ago.

There is absolutely no way you're going to prevent folks from randomly talking to each other about every bright-and-shiny thing that's going on in your company. In fact, you want to encourage it. One-on-ones and meetings are only going to get you so far. The thing you can change is the quality of the information that's wandering around the company.

In the absence of information, people make shit up. Worse, if they at all feel threatened, they make shit up that amplifies their worst fears. This is where those absolutely crazy rumors come from. See, Kristof is worried about losing his job, so he's making up crazy conspiracy theories that explain why *the man is out to get him.*

Without active prevention, the Grapevine can be stronger than any individual. While you can't kill the Grapevine, you can dubiously stare at it when it shows up on your doorstep and simply ask the person delivering it, "Do you actually believe this nonsense? Do you believe the person who fed you this trash?" Rumors hate to justify themselves, so give yourself a point if you make it a point to kill gossip.

Magnitude and Direction

There is a higher-order goal at the intersection of these two questions on the Rands Test: *Where am I?* and *What the hell is going on?* While understanding the answers to these questions will give you a good idea about the communication health of your company, the higher order goal is selfish. I'll explain.

I think of the two lines of questions as a vector. A simple vector can be drawn as two points connected by an arrow, but a vector is far more interesting. It's a geometric object that describes both direction and magnitude. Understanding how information moves, how you communicate with your boss, and being able to describe both your career strategy and that of your company sketches a vector in your head. The first point is you at this very moment, and the other point is where you want to be. The distance and direction between the two start to explain how you're going to get there. I love vectors because they draw a picture about a complex problem, and I hope as you were answering the questions above that this mental picture began to appear in your head.

Like the Joel Test, the point of the Rands Test is not the absolute score, but the score is good directional information. If you got an 11, I'd say you're in a rare group of people who have a clear picture of their company and where they fit in. Between 8 and 10, you are likely troublingly deficient in either communications, strategy, or your development—it depends where the points are missing. Less than 8 and I think you've got a couple of problems.

There are a lot of different scenarios I expect folks to find themselves in as they explore these questions, which is why it's tricky to prescribe specific action. Your company may be doing well, but you may be unhappy and have no clue what you want to do next. You might love your job, but have no idea whether the company is actually growing. Your course is dependent on what you care about, and the Rands Test points out good places to start.

How to Run
a Meeting

I bag on meetings.

I bag on meetings because, like any nerd, I expect the universe to be efficient and orderly, and there is no more vile a violation of this sense of orderliness than a room full of people randomly bumping into shit and calling it a meeting.

There are solid meetings out there. There are meetings that build a sense of structure, move forward for the entire hour, and finish with a sense of accomplishment. The question is, How do we make sure every meeting is like this? Let's start by understanding why meetings showed up in the first place.

You're sitting in your office eating a sour-apple saltwater taffy, and you're fully in the Zone. It's great forgetting there are other humans on the planet Earth; it's blissfully productive until Richard walks in the room, and Richard *wants to talk*.

"Stan is one day away from totally screwing our performance ..."

Maybe if I ignore him, he'll go away.

"No one is code-reviewing his stuff ..."

Maybe if I offer him a sour-apple saltwater taffy, he'll go away.

"And he just checked into your component."

"He what the fuck what? *Stan!*"

Now, an important transition is occurring as you and Richard are running down the hallway to grab Stan. When Richard was rambling in your office, the two of you were talking, and talking is a conversation. Anything goes when it comes to a conversation. It's a simple negotiation: make a point, get a response, retort, retort back.

A conversation is verbal Ping Pong: There are many different styles, but for two players, you bat the little white verbal ball back and forth until someone wins.

When you and Richard walk into Stan's office, the conversation now becomes a meeting, and the core difference between a conversation and a meeting is that it needs rules so people know when to talk.

Alignment vs. Creation

There are two useful types of meetings: *alignment meetings* and *creation meetings*. Briefly, alignment meetings are tactical communication exchanges that rarely dive into the strategic. These are fine meetings that have a weekly cadence, and while there are lots of ways to screw up these meetings, their tactical repetition often keeps them on the rails.

Creation meetings—diving into solving a hard problem—involve, well, more creativity. Each hard problem requires a unique solution, and finding that solution is where creation meetings can go bad.

I've documented many of the rules for meetings in other chapters. In this piece, I want to talk about some of the obvious and non-obvious rules around meetings.

A meeting has two critical components: an agenda and a referee. Let's start with the obvious—the agenda. The agenda answers the question everyone is wondering as they sit down: how do I get out of this meeting so I can actually work?

Different referees have different agenda strategies. They vary from sending the agenda out in an e-mail before the meeting to writing it down on the whiteboard at the beginning of the meeting. Whatever the move, the agenda exists in everyone's head. Everyone can answer the question, "What do we need to do get the hell out of here?"

The other component is the referee. I originally thought the owner was the critical component, and while an absent owner is certainly a meeting red flag, the lack of a referee is a guaranteed disaster.

All active participants in a meeting can instinctively sense progress, and when progress isn't being made, they get cranky and start looking for the exit. A referee's job is to shape the meeting to meet the requirements of the agenda and the expectations of the participants. Style and execution vary wildly from referee to referee, but the defining characteristics are the perceptions of the meeting participants. A good referee not only makes sure the majority of the attendees believe progress is being made, but they're aware of anyone who doesn't believe that progress is being made at any given moment. And they're looking for one thing . . . people checked out.

If they're doing anything except listening, they aren't listening. There are lots of exits from a meeting that look nothing like a door. Every single moment of a meeting is not going to be interesting to you. When Stan and Richard dive deep on that one piece of code you care nothing about, you mentally wander. You reach into your back pocket, pull out your iPhone, check your mail, and think, "Let 'em wander ... they'll be back to the interesting shortly." Two screw-ups here:

1. You're the referee and you're checked out. You're the guy running down the hallway to figure out whether Stan is going wreck your weekend with crap code. You're the referee because you have the incentive to drive this meeting to some reasonable conclusion and ... you're checking your mail.

2. You aren't listening. This is what you're hearing: "Blah blah blah Jira blah blah scales linearly blah blah." Thing is, there might be value in the blahs, but you will never know because you're checking your mail rather than understanding where this meeting is headed. Worse, when the meeting goes off the rails due to your lack of attention, you have less of a chance of bringing it back because you were mentally elsewhere.

The rule is for everyone in the room: if their attention is elsewhere, they aren't listening. Frank, the guy who plays Plants vs. Zombies during staff meetings and swears he's listening? He's not. He's getting 50 percent of what's being said, and worse, he's giving everyone else in the room permission to slack.

However, the problem here isn't with Frank, it's with the referee. Frank is not sensing progress, so Frank has left. The referee has forgotten that ... *if steam isn't coming from their ears, they might stop listening.* It is the responsibility of the referee to constantly surf the room visually to determine who is and isn't engaged. This is hard.

Referee. Solid agenda. Seven people. At any given point in the meeting, three of these people are verbally sparring about the topic. In addition to making sure the three active participants don't kill each other, the referee—in real time—needs to figure out whether the other four are mentally present, and, if not, what to do about it. This is really hard.

This is really hard because refereeing these meetings is incredibly situational. You've got seven people, each with their own personality and agenda. You've got whatever mood they happen to be in at that precise moment. And you've got whatever topic merits this meeting in the first place. Given all of these fuzzy variables, what possible relevant advice can I give you to keep everyone engaged? Here are a few small tips:

- Pull them back. If they don't look engaged, steer the conversation toward them and ask them a question relevant to the current state of the topic: "Stan, no code reviews? Really?"

- Reset the meeting with silence. If several folks have checked out, one of my favorite moves is referee silence. When all eyes are on you, count backward from 10 and watch what happens—Frank is going to look up from Plants vs. Zombies and wonder, "Why's it so quiet? What'd I miss?"

- Change the scenery. Are you sitting down? OK, stand up. Have you been writing stuff on the whiteboard? No? Try it. Small tweaks to the scenery might change nothing, or they might give someone a nudge out of their mental haze.

A meeting's progress is measured by the flow, and the referee's job is keep it moving along at a good clip, which is why the referee sometimes needs to . . .

Own it: There are a variety of meeting denizens you're going to encounter as both a referee and a meeting participant. The one I want to talk about is the person who believes it is their moral imperative to contribute to the meeting simply because they were invited. Yes, talking is a sign of active engagement. Yes, you never know what random verbal curveball is going to magically improve a meeting. Yes, this person always talks . . . every meeting . . . like forever.

There is a point where the referee becomes the dictator and owns the meeting. They own it. They actively demonstrate control of the meeting, and when you're the person who gets owned, it stings a bit, but this meeting is not about you. It's about each and every person sitting in the room wanting to get out of this meeting and go to where real work is done.

For the referee, the decision to step in and shut someone down during a meeting isn't one taken lightly. A good referee knows that abuse of the dictator role eventually results in everyone shutting down, which is just as inefficient as that one person who never shuts up. Summoning the dictator is a last-ditch effort geared at fixing the problem right now, but in such a way that the problem doesn't show up again. It's a gut referee call that you're going to screw up before you perfect; however, an important and immeasurable part of running a good meeting involves . . .

Improvisation: The solution to whatever the hard problem might be is going to show up via one of two things: random brilliance or grindingly hard work. The path to either involves a competent referee doing everything I just described while also knowing when to ignore it.

A good referee knows

- When the meeting is nowhere near the stated agenda, but everyone in the room is showing all the nonverbal signs of progress—so screw it, let's see where it goes.

- When this person who appears to be rambling and wasting everyone's time is onto something that might lead to random brilliance—so let them ramble.

- The glaring danger signs for a meeting that is doomed, whether it's a lack of preparation, the absence of a key player, or the fact the team is wound up about another issue entirely.

- The courage it takes to stop this meeting five minutes into the scheduled hour because there is no discernible way to make progress.

Meeting management, like people management, is often the art of managing a moment, which means that the only rule that applies is entirely dependent on the snowflake-like context of the moment.

A Culture of Meetings

Somewhere in the evolution of a growing company, meetings take over. At the time, it seems like a good idea, because the product roadmap is all over the floor, key people are quitting, or there's lots of yelling in the hallways. Whatever the disaster, a single well-led, efficient meeting with the right people provides a solution to a hard problem. Those who are watching notice and think, "All right, we now have a new tool to solve problems—it's called a meeting."

With this fresh sense of validation, meetings spring up all over the place. They become the fashionable solution to problem-solving—to making progress. More folks are invited to these affairs because everyone believes that *if you're invited to a meeting, you are somehow more professionally relevant.* People start becoming scarce around the building, checking someone's free/busy schedule becomes part of the culture, and suddenly *we're worrying more about the care and feeding of meetings than getting shit done.*

Meetings must exist, but meetings cannot be seen as the only solution for making progress. If you must meet, start the meeting by remembering that the definition of a successful meeting is that when the meeting is done, it need never occur again.

The Twinge

You know this meeting, and you know it the second you hear the attendee list. Something is up: a product is at risk, a strategy is being redefined, or a decision of magnitude is being considered.

Slide reviews are conducted via e-mail, rehearsals are performed, and demos are fine-tuned. When the day arrives, the room fills, nervous glances are exchanged, and it begins. Your practice pays off. Expected questions appear and are quickly answered. The project is solid; perhaps there is no need for that massive decision. We're in good shape—except that Allison, the SVP, has a question. Allison?

"Has anyone talked to Roger's group about this? Can they support this load?"

Shit.

There is an impressive silence in the room when everyone understands the colossal gap that Allison's questions unexpectedly illuminate. The question I want to answer here is how in the hell an SVP who isn't even part of this project, who was invited as a courtesy, and who has never even see the project proposal finds the biggest strategic gap in our thinking after staring at our slides for 13 minutes?

She had a Twinge.

Twinge Acquisition

As a manager, you manage both yourself and your team, and the simple fact is there will always be more of them than of you. Unless you're the guy managing a single person (weird), you've got multiple folks with all their varied work and quirky personalities to manage.

Rookie managers approach this situation with enviable gusto. They believe their job is to be aware of and responsible for their team's every single thought and act. I like to watch these freshman managers. I like to watch them sweat and scurry about the building as they attempt to complete this impossible task.

It's not that I enjoy watching them prepare to fail. In fact, as they zip by, I explicitly warn them: "There is no way you're doing it all. You need to trust and you need to delegate." But even with this explanation, most of these managers are back in my office in three weeks saying the same thing: "I have no idea how you keep track of it all."

"You can't, and I sure don't."

In addition to trusting those who work for you by delegating work that you may truly believe only you can do, you must also understand the art of evaluating a Spartan set of data, extracting the truth, and trusting your Twinges. When you listen to and act on your Twinges, well, you look like a magician, but when you ignore them, the consequences can be far ranging and damage the project as well as your reputation with those involved.

Twinges: Built on Experience

Before I explain the cost of ignoring a Twinge, let's first understand why rookie engineering managers aren't listening to me. Remember, I'm talking about engineers here: a class of human being that derives professional joy from the building of things—specific things. Things they can sit back and stare at—look there!—I built that thing.

The building of things scratches an essential itch for engineers. It's why they became engineers in the first place. When they were six, their dads handed them two boards, a nail, and a hammer, and they started whacking. *Blam blam blam!* Even with the nail awkwardly bent in half, the wood was suddenly and magically bound together: a thing was built. At that moment, this junior engineer's brain secreted a chemical that instantly convinced them of the disproportionate value of this construction: "This is the best wood thing in the world because I built it." And then they looked up from their creation and pleaded, "Dad, I really need more nails."

Dad handed them three more nails, showed them where to hold the hammer, and demonstrated how to hit the nail. More whacking. *Blam blam biff!* This time the nail wasn't bent; this time on the last hit the nail slid effortlessly into the wood. This engineer in training had now experienced two essential emotions: the joy of creation and the satisfaction of learning while gaining experience, perfecting the craft.

Engineers are wired to learn how to build stuff well. And as they continue to do that, someone eventually thinks it's a good idea to promote them to the ranks of management. These new managers initially believe the essential skills of building that made them successful as engineers will apply to the building of people, but they don't. It's their experience that matters.

Management is a total career restart. One of the first lessons a new manager discovers, either through trial and error or instruction, is that the approaches they used for building products aren't going to work when it comes to people. However, this doesn't mean all of the experience is suddenly irrelevant. In fact, it's that experience that creates the Twinge.

A Manager's Day: Full of Stories

As a manager, think of your day as one full of stories. All day, you're hearing stories from different people about the different arcs that are being played out in the hallways and conference rooms. As these stories arrive, there is one question you need to always be asking: do you believe this story? Before you make that call, there are a couple things you need to know.

First, this story is incomplete, and you're OK with that. Here's why: for now, you need to trust that those who work with you are capable of synthesizing a story. Part of their value is their judgment in presenting you with the essential facts, and until they prove they can't synthesize well, you assume they can.

Second, and contradictorily, while I believe that folks don't wake up intending to construct lies, I also know that for any story you're hearing, you're getting the version that supports their chosen version of reality. As a story is being told to you, the opinion of the storyteller is affecting both the content and the tone. Their agenda dictates what they are choosing to tell you. Again, malevolent forces are not necessarily driving the storyteller. They are hopeful and they want to succeed, but this story needs judgment, and that's where you come in as a manager. I'll explain by example.

A Familiar Nail

"OK, Project Frodo—we're two weeks from feature complete. Our task list is down to seven items, but as you can see from this chart, the work is spread out among the teams. I'm confident we'll hit the date."

This sounds like good news. This sounds like the truth. Nothing in those three sentences is setting off any alarms in my head, but I'm a manager and it's my job to sniff around.

"Is the design done?"

"Yes, except for items six and seven."

OK, so it's not done. "When will they be done with design?"

"In a week and half."

"And you can get the tasks done in the two days after we receive the designs?"

"I, uh ..."

Sniffing around pisses people off. Sniffing around is often interpreted as micromanagement, a passive-aggressive way of stating, "I don't believe you can do your job."

While there are a great many managers out there who pull this move as a means of pumping up their fading value, this is not what I'm doing—I'm trying to figure out if this story is familiar.

I've built a lot of teams that have built a lot of software. I know that what we receive as a complete design is usually 80 percent of what we actually need, because I've been the engineer staring at the Photoshops in the middle of the night with two days to feature complete, thinking, "It's sure pretty, but what about internationalization? And error cases? You know that's work, right?"

It's not that I know all the intricacies of Project Frodo, and I don't want to know them. It's a team full of personalities, tasks, and dependencies that I could spend my entire day trying to understand, and I've got two other projects of equal size that are running hot. As I'm listening to this story, I'm listening hard and trying to figure out ... have I seen this nail before? I have, haven't I? I don't remember when, but I do remember the Twinge.

Do you remember every success and failure? No. You can recite your greatest hits over a Mai Tai, but I don't think you can actually recollect them all. However, this doesn't mean you don't remember the experience. I've long since given up trying to understand why one story rings true to me while another triggers the Twinge. My belief is that my brain is far better at subconscious analysis, pattern matching, and teasing out apparently essential details from the noise than I'll consciously ever be. My belief is that my experiences drive my sometimes subconscious instincts, and this is why I've come to trust the Twinge.

A Twinge Catastrophe

A Twinge is your experience speaking to you in an unexpected and possibly unstructured way, and while I'm not saying you should base your management strategy on these amorphous moments of clarity, I do want to explain their importance in the organization.

This storytelling—the careful selection of facts, ideas, and data—is going on everywhere in the company. Everyone is building a story about what and how they're doing, and they're often optimizing in their favor.

While many of these stories involve the mundane day-to-day operations of the company, some of these stories are terribly important. While it might not sound like it right now, that story Bob just explained about a small performance issue on one server is actually a massive performance debacle in the making. Joe's story about that annoying interaction design problem is actually the description of the absence of a feature you don't even know you're missing.

When these seemingly benign stories are not judged, when they are not questioned, the story is over. Bob's conscience is clear because he gave you a heads-up. Your conscience is clear is because you listened to Bob's concern, and, yeah, you had a Twinge, but Bob's delivery record is impeccable, so Twinge be damned, it'll sort itself out in the end.

Your failure to heed your Twinge is a management failure.

It gets worse. This story optimization is happening at every layer of management and in every group of people. Each time an unheeded Twinge story jumps from one person to the next, a lie is being propagated throughout the organization. And if the story started in your group, it's your fault this misinformation is running amok. Now, there are other people in the building who might get a Twinge and save your team's collective professional ass, but again, if it's a story that originated in your group, the responsibility is yours.

Just Another Nail

New engineering managers wrestle with the gig because they miss building stuff. The powerfully addictive act of building is no longer part of their day, and they bitch, "You know, I don't know what I actually do all day." Finding other ways to scratch this itch is a topic for another chapter, but for now, one of your jobs is to listen to the stories and map them against your experience. And when there's a Twinge, you ask questions, and you need to believe the asking of these questions is a form of building.

As a manager, when the story doesn't quite feel right, you demand specifics. You ask for the details of the story to prove that it's true. If the story can't stand up to the first three questions that pop into your mind, then there's an issue.

You don't run a team or a company on a Twinge. The ability to listen to random stories and quickly tease out a flaw in the logic or the absence of a critical dependency is just one of the skills you need to develop as a manager. Like building, both the discovery and the asking of these questions are arts; they're just more nails you need to figure out how to hammer.

The Update, the Vent, and the Disaster

Business is noisy.

Business is full of people worrying loudly about projects, process, and other people. These people have opinions and they share them all over the place, all the time. This collective chatter is part of the daily regimen of a healthy business, but this chatter will bury the individual voice unless someone pays attention. And paying attention is best done in a one-on-one with the people you manage.

Your job in a one-on-one is to give the smallest voice a chance to be heard, and I start with a question: "How are you?"

The Basics

Before we start, let's go over the basic rules I follow regarding one-on-ones:

> *Hold a one-on-one the same time each week:* When you become a manager of people, an odd thing happens. You're automatically perceived as being busier. Whether you are or not is irrelevant; folks just think you are. Consistently landing your one-on-ones at the same time on the same day is a weekly reminder that you are here for them— no matter how busy.

Always do it: OK, so you are really busy. You're running from meeting to meeting. It's easy to deprioritize a one-on-one because, unlike whatever meeting you're running to or from, a one-on-one doesn't represent an urgent problem that needs solving. I'll beat this perceived-lack-of-value opinion out of you later in this piece, but for now, understand that each time you bail on a one-on-one, the person you're managing hears, "You don't matter."

Give it 30 minutes, at least: Another favorite move of the busy manager is to schedule a one-on-one for 15 minutes or less. *It's the best I can do, Rands. I've got 15 people working for me.* First, those 15 people don't work for you; you work for them. Think of it like this: if those 15 people left, just left the building tomorrow, how much work would actually get done? Second, if you've got 15 people working for you, you're not their manager, you're just the guy who grins uncomfortably as you infrequently fly by the office, ask how it's going, and then don't actually listen to the answer.

Having a meaningful conversation with anyone takes time. As you'll see in a moment, you start with an opener where you figure out where everyone is mentally, which builds momentum into having a conversation of consequence. In your 15-minute one-on-one, all you learn is that you don't have time to care.

How Are You?

It's a softball opener. I recognize that, but I lead with a vanilla opener because this type of content-free question is vague enough that the recipient can't help but put part of themselves into the answer, and it's the answer where the one-on-one begins.

What's the first thing they say? Do they deflect with humor? Is it the standard off-the-cuff answer? Or is it different? How is it different? What words do they choose and how quickly are they saying them? How long do they wait to answer? Do they even answer the question? Do you understand the answer isn't the point, either? The content is merely a delivery vehicle for the mood, and the mood sets your agenda.

As I'm listening to the answer, I'm discerning your mood, and I'm throwing you into one of three buckets regarding the type of one-on-one we're about to have:

- The Update (all clear!)
- The Vent (something's up . . .)
- The Disaster (oh dear . . .)

The majority of the one-on-ones fall into the first bucket. The answer to my softball opener is pleasant and familiar. We're going to walk through the facts, dig a little bit here and there, wander, and then it'll be over. Great. The other two buckets are trickier to assess with a single question. Your answer to my question is ... off. You either state this up front with the alarming, "We need to talk" proclamation, which immediately throws you in the Vent bucket, but this could also easily be a Disaster. By far, the worst answer to the opener is the quiet one, the answer that contains something hidden and insidious. Oh dear.

The Update

You get exactly what you expect from the Update—it's status. These are my projects and these are my people and this is how it's going down. I believe most folks consider this type of one-on-one to be a success, and they're wrong.

A one-on-one is not a project meeting. A one-on-one is not status report. See all those project managers scurrying to and fro? Their job is the maintenance of the facts and the discovery of project truth. If you're drawing the line for success in your one-on-one as the discussion of data you could find in a status report, you're missing the point. A one-on-one is an opportunity to learn something new amidst the grind of daily business.

When a one-on-one starts and is clearly an Update, I start listening twice as hard for a nugget of something that we can discuss, investigate, and explore. It's not that I don't care about status, it's just that we've got 45 minutes here, and if we fill that time with data I can find scrubbing the bug database and the wiki, we're both wasting our time.

So, I listen, I take it on myself to find a meaty conversation, and if I don't find it in the first 15 minutes, I've got three moves:

> *Three prepared points:* While I believe part of a good organic one-on-one is improvisation, I usually have three talking points in my back pocket that have shown up over the past week regarding you or your team. If we can't find a good thread of conversation in the first 10 to 15 minutes, I'll start with one of these points and see where that takes us.

> *The mini-performance review:* You read that right. If we're 15 minutes into a lifeless, redundant, status-based one-on-one, and I don't have anything sitting in my back pocket, I'm going to turn this into a performance review. It won't be your actual performance review; it's one aspect of your review that somehow strikes me as more appropriate conversation than an update on your bug counts. *I see you've got a handle on your bugs, but one thing we talked about*

at your last annual performance review was getting a better handle on the architecture. How's that going?

My current disaster: Chances are, in my professional life, something is currently off the rails. It's selfish, but if you're leading with status and I can't find an interesting discussion nugget, let's talk about my current disaster. *Do you know how many open reqs we have that we can't hire against? Who is the best hiring manager you know and what were their best moves?* The point of this discussion is not to solve my Disaster; the point is that we're going to have a conversation where one of us is going to learn something more than just project status.

Business is noisy because there is always stuff to do, and the process of doing stuff is called *tactics*. It's tactical work, and while tactics are progress, the real progress is made when we get strategic. A productive one-on-one is one where we talk strategically about how we do stuff, but more importantly, how we might do this stuff better.

The Vent

A really good Vent starts with a disarmingly long period of silence. I've just asked my soft opener and you're quiet. Really quiet. I can see you mentally gathering steam. I take this time to ground myself, because while I know a Vent is coming, I likely don't know the content or the severity. Vents vary from a semi-tense "I can't stand QA today" to a full-on explosion: "If I have to listen to Thomas grind his goddamned Fair Trade–Certified Peruvian coffee beans in his office *one more time*, I might lose it."

When the Vent begins, you might confuse this for a conversation. It's not. It's a mental release valve, and your job is to listen for as long as it takes. Don't problem solve. Don't redirect. Don't comfort. Yet. Your employee is doing mental house cleaning, and interrupting this cleaning is missing the point. They don't want a solution; they want to be heard.

A Vent does have a conclusion. There is a point where you need to jump in, but these conclusions and your actions vary.

> *It's done:* The Vent starts to lose steam and the venter finds themselves panting and staring at you with nothing to say because they've said it all—probably a couple of times. It's in this moment that you begin your triage. *Great, now we start talking . . .*

> *It's a rant:* A Vent can repeat itself. The same facts and content might be thrown at you in a couple of different ways. I see this repetition as healthy way of chewing on

the problem, but there's a point where this Vent becomes a rant. After a couple of Vent cycles, you might try grabbing hold of the conversation and starting with triage, but brace yourself—the venter might not be done. My suggestion, in the face of resistance, is to give them the benefit of the doubt and let 'em go another round.

The Vent that wants no help is a rant. The ranter somehow believes that the endless restatement of their opinion is the solution. Perhaps they have no clue what a solution might be or how to find it, or perhaps they've been stewing on the topic so long that they've lost all sight of logic.

Whatever the backstory, the ranter is finding some weird mental satisfaction in the endless restatement of the problem, but they have no interest in solving the actual problem at this point. Annoying. When you've got a confirmed rant on your hands, it's OK to jump into the middle of the Vent—you're saving everyone a pile of time, and you're teaching the ranter that the incessant restatement of the rant is not progress.

It's a disaster: You're listening carefully to the Vent. It's moving forward and it's not repeating itself, but . . . something is up. Perhaps it's their demeanor or maybe it's the topic, but your radar is pinging. The venter is not standing on their usual soapbox. They're out of character and, as time is passing, they are becoming less themselves.

At its core, the Vent is motivated by emotion. That's the key difference between the Update and the Vent. The topic has triggered an emotional response, and the venter's therapy is the verbal statement and restatement of the situation. Emotion is a slippery slope, and what can start as a Vent has a chance of spiraling into a Disaster. It's rare in business, but it's a risk when you're dealing with emotionally slippery human beings.

The Disaster

If a Vent feels like a speech, a Disaster feels like an attack. What started as an emotional conversation has transformed into a war, and you're suddenly and unexpectedly on the battlefield.

Until you've seen the Disaster once, it's hard to predict how you're going to react to the perception of being attacked. For better or worse, it's happened enough to me that when I see the Disaster approaching, I carefully tuck all of my emotions in a box, lock the box, and magically transform into a Vulcan.

When the Disaster arrives, the absolute worst response is any semblance of emotion. See, in this case, the venter wants to fight. They literally want to go a couple of rounds on this particular topic. What was a high degree of frustration has transformed into pure aggression and if you so much as blink improperly, you're contributing to the escalation of this situation.

Here are some tips on recognizing and handling the Disaster:

- The person you're talking to isn't him- or herself. As you're sitting there weathering the Disaster, remember that you are experiencing an anomaly—a bizarre emotional version of the person that only shows up when they're on the edge. The person you're familiar with will show up ... eventually.

- Shut up. Really. Your primary job during the Disaster is to defuse, and you start defusing by contributing absolutely nothing. If you're a logical, reasonable management type, you'll be tempted to ask clarifying questions—to try to shape the problem. Don't. Be quiet. Let the emotion pass. Here's why ...

- It's not about the issue anymore. You're no longer experiencing the problem. You're experiencing the employee's emotional baggage regarding the problem. Sure, there's the core issue, but that's not what you're currently observing. You're seeing the extreme negative reaction to the issue, and that's the first order of business.

As with the Vent, success comes with traversing the emotional explosion. There will, hopefully, be a point when the majority of the emotion has passed, and the aggrieved will be willing to having a rational discussion. Unlike with the Vent, the discussion won't be about the core issue. It will start with the Disaster, with understanding the intense emotion surrounding the topic.

A Disaster is the end result of poor management. When your employee believes totally losing their shit is a productive strategy, it's because they believe it's the only option left for making anything change.

Assume They Have Something to Teach You

The cliché is, "People are your most valuable resource." I would argue that they are your only resource. Computers, desks, buildings, data centers ... whatever. All of those other tools only support your one and only resource: your people.

People mentally wander. It's in their nature to make off-the-cuff observations— "Why does Phil get the choice features?"—and to let those observations fester, mutate, and sometimes transform into a Disaster. I'm not suggesting that every one-on-one be a tortuous affair to discover deeply hidden emergent disasters, but that they offer a weekly opportunity for you to see where dissatisfaction might quietly appear. A one-on-one is your chance to perform weekly preventive maintenance while also understanding the health of your team. A one-on-one is a place to listen for what your employee isn't saying.

The sound that surrounds a successful regimen of one-on-ones is silence. All of the listening, questioning, and discussion that happens during a one-on-one is managerial preventative maintenance. You'll see when interest in a project begins to wane and take action before it becomes job dissatisfaction. You'll hear about tension between two employees and moderate a discussion before it becomes a yelling match in a meeting. Your reward for a culture of healthy one-on-ones is a distinct lack of drama.

The Monday Freakout

Mondays start on Sunday. It's the moment you realize that the weekend is over and you begin staring at the endless list of things to do that you began to ignore early Friday as the sweet, sweet smell of the weekend filled your office.

As a rule, the earlier on Sunday that you think about Monday is an indication of how much you neglected to do on Friday. Worse, the more time you spend during your weekend fretting about your weekdays, the more pissed off you're going to be when Monday actually arrives. The extreme case is when someone spends the entire weekend working themselves into a frustrated knot of stress regarding their work situation, and that means, when Monday arrives, they might freak out.

This Monday's freakout was courtesy of my QA lead, Dingfelder. He was simmering in the hallway all morning. He was talking in sharp, hushed tones to anyone who would listen. I already knew about the topic, but I was surprised by his verbal intensity. Right after lunch, he struck. Hands tightly folded in front of him, Dingfelder stood in my door, lightly bouncing on the front of his feet.

"Rands, can we talk for a minute?"

Shit.

I gripped the table and braced myself.

"Dear lord," he said. "We're going to ship horrible product and you're setting unrealistic deadlines and QA always gets the shaft and do we support Internet Explorer 9 and my credibility is on the line here and Jesus Christ didn't we learn our last time please I hate HTML and this developer keeps on diddling with shit."

Rands Rule of Software Management #27: If someone is going to freak out, it's going to be on a Monday.

Freakouts are unique because of their intensity. The first time you're on the receiving end, you'll be unable to catch your breath because of the shock. How did this usually calm person end up yelling in my face? Let's not worry about that right now. Let's first understand how to deal with the freakout in front of you, and that means following the rules.

Don't Participate in the Freakout

The worst type of freakout is one that is purely emotional, illogical, and based on little or no fact. It also lacks any type of solution because there really isn't a well-defined problem except that this person really needs to freak out. The volume and intensity of this type of freakout can be negatively intoxicating and you'll be tempted to jump on the freakout bandwagon.

Don't.

The best move here is to simply listen and maintain eye contact. Your calmness is a primal attempt to telepathically reflect the insanity back to the freak so they'll realize they've gone off the deep end. This can be rough because the freakout may be pointed directly at you, but even under attack, your job is the same: Listen. Nod. Repeat.

Give the Freak the Benefit of the Doubt

Chances are, your freak really does have something to say, but maybe they've lost perspective spending every waking moment stressing since last Friday at 5 p.m. Perhaps their freakout has nothing to do with what they're saying and has everything to do with an unrelated series of events the previous week that ended poorly and has mutated into this freakout. Maybe they drink too much coffee, but remember, they have a point.

In any freakout, there is normally a very noisy preamble which is designed to get your attention. Dingfelder's comments above are all preamble. I know after he stops to take a breath that we're going to get to the heart of the matter. He's probably already said it, but when he says it again, "Unrealistic deadlines," I know we have progress because we've hit on the foundation of the freakout and we can begin a conversation which is the first step to defusing this situation.

But, it's not always that easy . . .

Hammer the Freak with Questions

Sometimes the preamble just doesn't end. Sure, there's content in there somewhere, but some freaks really just like the freakout. They like that they have your attention, or maybe they just like to hear their voice, but if it's been a couple of minutes and all you're hearing is preamble, it's time to grab the reins.

Ending the preamble and starting the conversation starts with a question. Why is the product going to be horrible? Should we care about IE 9? Properly timed and well-constructed questions lead your freak away from emotion because they force them to the other side of their brain where they don't freak, they think.

I was lucky; I knew Dingfelder was about to drop the bomb a good two hours before he got around to it. In that time, I leapt into our bug tracking system to figure out how many bugs each person had filed; I glanced at bug severities, arrival rates, and any other juicy bug tidbits that might help me defuse the bomb.

Once the Dingfelder freakout began, I calmly pulled my bug notes out. The moment he took his breath, I asked, "Hey, so how many bugs showed up this weekend? How many did we fix? How many of those fixes didn't take? Wow, why do you think that happened?"

The key with a question offense is to move your freak from the emotional state to the rational one. I know I know and I know how good it feels when you're stressed out to attack the source of that stress in what looks like a rational manner, but, um, you're yelling, pointing your finger at me, and jumping up and down. Do you want me to react to the yelling or to the facts?

Get the Freaks to Solve Their Own Problems

One pleasant side effect of attacking freakouts with questions is that you discover the freak is often already close to a solution. Remember, they've been simmering since Friday and, in that time, they've been chewing on the problem from every angle possible. In that time, their understanding, while soaked in emotion, has more depth than yours.

Even if you haven't successfully predicted a freakout, you can still use your experience as a means of exploring the freak's understanding of whatever the issue might be. Heck, you don't even need experience; all you need is the desire to understand what this person is freaking out about. Sometimes, you get lucky. Your simple clarification questions end up with an "And *dammit Rands*, the engineering managers should be *scrubbing their bugs every morning!*"

OK.

Let's do that.

You Still Have a Problem

Being emotionally invested in what you are doing is an absolute requirement for caring about your job. What I hear when you walk into my office and freak out is "I'm caring about my job here, Rands, please listen." It's taken years of weathering these explosions to hear this and not to take it personally, but I've come to expect that freakouts are a normal event in passionate engineering teams.

It's still a management failure.

It's great that your freak has chosen to freak out. The alternative is that they're not saying a thing and have decided to leave the company. The fact that your particular Dingfelder is screaming at you in your office is a good sign that he's not leaving because he clearly, loudly cares.

But you screwed up. Someone is screaming in your office, and once you successfully defuse the situation, you know two things. First, there is a problem that needs to be solved. Second, and more importantly, someone believes the best way to get your attention is by freaking out.

Lost in Translation

Early on in your mastery of a complex thing, you are going to catastrophically overestimate your ability.

Your confidence is going to be artificially high. This new job, hobby, or sport is going to appear magically easy. You're going to feel gifted. Those watching your miraculous aptitude keep saying "beginner's luck," but that's neither what you're hearing nor what they're actually saying. What you're hearing them say is, "We are jealous that you are gifted at this thing you totally don't understand," but what they're actually saying is, "We understand it's intoxicating to instantly feel like an expert and we will most certainly bite our tongues when you painfully discover how much you have to learn."

Learn schmearn. I'm a genius.

The gift of the enthusiastic beginner is blissful and empowering ignorance. Beginners are not burdened with the depth and complexity of understanding; they shine brightly with enthusiasm . . . until the Fall.

Wallace Hates Me

I wasn't even a manager. I was a lead of two engineers, but titles don't matter. It was the change in attitude of one the engineers that got my attention. Harold didn't miss a beat after I became his lead. He was in my office on Monday morning: "Where do we start?"

"Maybe we should, uh, fix error-handling in the test framework? Maybe?"

"It'll be done by Wednesday." *Cool. I can so do this.*

Wallace, on the other hand, was indifferent. I waited until Wednesday to walk into his office to ask, "Hey, I was wondering what you were working on?"

"Same as last week. Endless bugs."

"OK, great . . . super. Uh, holler if you need anything, OK?"

Silence. *OK, fine. I've never really gotten Wallace; he's done his own thing and he seems to do it well, so let him do it, right?*

Besides, I was a lead. Look at Harold—he bolts into my office every morning in his bright orange Philadelphia Flyers jersey and asks the same question: "What's next?" He and I were cranking, so much so that three weeks after I became a lead, they added Stan to the team. Stan was a Boston Bruins fan, but he and Harold were birds of a feather. They grabbed coffee together in the morning, argued about hockey, and then darted to my office: "What's next?"

I can so do this.

Three weeks turned into three months, and Harold, Stan, and I were nailing it. Yes, I'd dutifully check in on Wallace each week, but the action was with the three of us. I figured that when Wallace was ready to climb out of his shell and join the productivity party, he would.

Three months to the day, my boss walked in my office with a paper in his hand. "Wallace has been keeping a daily log of every interaction with you and claims, outside of meetings, that you've collectively spent 30 minutes with him in the last three months. Is that true?" He handed me the paper:

> *3/21:* Asked about bug status—47 seconds

> *3/22:* Question about performance—doesn't know
> what he's talking about and/or asking for—1 minute,
> 12 seconds

> *3/23:* No interaction

> *3/24:* No interaction

Six pages of meticulous, single-line entries documenting every single minute of my managerial incompetence. My thought: "I thought he didn't care."

It's called the Fall because in an instant the normally predictable floor upon which you stand vanishes and you enter a mental free fall where you feel like throwing up because you no longer know which way is up.

The Fall Is Not the Lesson

The sensation of the Fall is disproportionate to the size of the lesson. You experience not just the sense of failure, but also the colossal irrational disappointment that you are no longer an expert at this task with which you have no previous experience—which is goofy. Here's the kicker—you now have just enough experience to understand the actual work involved in becoming proficient at a task you previously thought you could magically improvise.

A Wallace-class Fall is common with freshly minted leaders, and it's one exacerbated by the commonly introverted tendencies of engineers. It's the discovery that not only is someone you lead not following, but that there is a complete and total personality disconnect with this person. None of your usual networking moves work. They stare blankly at your witty repartee, and when they do talk, it's as if they haven't heard a single word you've said.

It's a frustrating discovery, because part of the reason you became a leader was due to your natural and proven people skills. But it's an enviable discovery, because on a planet full of people, most of them aren't like you, and your first Wallace will not be your last.

Your Instincts Are 100 Percent Wrong

A complete personality disconnect with someone you intend to lead, like in a Wallace situation, is rare, but for the sake of figuring how to tackle it, let's assume this worst-case scenario.

In a normal getting-to-know-you situation with an employee, the first question I want to be able to answer is, "What do they want?" What is their core motivation with regard to their current gig? Are they working on a promotion? Are they just figuring out the gig? Are they adrift? Are they OK with being adrift?

Understanding core motivation does not give me a complete picture of a person, but it gives me a place to start. When I know where they want to be, I can start to figure out how to get them there. Unhappily adrift people want immediate action. Those seeking promotions are eagerly seeking opportunity and will own anything to get it. However, this is Wallace, and Wallace stares blankly when I blithely ask, "What floats your boat, Wallace?"

Give up on the idea that you're going to finesse Wallace into telling you his secrets. Nothing that comes to you naturally is going to work with someone who honestly believes you are an alien. Your first job isn't understanding core motivation, it's basic communication.

In any situation where communication is suspect, I rely heavily on clarification. Whenever I say something that might be ambiguous, I ask, "What did you hear?" In return, when I'm listening, and the topic or intent is not abundantly clear, I restate: "OK, what I heard was . . ."

It sounds like this:

> *Me:* . . . and new requirements came in this weekend, but Jennifer still wants to see an initial spec by Thursday. Wallace, *what did you hear there?*

> *Wallace:* Jennifer wants a spec on Thursday.

Now, if this were Harold or Stan, we'd be done. A verbal commitment was made and we'd move on, but this is Wallace and I can assume nothing.

> *Me:* Yes, a spec on Thursday. And what does that mean for your work?

> *Wallace:* I was planning on finishing doc review on Monday and building out test data on Tuesday and Wednesday. I won't get to that if Jennifer needs a spec on Thursday.

> *Me: What I'm hearing is* that you've got a pile of work that will need to be rescheduled, right?

> *Wallace:* Right.

> *Me:* And if we do that, do you think you can have the spec done?

> *Wallace:* Maybe.

I know it feels like the passive-aggressive Olympics, but I swear this is how Wallace thinks. In his world, a work commitment is never implied and must be verbally stated. We need to go back and forth until he states, "I will reschedule all of my planned work from this week until next week. I'll relay the implications of these changes to the docs and QA teams, and I have moderate confidence there will be no issue in delivery of a first draft of the revised spec by close of business on Thursday."

It's pedantic, annoying, and inefficient, but when personalities are disconnected, you don't know how to communicate, so that's where you start. With practice, you'll learn the unique rules of engagement. You'll discover the words and the ideas that people use to describe both their happiness and their displeasure. You'll learn the visual and verbal cues they employ when they have no idea what you're talking about. In time, you'll develop a mental map of this person who is decidedly not you.

The sensation of interacting with these aliens will never feel natural. It will always feel deliberate and foreign, but practice will provide you with a guide into how they think and a map that might provide insight for you into what they want.

The Size of the Lesson

It took months. It took months of conscious and intentional conversations with Wallace for us both to subconsciously agree to a communication peace treaty. It was painful—each time Wallace and I would drop into that primitive conversation dance, Harold and Stan would stare at each other and shake their heads. This nonsense again?

The nonsense was the essential lesson I learned from my first managerial Fall: when communications are down, listen hard, repeat everything, and assume nothing. The Wallace situation was the first of many Falls, and the beginning of my understanding something fundamental to making future Falls less catastrophic: that people are the best puzzles you'll never solve.

Agenda Detection

I hate meetings.

Everyone hates them because we've all been to so many that have sucked unequivocally that we now walk into a conference room, sit down with our arms folded, and think, "OK, how long until this one is officially a waste of my time? How long until *this* one sucks?" And then it does. Time is wasted. Hot air is generated and everyone sits around the table wondering when someone is going to stop the madness.

If you've ever been frustrated in a meeting—if you've sat there wondering why in the world these people, these managers, who are paid the big bucks to move the company along, simply can't do or say the painfully obvious—then keep reading.

There is a basic skill you need whenever you walk into a meeting that has suck potential. This skill is important whether you're a participant or the person running the meeting. The skill is called *agenda detection.*

Simply put, agenda detection is the ability to discern

1. Typical meeting roles and how meeting participants assume them.

2. Explanation of what these distinct meeting roles want out of a meeting.

3. How to use this understanding to get the hell out of the meeting as quickly as possible.

Meeting Bail Tip #1: Identify the Type of Meeting

The first step in getting out of a meeting is to identify what kind of meeting it is. A meeting agenda would help, but as most meetings proceed without one, you're on your own. Chances are you're either in an informational meeting or a conflict resolution meeting.

At informational meetings—big surprise coming here, folks—information is passed on. Think your favorite quarterly all-hands meeting. Staff meetings. Any meeting where there's a standing assumed agenda. There are two kinds of participants in these meetings: talkers and listeners.

Roles and agendas in these meetings are simple. Talkers are talking and listeners are listening. Get it? There is no problem to be solved other than the transmission of information. The quicker it happens, the sooner everyone is back to work.

You can quickly identify those folks who don't get this. They're the whack jobs who always ask the same (or random) questions during an all-hands with the hope that simply by asking, they're going to change something. It's a noble act, speaking your mind in front of all your peers. But it's also a waste of time. This is an informational meeting, people. The talkers are here to pass on whatever organizational knowledge they need to so as to prevent a rebellion. Folks are here to nod, not solve problems. When the whack job speaks up, everyone who understands the nature of the meeting is thinking, "OK, another useless question that's going to keep me here longer. Crap."

At a conflict resolution meeting, some problem needs to be solved. Apparently, it could not be resolved via e-mail, instant messaging, or hallway conversations, so some bright fellow decided to convene a face-to-face meeting where the bandwidth is high and the time wastage is significant.

Agenda detection in the conflict resolution meeting is more complex. To see it in action, let's create a meeting:

Tuesday, 4 p.m. List of suspects: You (Joe Senior Engineer), two other random engineers, one product-management person, and a program manager. The program manager called the meeting to solve a problem your team had nothing to do with, so you're already resentful of being here in the first place. See, the sales folks sold something that your company does not make. You're here to explain how much it would cost to build this thing that you've never built before but that's already been sold. Been here? Thought so.

Meeting Bail Tip #2: Classify the Participants

Agenda detection starts by first classifying the participants. There are two major types that you need to identify: *players* and *pawns*. The simple distinction between the two types is that players want something out of the meeting. This is their incentive to participate. They'll be leaning forward, actively nodding, barely able to hold themselves back from spilling their agenda all over the table.

Pawns are either silent or instruments of running the meeting. In either case, they're adding very little to the meeting and can be removed from strategic consideration. The term *pawns* is not intended to be derogatory, of course. Pawns very well might be running your company, but in meetings, they don't contribute. . . it's just not their key skill.

Meeting Bail Tip #3: Identify the Players

The bucketing of players and pawns is simple. You can do it with the attendee list and a bit of organizational knowledge. Let's try it with our hypothetical meeting mentioned previously.

First, you can assume all the engineers are players. They obviously have technical knowledge they may throw on the table, otherwise why were they invited? The product-management person is also a player as she represents the sales folks in this meeting. Program managers in these meetings are pawns. They'll make sure action items are recorded and that the meeting ends on time.

If you're sitting in a meeting where you're unable to identify any players, get the hell out. This is a waste of your time. These are meetings traditionally called by windbags who like to hear themselves talk, but hold no real influence over the organization/product/whatever. Unfortunately, if you're new to a group, you need to get burned by the windbags a few times before you learn to avoid these totally fucking useless meetings. It's tough being the new guy.

Meeting Bail Tip #4: Identify the Pros and Cons

The next step in agenda detection now kicks in as we look at the players. This is when you figure out each player's position relative to the issue on the table. For whatever that issue is there are two subclasses of players: the *pros* and the *cons*.

The pros are the players who are currently on the winning side of the issue. They're getting what they want and are not incented to negotiate. They don't even have to be here, and yet, they're here and appear willing to listen to the cons, right? Maybe. Maybe they're just here to watch the cons squirm.

The cons, clearly, are the ones who are being screwed. They're likely the ones who yelled loudly enough to get the meeting set up in the first place. Cons are usually easy to pick out because they're expressing some degree of pissed-off-ed-ness.

Like our player requirement, both pros and cons must be represented for any progress to occur, otherwise you're just going to talk and talk and talk. You're guaranteed the cons are going to be present because they're the ones screaming and shouting. If you want the meeting to produce something useful, the pros must be represented. The specific pro does not need to be in the building, but they must have a designated proxy, or the cons will bitch, heads will nod, and *nothing* will happen.

Let's take a stab at identifying the pros and cons in our hypothetical meeting.

In the previous example, it's clearly engineering that is being asked to build a product *that does not exist.* They're pissed and they've called this meeting to quantify this frustration. Hello, cons.

As we've already identified our program manager as a pawn, we can only assume that our product manager is the pro. But wait, now you're in this meeting and she sounds like an engineer. "Those goddamned sales folks. What the hell were they thinking? This is the last time, blah, blah, blah . . ." She trails off into everyone's frustrations, and you're back to square one trying to figure out who's who in this mess.

Our product manager suddenly appears to be a con. Does this mean I think you should pull the ripcord and get the hell out? No, your product manager's the pro, all right; she's just bright enough not to let anyone know it. A common tactic of a good pro is to not acknowledge that they're the pro. This means that they don't actually have to take the heat for whatever the conflict is. The real pros, in this example, the sales folks who cut our brilliant impossible deal, aren't in the room, they're out in the field, cutting *more* unachievable deals. The product manager is attempting to fake out the engineers in the room by saying, "Hey, this is a tough problem that *they* have put *us* in. What are *we* going to do?" Brilliant bait-and-switch, no? Don't sweat it. They make less than you.

The stage is set. Our pawns have been filtered out; our sneaky pro is nodding, placating cons with her feigned commiseration; the cons are yelling; and yes, you're still in the meeting.

Believe it or not, the hard part is done.

Meeting Bail Tip #5: Figure Out the Issue

If you've paid attention, you've got a pretty good map of who's who, and where the whos are, so now all you need to do is figure out what the whos want. The pawns don't want anything; they were just happy to be invited. The pros are there to show off their complete and utter ownership of the issue. They'll leave whenever, and the sooner the better.

So the reason you're sitting there is the cons. What do they want? I'm convinced that the majority of meetings on this planet go long and do little because the people sitting around the table simply do not figure out who the hell they're talking to and what they want.

Stop. You've got a meeting in mind, some horrible meeting where the issue is so complex that there's no way the simple identification process I described could apply. Wrong. You're jumping to solve the issue and that's where everyone fucks this up. Who cares about the issue? Do you know who matters in whatever horrible meeting you're sitting in? Did you take the time to identify the people who actually care—the ones who can make a difference? If you didn't, you deserve every useless minute of that meeting.

Meeting Bail Tip #6: Give the Cons What They Want

So yes, the cons *do* want something here. You're going to meet their needs in order to get out the door and their needs are simple—so simple you're going to laugh. The cons need a plan, some assurance that will somehow address whatever the issue is. Doesn't matter if that plan comes from the pawn, the player, the pro, or the con. Someone needs to synthesize everything into constructive next steps and *communicate that to* the cons, and then you're done. You're out the door.

Doesn't need to be a great plan, or an honest plan, or even a complete plan. Cons will not let you out of that meeting until there is the perception of forward progress. If you've scheduled an hour and that hour is up, you're thinking, "Well, that's one way out." Again, incorrect, because the cons are returning to their desks and scheduling a follow-up meeting where the organizational ineptitude is going to continue.

Meeting Bail Tip #7: Figure Out the Issue

You might very well have the requisite players, pros, and cons, but then again, you might have too many. If it's 30 minutes in and you still can't figure out what the issue is, it's time to go: too many issues. Someone who cares more than you needs to distill this chaos down to a coherent statement so the pros and cons can argue about one thing.

Conclusion

Meetings are always going to be inefficient because language is hard. Getting folks in the same group, with the same organizational accent, to talk coherently to each other is hard enough. Meetings give us the opportunity to include other organizations with other accents. This makes the language chaos complete. Now, you don't care. You don't need to know what they're saying because with agenda detection, you can figure out who they are, what they want, get it for them, and get the hell out.

Dissecting the Mandate

In your quiver of management skills, you've got a couple of powerful arrows. There's the annual review, where you take the time to really explain, in detail, what a given employee needs to do to grow. That's huge. That can be life changing. That's a big arrow. How about the layoff? That's when you get asked who stays and who goes. You're going to lose some sleep when you've got to pull the bow back on that one.

Then there's the mandate. The mandate is when you gather the team together and calmly say, "This is the way it is." No Q&A. No collaboration. It's your dictate handed down from on high.

Most folks have learned to despise the mandate.

Rewind a few years back. I'm at my prior gig and we've just hired a new VP I really liked. This guy was sharp, experienced, had a litany of name brand companies on his resume, and he could tell a joke. Sold. Hired.

He was pretty quiet the first few weeks, checking out the landscape, sitting in on various meetings and listening. Engineering was in the process of discussing some drastic new directions for our products, and the incrementalists (ship it soon!) were doing battle with the completionists (ship it when it's done!). Tensions were high. There was finger pointing, yelling . . . all the things you aren't supposed to do in business, but *they feel so good* when you *know you're right.*

The VP's second month arrived and we were still yelling. Then, in one of my Wednesday one-on-ones with the VP, he simply told me, "We are going to do it like this. End of discussion."

Right, so of course I started spewing, "See, we still have to resolve issue #27 and, boy, are the completionists going to be pissed, and have you even thought about risk #12A?" He let me go on for a while, and then he repeated himself: "We are going to do it like this. End of discussion."

I might have nodded, I don't remember.

As predicted, the team freaked. One completionist assured us he was going to quit. He slammed his door. The incrementalists weren't happy either because they didn't like being told what to do. They like to run the show. We had a good solid week of organizational disarray and then we got back to work.

The new VP employed the mandate. He said, "I'm the guy who's telling you the way it is."

There is a fine line with the mandate. It is just as easy to convey, "Shut up and get moving," as it is, "This is the move and I'm the guy you can blame if it's a bad call." Your job as a manager is to move the team forward without hurting morale.

There are three distinct phases to the mandate: Decide, Deliver, and Deliver (Again). Since you are the ultimate decision maker regarding this particular matter, we're going to call this a *local mandate*. These are opposite of *foreign mandates*, which we'll talk about later. Let's begin.

Decide

Your first step is to decide when to employ the mandate and to also understand what the consequences are. There are thousands of little tiny decisions you and your team make during the course of a day. A majority of these decisions come and go and no one is the wiser. Every so often, a big decision comes along. Doesn't matter what the content is, what matters is that some portion of your team is on one side of the decision and another group is on the other side. And they're arguing.

Collaboration, cross-pollination, debating, arguing. Whatever you want to call the process, well, it doesn't always work. Sometimes the team is so polarized that they start confusing the emotion with the decision. Rather than arguing the facts, they begin to argue from their heart and that is when you need to consider the mandate. Rule of thumb: When the debate is no longer productive, it's time to make a decision.

My management style is to allow the team to argue as long as possible. I've got a collaborative management style because I know that the more brains and more time the team spends staring at an idea, the stronger the idea becomes. This means that decision-making in groups that I manage tends to be slower because I'm busy cross-pollinating. Consequently, I'm certain it means our output is higher quality because we've taken the time to consider what the hell we're doing.

Remember that for every person on the team who has a strong opinion regarding the decision, there are probably four other coworkers who just want someone to make a decision so that they can get back to work. We've each been part of the silent majority before. It's the time when you choose to not engage in the heated debate. Maybe because you're doing actual work or perhaps you just don't care. You appreciate your silent status as you see the debate rage in the hallway and realize how much pain, sweat, and tears you saved by staying out of it. When the team is still yapping away two weeks later, you start to wonder when someone is going to shut these people up.

Mandates are the friend of the silent majority. Even if you really annoy the concerned parties, the silent majority will appreciate the peace and quiet once you've delivered your verdict.

Deliver

The purpose of this chapter is not to explain how to make whatever hard decision you need to make regarding the heated topic in your organization. I don't know what the topic is, so you're on your own. I will say that if you don't spend time considering both sides of the issue before you deliver, then your team will know it and your credibility will be suspect. Those on the losing side will wonder why they weren't consulted and then they'll start wandering the halls murmuring that you're either lazy or a tyrant. Ouch.

The goal of the Deliver phase is straightforward. You need to explain to the team that a decision has been made. Sounds easy, right? Well, this is where junior managers blow it. They do a good job of explaining the decision, but they fail convey that this is the decision and further debate is not necessary. A good sign of poor mandate delivery is when the delivery degrades into another debate of the issues. Delivering a mandate takes moxie. The team has got to leave the room knowing the decision has been made. They don't have to like it, they may hate it, but they can't leave the room thinking there's wiggle room in what you decided.

Again, an added benefit of my collaborative management style is that delivering mandates is less controversial because I've already vetted the various flavors of the decision with all the folks who have an opinion. When the mandate lands, it feels less like laying down the law and more like I'm relaying the results of our investigation. I still piss off those who disagree with the decision, but they know they were heard.

Deliver (Again)

Congratulations. You've delivered your first mandate and now you're staring at a room full of heads nodding in the affirmative. Even the folks who have been screwed by your decision are nodding. Well done!

There's more work to do.

All that head-nodding is a big ego boost, but the fact of the matter is that each person walking out of meeting has one of three distinct opinions:

- **Yay:** You are a great motivator. The winners will have this opinion of you and you still you need to deliver (again).

- **Boo:** You are a tyrant. Commonly held by those who've been screwed. You must deliver (again).

- **Yawn:** What took you so damned long? Silent majority here. Don't sweat them.

The Deliver (Again) phase might be better called damage control, but that makes it sound like you screwed up by pushing the team forward and you didn't. Maybe. Delivering (again) is taking the time to individually express your reasoning to the concerned parties—both the winners and the losers. This not only gives you a chance to re-enforce what you mandated, but also gives coworkers the chance to respond in a non-team setting. Expect more venting. In fact, insist on it. If you're sitting with someone who was on the losing side of the decision and they're still nodding their head, *they don't believe the battle is over.* They're sitting there figuring out their next move to erode the mandate. If you fail to get this person to open up, you will be mandating (again) in a few short weeks.

Delivering (again) is not going to quench discontent in your team, but it's going to give everyone involved a chance to speak up, and that should push your management karma toward motivator and away from tyrant.

Foreign Mandates

I've been talking about the ins and outs of local mandates so far. These are situations where you are the decision maker, which gives you access to a wealth of information as well as all of the players. In any decent-sized organization, you are equally likely to be on the receiving end of foreign mandates. This is a mandate that occurs way outside of your sphere of influence. *We have a brand new strategy. Ready. Go.*

Yes, the tables are turned. Mandates might just randomly show up and there isn't a thing you can do about it.

Guess what? The same rules mentioned previously apply, with one exception. Just like your team, you are going to have one of the three opinions (yay, boo, or yawn) regarding the mandate. Regardless of what your opinion is, you must figure out the justification behind the mandate. You might have a yawn opinion about this, but what about the rest of your team? They might hate the mandate, and you are going to look lame when you relay the mandate without a clue as to why the mandate showed up.

Here's the rub—mandate justification often does not travel well through a large organization. Either someone in your management food chain had a yawn reaction to the mandate and didn't bother to gather a justification, or the grapevine has tainted the justification to the point that it no longer makes any sense. Either way, you're going to be delivering news to your team sans reasoning. This blows. I'm certain that companies that exhibit this poor communication structure are the same ones that have reputations for notoriously tyrannical CEOs. Maybe they're not tyrants. Maybe they're surrounded by poor communicators. Or maybe they are tyrants. I can't tell from where I'm sitting.

The good news is that if you ever have to deliver a mandate without the facts to back it up, you're less likely to pull a rookie mistake and land your local mandate without the reasoning … the justification. You're also not going to forget to deliver (again), because you know that each time you stand in front of your team, trying to be a leader, they are watching and they are listening. They want to know if you deserve the title of manager.

Information Starvation

There's someone standing outside your office, and he's not saying a thing.

It's a freakout, but for now he's just standing there. Or maybe he's not. Maybe he's employing the Hover—where he walks by every few minutes. It could be the Long Stare, where he stands outside and just glares. My favorite is the Avalanche, when you look up from your screen and have mere seconds to brace yourself before the tumbling heap of frustration piles into your office.

What you call these freakouts is unimportant. What's essential is that you figure out how you, the manager, could have prevented them. It probably has to do with a lack of information.

Information Conduit

One of your many jobs as manager is information conduit, and the rules are deceptively simple: for each piece of information you see, you must correctly determine who on your team needs that piece of information to do their job.

Easy, right? An e-mail shows up, you read it, and you decide it needs to go to one of your developers. So you forward it. Here's the wrinkle: there's vastly more information than you think; there are more people who need it than you expect; you're going to screw up your assessment of who needs it more often than not; and you've got a lot of other essential crap to do.

First, let's worry about the consequences of poor information management, because that's how I'm going to get your attention.

So, a not-so-average day at the office. There are rumors of layoffs wandering the hallway and the rumors are correct. Now, there's a Long Stare outside your office, and, of course, the first thing you do is invite her in so you can triage Long Stare's issue.

"Why the long stare?"

"The what?"

[Denial.]

"You've been outside my office for two minutes staring at me."

"I have?"

[Wow, total denial.]

"So, what's up?"

"Um, am I going to be fired?"

Now, this is your best developer. She's your rock star. She's the one you throw the vaguest of ideas at and you know she'll turn that hand-waving into a feature, a product. She's done it *five times* and now she's in your office wondering if she's about to be fired.

What happened? How is it possible your single most valuable engineer believes she's so irrelevant that she could be let go?

She's starved for information, and in the absence of information, people will create their own.

Nature Abhors a Vacuum

Think back to your last layoff. What happened? Well, first you heard the rumor that "layoffs are coming," which, as it turns out, wasn't a rumor and was the last factual thing you heard for the next three weeks.

See, the management team was spending those three weeks trying to figure out what was going to happen and who was going to get laid off. But they didn't actually know yet so they weren't saying anything, which was precisely the wrong thing to do.

Everyone else was wondering whether they have a job or not, and in the absence of knowledge, they were making up some pretty crazy shit.

It's the rumor mill, it's the grapevine, and its existence is directly related to how well you, the manager, are communicating.

The creation of information is the act of creating context and foundation when there is none. Call it a rumor or gossip, but what it really is is a reaction to a failure to communicate. When I hear a fantastic piece of gossip, I'm listening for two things. First, what is actually being said, and second, what informational gap in knowledge is being filled by this fantastic fabrication.

Back to the rock star who thinks she's about to be fired. Given that I know there is no chance she's about to be fired, what am I hearing? First, I'm hearing, "I don't know where I stand in the organization." It's not that she actually thinks she's going to be fired—she doesn't understand her value. Second, I'm hearing, "Given that I don't know my value, I'm going to make up a crazy consequence, which isn't actually likely, but boy, will it get someone's attention."

Gossip, rumors, whatever the creation is, it means that someone, somewhere in your organization is asking for help.

Starvation Prevention

You're going to need damage control with the rock star. You're going to need to sit her down and remind her of the five different times she created great products out of your hand-waving. You're going to need to check in multiple times to make sure she knows she's valued, but mostly, you're going to need to figure out how she got starved in the first place.

Well, it started with you not conveying information, we know that, but the question is, why? Here are some common failures.

"Don't worry, I'll remember to pass that on."

Perhaps the biggest loss of essential information is when managers rely on their brains as to-do lists. This is a common mistake made by green managers who haven't figured out their conduit gig yet. They sit in a meeting and hear a to-do they need to pass on to one of their engineers and they think, "Got it. Remind Bob that Phil is going to break the build unless X happens. I can remember that."

If that was the only item on the list, this manager would be in good shape, except he's got four more meetings and ten other to-dos to remember before he sees Bob in the hallway and remembers, "Phil . . . something."

Write it down. Keep a notebook with you all the time and anything that sounds remotely interesting goes in that notebook. This leads us to . . .

"I don't think anyone needs to know that."

Bill was a new manager on my team and he was just happy to be attending the staff meeting. My staff meetings are broken into two parts. Part one is the recital of all the information I've gotten from my boss's staff meeting combined with my thoughts and opinions. Part two is quick status and relevant bits from each of the folks in the team.

There is a lot of redundancy in part one. How are products doing, who has been promoted, what were the latest customer wins. If you listened to it each week, you'd be bored, but I recite the same thing. Every week.

Bill picked up on the boring immediately and stopped taking notes during part one. When I asked him about it, he said, "I don't think my team cares about customer wins for a product they're not responsible for."

"Really? Why don't you ask them?"

The following week Bill was furiously taking notes. His comment: "Yeah, they want to hear it all."

Especially in larger organizations, you need to pay careful attention to maintaining a consistent flow of organization information. It might feel like you're passing on useless information, but the rule of thumb is that you never know what your team is going to care about. I had an engineer who faithfully kept a running diary of who our new customers were, and, after a few months, he knew more about our customer base than most of our sales folks.

I realize it could be a full-time job relaying every piece of information that you're exposed to, and part of your job as a manager is to make judgment calls regarding what gets passed on. My rule of thumb is that if I'm debating whether to pass something on for more than a few seconds, I might not be qualified to decide, so pass it on and see what happens.

"My employees can read my mind."

Maybe you're doing a good job of relaying information. You've got content-rich staff meetings and a steady flow of forwarded e-mails. That's terrific. I'm glad you're passing on all the information, but the question is, "What are your employees hearing?"

The last VP at the startup did a stunning job of forwarding every single e-mail that showed up in his inbox. Every e-mail. It was great to be included in all the VP's communications, but it was a borderline spam situation. What was worse was his cryptic brief additions to the beginning of each e-mail.

"Interesting."

"We should."

"Hah. Told you!"

More often than not, I could dereference his one-word thoughts based on recent conversations, but there were times I had no clue what I was supposed to do with an e-mail.

Simply because an e-mail or thought makes sense or has some interesting context in your head doesn't automatically mean the insight is going to be obvious to anyone else. It's a goal of mine to have a team that is working closely enough together that they share a common mind, but taking the time to give each piece of information that you're passing on a bit of your personal context never hurts. It takes time, but it maintains the quality of the information while preventing a slow mutation into confusion.

The good news is, if you're ever wondering what your team heard or read when you pass on your information, you can ask one of my favorite follow-up questions: "What did you just hear?"

Aggressive Silence

A structured regimen of information dispersion is the first step in keeping the team in touch with the rest of the organization, but you're still going to screw up. Whether it's one of the failures I described previously or a totally different failure, your job is to constantly assess what your team needs, and I've got really good news.

Your team is going to tell you what they need. Whether it's gossip, rumors, staring, pacing, or yelling, your team is always telling you what they need to know. This means your job is not just to be an information conduit; it's also to employ a policy of aggressive silence.

In my staff meetings, I throw in the occasional long pause. Maybe I've just said something controversial and received no pushback. Perhaps I know one person at the table is seething about our most recent discussion. So I wait. I fill the room with silence.

In this uncomfortable quiet, if they're about to say it, they just do. Try it; just shut up and see what your team says when you're saying nothing.

Subtlety, Subterfuge, and Silence

Managers, wannabe managers, and folks who want to understand managers simply need to read *The 48 Laws of Power*, by Robert Greene and Joost Elffers.

I've purposely not done any background research on this book, because my first reaction to this list was profound and I wanted to hold onto that reaction. There's some pretty evil shit documented there as well as some basic truths about what managers are up to on a daily basis. At first I couldn't tell if the guys who wrote this were serious when they write things like: "Keep Others in Suspended Terror: Cultivate an Air of Unpredictability." But after several readings, yeah, I think they're serious.

My problem with this list and how it relates to managers is that so many of the "rules" involve psychological torture of those you're trying to lead, and that strikes me as a good way to further the intense negative knee-jerk reaction regarding managers: "That guy is a power-hungry jerk."

Still.

Part of management is navigating your way through some tricky political jungles. It's about getting folks to comfortably bend in an uncomfortable direction. A good manager is a person who is playing to a strategy and isn't merely stumbling around squashing fires all day.

Management is chess. When you're presented with a problem, you sometimes need to sit back and take a look at the board, figure out the consequences of each of move, and, most importantly, pick a move. In my experience, the move and how you pick it does not involve 48 laws, but only three words: subtlety, subterfuge, and silence.

Subtlety

I've just delivered a painful performance review to an employee and he doesn't get it. Two weeks I spent writing this thing, gathering different perspectives from peer feedback, rereading relevant e-mails from the past year, and rewriting, rewriting, and rewriting. Worst performance review ever. And he's sitting there like everything's dandy.

I'm not about to fire this guy, but given his current trajectory, he's two years from becoming irrelevant. I want to nip this in the bud, but all I'm getting is radio silence.

"Any questions on your review?"

"Nope."

"Are you clear about the areas I want to work with you on?"

"Yup."

Now, the point of a performance review is not the review itself but the conversation that stems from it. It's about constructively conveying information about the performance of the coworker and then chewing on it a bit. You want to see the person processing the information you just presented; you want to see them asking questions.

This guy gave me nothing.

OK, so maybe the performance review wasn't the right place to course correct. Maybe I needed to use a subtler approach. A week later, we were in our one-on-one and I had a list. It had each and every discussion point I had for this gentleman rewritten to support the areas of improvement I called out in the performance review.

The employee in question wasn't comfortable with the strategic broad strokes I'd painted in the review, but when I carefully mapped the review into our tactical day-to-day work, he was listening. By the end of the one-on-one, I'd piled his to-do list so high we were actually back to talking about the performance review because it was that advice that was going to help him get the work done.

Subtlety starts with humility. Exhibiting your power and knowledge as a manager isn't always the best method of communicating. Sometimes your approach needs to start small, humble, and in a place in which you admit that you don't have all the answers. I know it feels great to make that snap decision and show the team you're the guy in charge, but was it the right decision or was it ego?

Subtlety finishes with elegance. It's not just successfully solving whatever hard problem you're staring at, it's that you solve it in an ingenious, novel way that builds and refines your management aptitude.

Subterfuge

Say it with me: "sub-ter-fyooooooooj." We should make shirts; it's that fun to say. But what does it mean? *Subterfuge* means "intrigue, deviousness, deceit, deception, dishonesty, cheating, duplicity, guile, cunning, craftiness, chicanery, pretense, fraud, fraudulence." Those synonyms cover a lot of territory, so let's refine it for the sake of this piece.

Relative to management, subterfuge does not mean "deceit, dishonesty, cheating, fraud, or fraudulence." It's everything else. I'll explain.

We were at a crossroads at the startup. Too much to do, two vastly different directions in which the team wanted to head. There were the infrastructure folks who wanted to spend three months replacing the application server, and then there were the interaction folks who wanted to improve the usability of the application. The VP listened to both sides and then he decided, "Infrastructure! Long-term scalability!"

The interaction folks were pissed. Their response: "Who cares about long-term scalability if no one wants to use the product?" Oh yeah—I was also the manager of the interaction folks and I agreed with them, but I had to throw my engineers on the infrastructure work because we didn't have the capacity. I was talking with existing customers and they weren't pulling their hair out because the application was sluggish, but rather because it was an interaction nightmare. They were spending most of their time trying to figure the damned thing out.

Grrrrrrrrr.

The lead interaction designer, an engineer, and I sat in a conference room fuming in silence when it popped into my head: "Hey, people are visual creatures. How long would it take to throw together a prototype that shows off what we were thinking?"

My engineer: "A week!" Good time to point out how enthusiasm reduces all engineering estimates by a third. My engineer continued, "But I'll need Frank."

Hmmmmm.

"Here's what we're going to do. I want you and Frank to work on this after 5 p.m., after we're done with our infrastructure work, and I want you to keep this on the down low. If, after a week, we like what we see, we're going public."

Herein lies the hard part of subterfuge. Depending on where you were standing, my plan could have been viewed in any number of ways. The other engineering director would have called it "disobeying a direct order," whereas my boss, who got wind of the effort two days in, called it a "skunk works project" and told us to proceed. Phew.

Our skunk works took us three weeks, not one, but when we showed off our work, the VP of engineering and VP of marketing were impressed and wanted to see us finish the work. Rather than sacrificing the infrastructure effort, they gave me two requisitions so I could hire a team to do the job right.

Subterfuge is a risk. The infrastructure director never quite trusted me after that even though I still went out of my way to keep him in the loop after we went public with our work.

The use of subterfuge for good means keeping the intent honest. If you're going commando to do what you believe is right, it doesn't mean someone isn't going to be pissed, but it should allow you to sleep at night.

Silence

Your most annoying employee is sitting across the table and he's on a roll. This guy's personality totally and completely clashes with yours and he's in his second hour of rambling about something you don't understand. My advice is simple:

Shut up and listen.

I mean it.

Now, if you know what he's trying to get at and you've continued to let him blather, OK, you can start talking and directing him elsewhere, but if he's valiantly trying to get to the point, you must shut up and listen. Your silence is giving him a chance to get something out.

I'm not a fan of public speaking. I'm not comfortable with the all-hands meeting where I'm laying out the next six months of work. My natural state is one of introspection where I'm soaking in the world, and the skill has taken me far because so many folks out there just can't shut up. While all this talking is going on, I sit quietly and nod while learning what all these yammering people are about and carefully file it away for future reference.

Managers lead, and a lot of managers translate that into "managers lead by talking." Combined with the tendency of employees to not say no to these managers, you can see why a lot of us have turned into professional windbags. We think we're guiding you by filling the air with our thoughts. There's a time and place for that, but in order to fill the air with something relevant, you've got to gather and process data.

In silence, you can assess.

My favorite use of silence is in a huge cross-functional meeting with a group I've never worked with before where I have no role other than listener. It's a table full of people I don't know and I feel like I'm sitting at the most profitable poker table ever because everyone tells you what they got.

Remember this: in most businesses, everyone's basic agenda is visible after they've talked for about 30 seconds. I'm not talking about who they are as a person; I'm talking about figuring out what they have and what they need. In poker, you keep this information hidden as best you can because your money is on the line. In business, everyone throws their hand on the table, stands up, points at their hand, and says, "People, I'm one card away from the nut flush. Who's going to give the queen of hearts?"

Asking for what you need is a good strategy in business; it's called collaborating. Each time I hear "I need," I learn another bit about those I work with and, in time, I can construct a better picture of how to interact with my coworkers. Still, I'm also wondering about that guy in the corner who isn't saying a thing. His eyes are darting around the room just like mine and I'm curious . . . what is he getting out of his silence?

Business Isn't War

The *48 Laws of Power* are the real deal, but they are focused on war, not business. Go buy the book if you want to know more, but read wisely. With each successful year on the job, I find myself adjusting to the ever-increasing complexity with which my peers play the chess game of management. Twenty years in, I can safely say there is one law—not in the book by Greene and Elffers—that is true: if you're only interested in building power, you're going to lose.

Managementese

One of my teams is facing a big, fat decision regarding future product direction, and the process has split the team in half: the Yes We Shoulds and the No Way in Hells. The manager of the team is facing a rebellion and spending much of his time trying to drive the team toward a decision.

I walked by his office, and he was talking with one of the No Way in Hells, trying to influence her over to the other side of the fence. I overheard a snippet of his conversation: "I think it's a key decision and I'm asking you to think outside of the box . . ."

I cringed.

Management speak.

Walking back to my office, I thought about my negative reaction to the term "outside of the box." What does that actually mean? Well, it means something like "Don't restrict your thinking to conventional avenues," but that's not what your team hears when you say it. They hear, "Hi, I'm a manager, and as a manager I'm telling you that you should be creative without actually telling you how to be creative."

No, that's not right. What they hear is, "Hi, I'm a manager and I've stopped thinking and I'm using throwaway phrases that obscure what I mean."

And managers wonder why no one trusts them.

As I sat in my office, a project manager came in for a one-on-one. With the observation fresh in my mind, I attempted to monitor my usage of managementese during our half-hour meeting. Here are my offenses:

"Can you *circle back* with her . . ."

"I want to *double-click* on that and . . ."

"These are the *action items* . . ."

What I learned: I've turned into a total dorkwad manager and can no longer communicate like a normal human being.

Management Metaphors

One of my favorite books on software construction is Steve McConnell's *Code Complete*. In the second chapter, McConnell describes the richness of language around computer science: "Computer Science has some of the most colorful language of any field. In what other field can you walk into a sterile room, carefully controlled at 68 degrees Fahrenheit and find viruses, Trojan horses, worms, bugs, bombs, crashes, flames, twisted sex changers, and fatal errors?"

He continues: "A software metaphor is more like a searchlight than a road map. It doesn't tell you where to find the answer; it tells you how to look for it."

I'd always assumed that management metaphors fell into the same bucket, and they do, but if your team doesn't know what you're talking about, you might as well be speaking in code.

Managementese is a language that is learned, evolved, and spoken by managers. For communication between managers, it's a convenient, high-bandwidth means of conveying information. Chances are, when you say "double-click" to a fellow manager, they understand that you are suggesting that they should pay attention to whatever it is you're doing.

There are unique spheres of language that exist in each part of the corporate organizational chart. Inside of each sphere is the language that is unique to the job. Engineers have one, marketing has another, and sales has yet another. In each of these groups, there are the managers who must speak their native language, as well as be able to translate between spheres in order to get the job done. I believe this is a legitimate reason for managementese. It's the cross-functional language of the company. Without it, the different parts of the organization aren't going to be able to communicate with each other.

Remember, managers are hubs of communication. (See Chapter 11.) The better they communicate across these sphere boundaries, the more people they can communicate with, and the more data they have. This consequently leads to better decisionmaking. Ultimately, stronger communicators make more informed decisions, and hopefully they are more successful because they waste less time wondering what to do.

Still, when you say "double-click" to an employee, they do know what you're talking about, but they also know that you've just self-identified as a manager. Why didn't you just say what you actually meant? My first guess is that you're in a hurry, but that's not what your team is hearing.

Language of the Lazy

In high tech, we're all in an incredible fucking hurry. We're working against an unreasonable deadline and we're over-committed on features. As a manager, your job is that of a bullshit umbrella. You need to decide what crap your team needs to deal with and what crap can be ignored. That means that you need to rapidly acquire information from a variety of people. In that rush, managementese can help you talk with your fellow managers to figure out what the hell is going on, but you're only half done. You still need to communicate to your team.

This can be tiresome because you, of all people, are absolutely sure what you're saying. This is why you might be tempted to use the readily accessible management metaphor-laced language that you're familiar with. Don't.

The main issue folks have with managementese is not that they don't understand what is being said; their issue is that they don't trust it. Think of the worst all-hands meeting you've ever been at and tell me why you hated it.

"Management is out of touch with what we're doing."

"They're all talk and no action."

"He's talking in generalities and what I want is specifics."

"He sure sounds like he believes what he's saying, but I don't know what he's saying."

Managers in a hurry need to remember that managementese puts you a few key metaphors away from sounding like a used-car salesman. Talking fast with confidence might make you feel like you're getting something done, but if the people you are talking to don't trust you, they're never going to understand what you're saying.

The "Bottom Line"

My advice is simple: when you're talking to individuals, talk to them using the familiar language of a friend. Dispose of the management hat and have a conversation in a common language. Ditch the managementese. This takes practice because it's a major context switch for you, but your goal is to have a conversation, and for that to happen, both people sitting at the table need to trust and understand what is being said.

Ninety-five percent of the people in a big company simply have no clue what corporate machinations are going down and how they might be affected and whether or not they'll be working in the next six months. How you will be judged as a manager by your team is based on how you communicate with them. That's not just about taking the time to have that quarterly all-hands, it's also understanding what they need to hear and being able to say it in a way they'll understand.

Fred Hates the Off-Site

The world of management has a set of power words that it has appropriated as a means of giving itself a sense of identity. This list is endless and entertaining. When these words are spoken, they are said in such a way that you are meant to wonder in awe, "What does that mean?" but you don't ask for fear of looking like an idiot.

Today's word: *off-site*. An off-site is a . . . meeting. There are some specific characteristics to an off-site, but it's really just a meeting with a group of people that likely lives up to its name in that it's elsewhere—it's off-site.

Now that you understand what it is, let's understand why you might hate it.

Why I Get in Fred's Face

The reason an off-site exists is simple: you, the leader of the people, need certain essential work to occur that cannot easily occur now under normal conditions within the building. It's a little sad. When it was only 20 of you, each of the three different off-sites I'm about to describe would just happen . . . organically. Fred would stand up in the middle of the office and say, "OK, we need a new UI framework. I'm going to do it, and anyone who wants to get in my face needs to do it now."

So you got in Fred's face. You argued. You debated. Fez and Phil jumped in, and in 17 very important minutes, you fundamentally changed the UI architecture of the product.

At an organizational size that varies for every team, natural cross-pollination and communication activities that used to happen organically, that allowed for cultural and strategic work to get done, and that allowed for big decisions to be made, can no longer occur. The team can no longer look around the room and get a sense for how everyone is doing because there are too many everyones.

Zeitgeist has become diluted. Random hallway error correction doesn't happen, because the right folks aren't bumping into each other. It's sad, especially for the folks who vividly remember standing up and getting in Fred's face. You need to recreate the space and place where a team can bond, a strategy can be devised, or you can begin an epic journey.

Who We Are, What We Need, and Our Epic Journey

The reason you invoke the off-site is going to vary from group to group. The following are three specific scenarios where I believe you need to employ the off-site, but there are more.

We need to understand who we are

If you're familiar with my writing, you'll know I don't think you really know what the hell is going on in a team for 90 days. You have moments of comforting clarity during the first three months, but you don't really know all the moving parts until a chunk of time has passed. Now, multiply that early confusion by every single person who has been hired in the last nine months.

During times of rapid growth, team members don't necessarily take the time to stop and get to know each other, because they arrive, and the first thing they notice is, "Whoa. Everyone is in a big fucking hurry, so I must hurry as well." Their normal instincts regarding getting to know those around them are buried in their goal of being recognized as a person who is also in a hurry.

You need an off-site not to solve a strategic product problem, but to give the team members time away from their hurry to get to know each other. Socialization will happen via each of the off-sites I'm about to describe, but the need for a team to understand itself is a cause worthy of an off-site all by itself.

We need a new direction and/or fewer disasters

Something significant is broken. Either disasters are occurring and the normal processes of detection and correction aren't working, or everything appears to be working but we're not achieving success—for whatever *success* means at that stage of the company. In either case, the status quo represents a legitimate threat to the company.

The purpose of this off-site is deep brainstorming. The group is tasked with discovering and refining ideas, proposing experiments to test these ideas, and finally stepping up to run with these ideas back at the ranch.

We are embarking on an epic journey

Nothing's broken; it's just time to start something. This last off-site might also be called a kickoff meeting. You generally know what you want to do and when you want to do it, but you need all the leaders responsible for making it happen to be in agreement about where you're headed and why.

This off-site is an alignment meeting. Strategy can be discovered as part of this meeting, but that isn't the primary goal. You are collectively pointing folks in the correct direction (*this is where we're headed*) and defining the urgency (*and this is why we're headed there*).

A Meeting with Certain Characteristics

While an off-site is just a long meeting, it is a meeting with certain characteristics that differ from your average daily meeting. I'll explain each, and I'm going to bring Fred along because Fred has no problem telling us exactly what he hates.

By definition, you can't invite everyone

Remember, the reason you need an off-site in the first place is that the team has grown to a size where they are consumed by hopefully essential tactics. They don't have time to step back and think about it later, because from the moment they walk in the door, there are meetings, phone calls, e-mails, and interviews that simply must happen. Everyone is consumed in the work. Yes, the individual has a free hour here and there to take a deep breath, but collectively the team doesn't have time to figure out what it is thinking or why it's working so hard.

Depending on the goal of your off-site, you need to pick the people who are both capable and willing to solve the hard problem sitting in front of you. If you're trying to understand who you are, you invite every person that you want to know. If you want fewer disasters, you invite both the folks creating them and those with the ability to fix them. You need to be able to look around the room and think, "These are the people who will solve the problem."

Fred hates it. He says, "Man, why are we being exclusive? I want everyone to weigh in on the important decisions that affect the company. We're all shareholders and we should all get a vote."

There's a name for a meeting where everyone is invited, Fred. It's called an all-hands, and if the all-hands isn't part of your regular company meeting regimen, I can see why you're pissed. However, your all-hands is 120 people, and my question is, When is the last time you saw 120 people efficiently propose, debate, and then make a decision? An off-site is not an opportunity to ignore opinion; an off-site is a chance to select a group of folks who are going to best represent the company on whatever huge problem we're solving. Yes, the selection process is hard.

Everyone presents, or at least speaks

Once you've got an initial list of folks, ask yourself this: What appropriate presentation would I ask each invitee to do? My rule of thumb is that each person at the off-site has a deliverable, and that usually means that they need to step up and present. This exercise teaches me two things. First, if I can't think of something I'd want this presenter to talk about given the problem at hand, then why are they invited? Second, I start to see duplication. *Well, Sarah and Frank are both great about talking about our lack of design process. Do I really need them both?*

This isn't a hard-and-fast rule. There are many times you need to invite folks simply because you know they'll speak up randomly and brilliantly. However, as you're building your off-site, this step illuminates both your agenda and your audience.

Fred doesn't really hate this, because he likes the democratic and flat feel it gives to the affair. Thanks Fred.

It's not in your usual building

The other word frequently associated with off-sites is *boondoggle*. When you learn that the senior leadership team is spending the weekend in Vail, I can assure you, yes, that is a boondoggle. I'm certain there is a clear business justification that explains why the company needs to fly seven executives to Vail in the middle of fall, but I'm also certain they could do the same work at a lower altitude.

Off-sites don't need to be swank, but they do need a sense of elsewhere. They need to be far from the tactical distractions of the office because people need a new view. One of your goals for an off-site is to create grounds where people feel comfortable speaking heresy. If whatever problem sitting in front of you could have been solved via the day-to-day, it would have been solved. Drastic measures call for creative thinking, and now that you've gathered these bright people together, you want them to feel comfortable saying whatever compelling ideas cross their minds. Speaking heresy is easier when you aren't surrounded by visual reminders of obvious constraints.

Fred hates it. "Do you know how much this is costing us? We could do exactly the same thing in the seventh-floor boardroom."

Yes, we could, Fred, but within two hours here's how it would play out: Someone is going to figure out we're hiding out in the boardroom, and they're going to find something that appears to be earth-shatteringly important that will pull one of us out of the room. Folks will return slowly from breaks and sometimes won't return at all. You are paying a premium to make sure everyone in the room can focus, but if you have an off-site—worthy topic, it's a small price to pay for this group's attention.

There's someone responsible for flow as well as action

With the correct group in the room, getting a healthy conversation started on the problem isn't hard. In fact, once the group gets started, the issue will be figuring out how to get them to stop. To manage this, there are two roles you need to designate before the festivities begin: a Master of Ceremonies and a Taker of Notes, and they are usually not the same person.

The Master of Ceremonies is the person responsible for not just moving the day along, but also knowing when to stop and pivot. Again, getting this particular group into a healthy conversation shouldn't be hard, but don't confuse a healthy conversation with progress. A deeply engrossing conversation is a great thing and a rich environment for finding the core of a great idea, but there are many conversations to be had, and this is just one. A good Master of Ceremonies knows when an idea has been explored as best it can and it's time to move on.

The Taker of Notes reads like an administrative job, but it's the most important gig in the room. Once an off-site really gets going, once the team really engages, it's all going to sound like great ideas. The Taker of Notes is tasked with not only capturing the bright ideas, but the right ideas. After years of off-sites, my observation is that you only find three new ideas that you act upon. These can be huge company-changing ideas, but there are only going to be three, and it's the immense burden of the Taker of Notes to not only find them, but assign them to the people who can and will drive them forward.

Fred hates it. "They're messing with the flow, man. Why can't we just have a conversation? A debate? Why are we on the clock?"

Fred, I understand that you hate process. You equate the appearance of process with a decrease in free will. You believe that process is slowly going to sap this company of the creative ninja spirit that got us from 12 to 120 people, and you're right. Blindly landing process without considering the culture it needs to support it is a recipe for disaster. However, believing that the loosey-goosey, make-it-up-as-we-go rebel spirit that got us to 120 is going to take us to 2,000 is absurd.

I believe that each time your company doubles in size, it needs to reinvent how it communicates, and each subsequent transformation is increasingly radical and foreign. *Fred, if we're going to grow, we need to constantly reinvent ourselves.*

No personality tests, no trust falls, and no outsiders

There are a couple of traditional moves that well-intentioned folks who have attended off-sites elsewhere are going to suggest, but that I want you to avoid.

Avoid personality tests. If you're working the team-bonding off-site, personality tests are going to be tempting. The idea of starting the off-site with perspective-altering personality tests feels . . . right. I want them to better understand each other, so have them answer a bunch of questions, and we'll explain ourselves to each other and—*wham!*—understanding. Personality tests in their endless variety do exactly that. They tell you which well-defined bucket you comfortably belong in and explain to others your bucket's intricacies. These buckets become social tent poles of the off-site, and suddenly everyone erroneously believes they've figured each other out. And while, yes, they now have convenient labels for each other, they haven't really figured each other out—they've cheated. You've bypassed the learning process via a set of clever labels.

If you want to understand someone, my advice is to sit next to them and solve a very hard problem together. You will learn who they are by watching how they think. Similarly . . .

Avoid trust falls. Another traditional off-site move is using staged games or activities to get folks socially and mentally limber. These are endless and not entirely useless. Just as being in a different place gives the team a sense of elsewhere, your initial content needs to get them thinking in unfamiliar ways. As with personality tests, my preference is that the learning we need to do be done in support of working on the problem. If you can find a goofball trust-fall-like exercise that is going to get us closer to figuring out how to have fewer disasters, I'm a fan. If you're putting the team through an uncomfortable and irrelevant social or strategic exercise because you're attempting to build trust, why not make it relevant? It builds trust faster and you get actual work done. Lastly . . .

Avoid outsiders. The last traditional move to avoid is the importation of outsiders. Facilitators, mediators—whatever. The justification for these external parties from the folks building the off-site will be, "I want to participate," or, more deviously, "Someone has to manage the flow and the action." An external facilitator gives a professional air, and they will move things along at a comfortable pace. However, while they would never admit this, they couldn't give a shit whether you solve your problem or not. It's not that they're callous people; it's that they're *other*. They don't know the culture, the problem at hand, the politics, or the personalities. They're simply not qualified to participate beyond holding a stopwatch. You need someone running the show who has skin in the game.

Fred, not surprisingly, is actually cool with all of this, too. Thanks again, Fred.

They need to sleep on it

There's a moment I like each person to have as part of an off-site, and I call it the bright-and-shiny inflection point. At some point after a compelling talk or brainstorming session, they start to believe. They finally let go of all the tactical things they need to do and allow their brains to jump into the creative soup that the organizers have been vigorously stirring. They see beyond the week and begin to see the next year. They have epiphanies and they start to see the beginnings of solutions to complex problems that have been nagging them for months.

How do you get them there? You've go to get them soaking in it, and that takes time. An off-site must be at least two days long. You need one evening where everyone gets away from what is hopefully a high-bandwidth conversation regarding whatever it is that ails the company, and gets a chance to process this conversation in the back of their heads. When they walk into the unfamiliar location the next morning, whether they've mentally made progress or not, the big huge problem is still sitting there on the whiteboard waiting to be attacked.

Fred hates it. "Since when do we need to spend two days solving this one problem? This company was founded by two guys high on Diet Coke at the Creamery. We had a prototype in a week, and that prototype was live the week after."

Fred, the curse of success is that we have to move slower, and it's a confusing curse. See, we've been successful, and the result of that success is that we're able to hire more people to do the seemingly impossible amount of work our success has created. But each person we add to do more work strategically slows us down. Each additional person levies a communication tax, and unless we figure out how to constantly improve our communication, we're just going to get slower. That's why we're here; even if perfect solutions came to us during caffeinated highs, we'd still need to vet them with the many bright people we've hired to help us grow.

What Fred Really Hates

The morning that Fred arrives at the off-site, which is at some nearby location. After a delightful breakfast, Fred and the rest of the off-site team gather in a room where someone important stands up at the front of the room and starts talking. As the morning's coffee kicks in, Fred's initial knee-jerk reaction to this talking is, "You know folks, I have essential stuff to do, and this yap-yap-yapping isn't helping me get this stuff done." Fred folds his arms, clenches his jaw, and resigns himself to simply waiting until it's over so he can get back to important work.

At some point during the first day, Fred silently has his bright-and-shiny inflection moment. He turns off his phone and furiously starts scribbling down ideas. That night at the off-site dinner, the conversation is about work, but it isn't about the shit he's been slogging through daily; it's about the strategic work he could do to make that shit go away—forever.

And then it's over. Fred returns to the office and he's pumped and ready to start changing the world, but the moment he walks in the door, everything he hasn't done is staring him in the face. As he starts rebuilding his daily work context, he realizes, "Not only do I have a lot to do, but now I'm behind." The bright-and-shininess of the off-site he's retained fades quickly.

A week passes and now he's angry. He's angry because now that he's caught up, he's never going to get ahead because no one is making any time for him to apply all of his bright-and-shiny epiphanies. In fact, after a week, nothing from the two-day off-site has survived except Fred's lasting opinion: "Well, that was a waste of our time."

The successful off-site is one that maps the discoveries of the off-site to the reality of the work. Bright-and-shiny inflection points are full of energy, but unless that energy is carefully channeled back into the building and immediately acted upon, all an off-site represents is a frustrating opportunity to dream, but not to act.

A Different Kind of DNA

Flat. It's an organizational meme in rapidly growing teams in Silicon Valley, and it contains a couple of noble ideas. Simply put, a flat organization is one with as little hierarchy as possible to encourage the individual voice. What's not to love?

The first challenge to the flat organizational mantra is the inevitable arrival of leads or managers tasked with organizing different aspects of the team. The flat religion's answer to this development is rebranding of the role: the lead or manager is no different from the individual. It's not a promotion, there is no raise; it's just a different gig. There is no difference between those responsible for building the product and those responsible for building the people.

I love this. I love this because it's the beginning of solving a core career problem in teams of engineers: How do we grow? As I wrote in my book *Being Geek* (O'Reilly, 2010), the curse of Silicon Valley is that great engineers are often promoted to leadership for their hard work. While many succeed in this role, an equal part fails because the skills required to lead are vastly different than the ones required to be an engineer. The curse is that we're often placing our most valuable engineers in a role where they're predisposed to fail.

Think of it like this: there's a large population of immensely talented engineers that should not be leaders. There is no amount of training that would make up for the talent we'd extinguish by teaching them how to write annual reviews.

But everyone wants to grow.

Unfortunately, in many companies the only perceived growth path is via management. Yes, there are job grades and cleverly phrased job descriptions that confusingly define the various states of engineering experience and growth, but these are a joke. These are a distraction packaged as a solution to the fact that we don't have a good idea how to systematically grow engineers outside the traditional management hierarchy.

No Ticker-Tape Parade

A solution begins with rebranding, by introducing the idea that managers and engineers are hierarchically no different. Keep the pay the same; don't throw a ticker-tape parade when a new leader is minted. They are peers. I support this religion because a flat organization is one where power, accountability, and responsibility are equally distributed. But I do not yet understand how this idea scales.

Even with leads and managers who have the best of intentions, the moment they become responsible for folks—the moment everyone realizes they (figuratively) sign the checks—the relationship changes. I can't yell at you because you sign the checks. This core change of perception isn't just based on compensation, it's based on a change of ownership and responsibility, and it's the beginning of all sorts of potential cultural turmoil that's worthy of an entire additional chapter.

We need leads and managers as a means of scaling responsibility and communication, but we need to dispel the idea that their roles are also the exclusive owners of decision-making.

As a solution, I offer the *DNA meeting*.

Five Kinds of Win

DNA stands for *design 'n' architecture*. At its core, DNA is just a meeting. It's a collection of bright engineers from across the team or the company sitting in a room tasked with a specific purpose. As the name *DNA* suggests, these engineers are responsible for deep analysis regarding decisions and directions core to the product. You probably already informally hold this type of meeting when faced with a big technical or design challenge. You gather together an informed set of eyeballs to vet the challenge. DNA makes the informal formal and it has five kinds of win:

1. *It shines a light brightly.* While the more eyeballs you get on any decision the better, the DNA meeting is scheduled when something technical is going down. Something big. Something of magnitude. It's not a bet-the-company decision, but it might be a bet-the-group—or the division—decision. If we fail at this, the consequences are extreme. This is why when a DNA meeting is going down, you ...

2. *Bring respectable firepower.* I'll talk more about the construction of the DNA team in a bit, but I want you to think of the three best engineers around you. I'm not talking just about those with ability, but also the folks who go out of their way to teach—the engineers who

not only know what they're talking about, but have the ability to explain their thinking. They shine a bright light on the idea by making the complex painfully obvious. The DNA team is not only the set of engineers who are the best candidates to vet the big idea, but those who have ability to talk about how to make it better, can constructively criticize, and are distinctly drama- and politics-free.

3. *It has teeth.* You can gather all the talented engineers you want, but what will make the meeting useful and memorable are two threats. First, the rule for all attendees in a DNA meeting is, *If you don't contribute, you won't be invited back.* A DNA meeting is not a regular meeting; it is an active and healthy debate about a bet big enough that we're gathering our bright minds to make sure we don't fuck it up. If you're in the room, it's because we believe you have something to add, and if you don't, we'll correct our misperception.

   Second, it needs to be culturally understood that if you don't bring your A game to the DNA meeting, the team is authorized to mentally kick the shit out of you. The end result of a healthy DNA meeting will have members of the receiving team sitting with their heads squarely planted on their desks, whispering, "Oh shit, I can't believe we didn't think of that."

   The DNA meeting is not cruel. It is a living, breathing example of a team of engineers who put the value of design and technical excellence above all else. They don't rule by mandate; they influence by being great at what they do. At a prior gig, the threat of a DNA meeting pushed us to prepare in extraordinary ways. Our goal was to predict every single question that might be asked and have every answer in our back pocket. Winning in the meeting was silence.

4. *DNA has absolutely nothing to do with management (and everything to do with leadership).* Pure managers are not considered for the team, because DNA is about cultivating technical leadership. A DNA meeting is a staff meeting of the influential engineers who don't want direct reports, but want to lead. They want to make decisions critical to the technology. If managers have anything to do with DNA, the meeting will become about the managers, not the technical leaders.

5. *DNA is achievable and aspirational.* Inclusion on the DNA team doesn't come from a popularity contest. It is the result of a well-defined journey that any interested engineer can embark upon. At the prior gig, you needed a combination of tenure and experience, shipped products, and visible technical contributions to the team. Some measures will be subjective, but the end result is that when someone arrives on the DNA team, everyone will agree that they belong there. It's not a club; it's an honor. DNA recognizes that the team members we want are examples of folks who live and breathe technical experience, who are selfless, and who contribute exceptional value to the company. DNA exists as an acknowledgment that a team is led not just by the folks who build the people, but also by people who build the product.

Flat Is a State of Mind

I didn't come up with the idea of DNA. It was a former boss at Apple who suggested the idea long before I arrived on the team. Since then I've adapted the idea twice, and each adaption has yielded different results. In the current gig, we split DNA into different tracks: UX DNA and system DNA.

You build a DNA meeting to suit your culture. You build a DNA meeting so your technical leaders have a platform where their ideas are heard, debated, and acted on. You build a DNA meeting to remind the team that all forms of leadership matter.

An Engineering Mindset

There's a very short list of new manager "must-dos" in the Rands Management Rule Book. The brevity of this list comes from the fact that a must is an absolute and, when it comes to people, there are very few absolutes. A clever way to manage one person is a disaster when applied to another. This makes the first item on the management must-do list:

Stay flexible.

Believing you've seen it all is a bad idea. Staying flexible is the only stance to adopt when constant change is the only constant.

Paradoxically, the second item on the list is surprisingly inflexible and it's a personal favorite of mine because I believe it helps set the stage for management growth. It reads:

Stop coding.

The theory is this: if you want to be a manager, you must learn to trust those who work for you to take care of the job of coding. This advice can be hard to digest, especially for new managers. It's likely that one of the reasons they became managers is due to their productive developers, and their first reaction when things go to crap is to revert to the skills that built up their confidence. That's writing code.

When I see a new manager fall back to coding, I tell the manager, "I know you can code. The question is, can you manage? You're no longer responsible only for yourself—you're responsible for the team, and I want to see you figure out how to get the team to solve this problem without you coding. Your job is to figure out how to get yourself to scale. I want lots of you, not just one."

Good advice, huh? Scale, management, and responsibility. Very buzzword-compliant. Too bad I'm wrong.

Wrong?

Yup. Wrong. Not totally, but enough that I might need to make some calls to past coworkers and apologize. "That 'stop coding' pitch of mine? Wrong. Yeah. Start programming again. Start with Python or Ruby. Yeah. I mean it. Your career depends on it."

When I began my career as a developer at Borland, I was part of the Paradox for Windows team, and this was a big one. Just on the application development team we had 13 developers. If you included the heads from the various other teams who provided essential technology like the core database engine, graphing engine, and core application services, you're talking 50 engineers directly contributing to the product.

No team that I've been on since then has even been close in terms of size. In fact, with each passing year, the size of the engineering teams contributing to my products has steadily shrunk. What's going on? Are we getting collectively smarter as developers? Nope, we're just distributing the load.

What have we, as developers, been doing for the past 20 years? Well, we've been writing a crap load of code. Piles of it. So much of it that we decided that maybe it was a good idea to make it easy to share by open sourcing it. Thankfully the Internet showed up, which made this sharing trivial. If you're a developer, try this right now. Go search Google or Github for your name and find some code you forgot about that everyone can see. Scary, huh? Didn't think your code lived forever? It does.

Code lives forever. Good code not only lives, it grows as those who value it make sure that it doesn't become stale. It's this pile of high-value, well-maintained code that is helping shrink the average size of the engineering team because it's allowing us to focus less on writing new code and more on integrating existing code to get the job done with fewer people and in less time.

There's a depressing line of reasoning here, the idea that we're all just a bunch of integration automatons using duct tape to connect different preexisting moving parts to create slightly different versions of the same thing. It's this train of thought that has a lot of senior management teams excited about outsourcing. "Anyone who can use Google and has some duct tape can do this, so why are we paying big bucks for our local automatons?"

We're paying these management types some pretty big bucks to think this crap up. Still, it brings up my final point that there are eager, bright developers all over the planet and they're eager and bright even though they haven't spent a moment in an accredited university. Oh yeah, and there lots more of them coming.

I'm not suggesting that you should be worried about your job because some bright fellow overseas is gunning for you, I'm suggesting that you should be worried about your job because the evolution of how software development occurs might be moving faster than you are. You've been working for ten years in your job, five years as a manager, and you're thinking, "I know how to develop software." And you do. For now.

Remove Yourself from the Code, But . . .

If you follow my original advice and remove yourself from the code, then you are removing yourself from the act of creation. This act is why I don't really sweat outsourcing. Automatons don't build, they process. While good process can save a lot of money, it's not going to bring anything new to the world.

With smaller teams doing more for less, removing yourself from the code strikes me as a bad career move. Even in a monstrous company laden with policy, process, and politics, you can't forget how to develop software. And how to develop software is changing. Now. Right under your feet, this very second.

You have issues. I understand. Let's hear them.

- *"Rands, I'm on the director track, and if I keep coding, no one is going to think I can scale."*

My first question to you is this: from where you are sitting in your soon-to-be-director chair, do you see software development changing within your company? If the answer is yes, my next question is: how is it changing, and what are you going to do about it? If your answer is no, then you need to move your chair because, I swear to you, software development is changing right this second. How in the world are you going to scale if you're slowly forgetting how software is made?

My advice is not that you start assigning yourself tons of features in the next release. My advice is that you take action so that you stay in touch with how your team builds stuff. You can do this as a director or a VP. More on this in a moment.

- *"Uh, Rands, someone has to referee. Someone has to have the vision. If I code, I'm going to lose perspective on my job."*

You still need to referee, you still need to massage decisions, and you still need to spend 30 minutes every Monday morning walking around the block four times with that engineer who needs to get through his weekly "we're doomed" rant, but you also need maintain an engineering mindset and you do not need to be a full-time coder to do this.

My advice for maintaining an engineering mindset:

1. Use the development environment to build the product. This means you must be familiar with your team's tools, including the build system, version control, and

programming language. This task is going to keep you in touch with the language your team uses to talk about how they get stuff done. And it will also allow you to continue to use your favorite text editor ... which rocks.

2. Be able to draw a detailed architectural diagram describing your product on any whiteboard at any time. I'm not talking about the three-boxes-and-two-arrows versions. You need to know the detailed one, the hard one that isn't pretty and is tricky to explain. This is your map for understanding just about everything about your product. It changes over time and you should be able to understand why those changes are occurring.

3. Own a feature. I'm literally cringing as I write this because it is fraught with danger, but I don't think you can really do #1 or #2 without a feature that is yours. Owning a feature not only forces you to actively participate in the development process, it also switches your context from "manager responsible for everything" to "person who owns a thing." This is a humble, unassuming perspective that will remind you about the importance of small decisions.

    I'm still cringing. Someone is already yelling at me, *"Managers owning features?!?!"* (And I agree.) You are still a manager, so make it a small feature, OK? You've still got a lot to do. If you can't imagine owning a feature, my backup advice is to fix some bugs. You won't get the joy of ownership, but you'll gain an understanding of the construction of the product that you'll never get walking the hallway.

4. Write unit tests. I still do this late in the product cycle when folks are losing their minds. Think of it as your checklist for understanding what your product does. Do it often.

Next concern?

- *"Rands, if I code, I'm going to confuse my team. They're not going to know if I'm a manager or a developer."*

Good.

I mean it. I'm happy you're about to confuse your team by swimming in the developer pool. The simple fact is that well-defined roles in software development are fading. User-interface guys are doing what can only be called development in JavaScript and CSS. Developers are learning more about interaction design.

Everybody is talking to everybody else and they're learning from each other's mistakes, stealing each other's code, and there is no reason that a manager shouldn't be participating in this massive global cross-pollination information cluster-fuck.

Besides, you want to be a part of a team of interchangeable parts. Not only does this make your team more nimble, it presents each person with the opportunity to see the product and the company from a vastly different perspective. How much more are you going to respect quiet Frank the Build Guy when you see the simple elegance of his build scripts?

I'm not wishing confusion and chaos on your team. I'm actually wishing better communication on it. My belief is that if you are building the product and touching the features, you'll be closer to your team. But, more importantly, you'll be closer to how software development is constantly changing in your organization.

Don't Stop Developing

A coworker at Borland once verbally assaulted me for calling her a coder.

"Rands, a coder is mindless machine. A monkey. A coder does nothing relevant except lay down boring lines of useless code. I am a software developer."

She was right and she would've hated my advice for new managers to stop coding. Not because I was suggesting that they were coders, but more that I was proactively telling them to start ignoring one of the most important parts of their jobs: software development.

So, I've revised my advice. If you want to be a good manager, you can stop coding daily, but . . .

Stay flexible, remember what it means to be an engineer, and don't stop developing.

Three Superpowers

Phil's team is adrift.

Phil is smart and meeting-friendly, but he's a crap people manager, and that crappiness is slowly poisoning his team. You know how bad it is because the star of Phil's team finds ways to schedule meetings with you where the story is always the same: "He's smart, but he is genetically incapable of managing people. We're three weeks away from full-on revolt unless something changes."

In the field, Phil's team waits . . . waits until whatever impending disaster has fully arrived before they grudgingly say, "Well, OK, huh, we should probably handle that . . . now?"

Frustratingly and confusingly, one-to-ones with Phil feel like progress. He says all the right things. He accepts responsibilities for failures and articulates compelling next steps that he assures you will improve the situation. But there is a wide strategic gap between those meetings and Phil's daily management judgment. The actions do not match the words, and each Monday morning arrives with the realization that *Phil still isn't getting things done, the stars on his team are about to quit, and I have no idea what to do.*

You need a new superpower.

Three Superpowers

You have a natural management state. This is the default state that is the foundation of how you make your decisions, the tone with which you run your meetings, and the personality you wear as you talk in the hallway. The state has served you well; you're comfortable with it because it is you.

Unfortunately, this natural state is the source of your Phil confusion. Your natural state is blinding you to the obvious course of action. Your instincts are wrong. You need to be someone you are not to radically change your perspective.

Here are three personalities, each with its own perspective, and, more importantly, its own superpower:

The Machine has the Debate

The Machine: Our classic mechanic.[1] Her mantra is, "Without a plan, there is no hope." She's convinced that the whole world is measurable. She follows the process because only by strict adherence to the process can we truly generate a meaningful measurement to clearly understand whether we are winning. The Machine's understanding of the process and the necessity of it are unparalleled. The Machine loves to debate; she loves to consider all options, but when she's decided, it's over. There's no changing her mind.

When the Machine wants something done, she uses the Debate. The Debate starts with data. *Each of you. Please explain to me in excruciating detail the last ten incidents of Phil being an incapable people manager, and understand that I will ask follow-on questions until our understanding is complete.*

The Debate continues with hypotheses. *Synthesizing our cornucopia of data, I put forth the following hypothesis, entitled "Three things we shall do to improve the blight of Phil." I expect everyone involved to challenge these hypotheses. But be warned, arguments based on feeling rather than fact will be terminated.*

If a hypothesis is successfully defended, it becomes law, and the Debate is over. If it fails, the Debate continues. A well-run Debate results not only in the truth being vetted, but, more importantly, a consensus being built around this truth, which sounds delightful, except for these caveats:

- If the natives are looking for action, the Debate can look like stalling. If your Phil situation is dire, a four-week analysis of the Phil blight may not be the response the folks who are about to quit are looking for.

- If the issue is deeply emotional, the Debate is a nearly insurmountable task. People are messy—especially a group of emotional, angry people—and while they'll be happy to vent about Phil's failings, turning the vent into a constructive Debate can take an intolerable amount of time.

- The Debate lacks art. While a good Debate thoroughly vets the validity of a hypothesis, it rarely leads you toward

---

[1] www.randsinrepose.com/archives/2005/02/20/organics_and_mechanics.html

innovation or a leap of faith. The whole point of the Debate
is to develop the best possible theory regarding how to
proceed, and, in my experience, that process leads you to
a credible, actionable plan that feels simply like common
sense, not inspiration.

This is why ...

The Jedi Master has the Nudge

The *Jedi Master* has magical people skills. His mantra is, "Help me help you." He's all
about the health of the people. He says, "People are our most valuable resource."
He's conflict averse because conflict is, like, a buzz kill ... man. He wants to be your
bud. His conflict avoidance has given him a healthy paranoia, but he buries that
paranoia beneath a pleasant veneer of caring. He listens with intent and usually
gets his way, but you're never quite sure how.

I'll tell you how—the Jedi Master employs the Nudge.

You won't even see the Nudge coming. In fact, you'll be hard-pressed to figure
out when it actually occurred. The Jedi Master will say something innocuous: "Phil,
what do you think of the design of Project X?" Rather than jumping on the question, Phil sits there staring blankly. He's chewing on ... something. If you could
hear what Phil was thinking, it'd be this: *The design? The design was signed off two
months ago. It's done. Why now? Is it because design was something we talked about in
my annual review? I'm sure it is. Why do I feel like I'm missing something? I need to talk
to the design team. Now.*

The Nudge is the smallest, most viral piece of constructive feedback you can give.
It is small enough to appear unthreatening, but it has enough intent, enough implications, that it plants itself in the receiver's mind and can't help but evolve.

The processing of a Nudge takes time—that's the point. The receiver of a successful Nudge suspects they have a hint of a something, but they have no specifics. They
have potential, and there's no telling when they're going to turn that potential into
action, but when they do, the action is all their own because they've done all the
work. And that's the point.

A well-constructed Nudge is a clever combination of everything you learned about
people, leadership, politics, and the person you intend to Nudge. It's the delicate
selection of a simple idea intended to slowly reveal a larger intent to someone
who, in this case, will not hear the truth from anyone except themselves.

A well-placed Nudge is a goddamned managerial work of art. A poorly placed
Nudge is a terrific way to get in trouble with your team:

- The Nudge is, by far, the slowest way to effect change. If
  time is of the essence, the Debate will move faster than the

Nudge. But if you're looking to effect permanent change, go with the Nudge.

- The Nudge is not a game. The goal is to not build a small, mysterious phrase with the intent to obscure. The Nudge is a seed you plant with the hope that it will grow in a productive direction. You monitor it, and when it seems lost, you Nudge again.

- Jedi Masters who rely entirely on the Nudge, who choose to speak in clever phrases, are intensely annoying. There are folks who are going to be pissed and ask you to tell it to them straight. Remember, a lesson is learned, not told. (Zing!)

Drastic measures may be necessary, so . . .

The Dictator has the Mandate

Finally, there's the *Dictator*. His mantra is, "I'm the one who's telling you how it is." It's his way or the highway. No one contradicts. No one argues, and while his imperatives are subtly molded and messaged as they are passed through the organization, he is oblivious to these small changes, because from where he sits, he believes directives are followed—word for word. The Dictator is allowed to exist because no one argues the fact that he gets results.

The Dictator's superpower is the Mandate,[2] and it sounds like this: *We are all climbing that hill right now, and we're not going to stop climbing that hill until everyone is at the top of the hill. Start climbing.*

And everyone does. There's no Debate. There's no Nudge. Even the avid non-hill-climbers drop everything they're doing to start merrily climbing as they sing, "We, the climbers of the hill, what a thrill."

The power of the Mandate is alluring. It requires none of the laborious cat herding involved in managing the Debate. It eschews the subtle inner dialog required in constructing just the right Nudge. The Mandate is immediate, undisputed action, and when misused the Mandate can get you killed.

When you employ the Mandate, you leverage a large part of your credibility. You're effectively saying, "Shut up and go," and if where they end up isn't where any-one expects, you're less of a leader than when you started. This is an important fact that actual Dictators often forget. They believe that pure charisma—absolute, unwavering confidence—is all you need to fuel a Mandate. However, while some

---

[2] www.randsinrepose.com/archives/2004/10/06/mandate_dissection.html

people will just be happy someone made a decision, if a Mandate produces the wrong result, there will be an equal number of folks ready to kill you.

Dictators are killed. The consequence comes with the title. It's not a messy death, it's a professional one—it's your employees ceasing to listen to you and eventually leaving when you've completely eroded your credibility, or it's the board of directors simply taking care of business when you've brazenly demonstrated you can't.

My Favorite Superpower

These are stark examples of leadership stereotypes, and while you might see aspects of you or your management in these colorful descriptions, it's more likely that each is already a part of you. You have a tendency to be a Jedi Master, but when cornered, you're the Machine. The Dictator can serve you well, but it leaves your Jedi Master feeling . . . cruel.

The solution to your Phil problem is likely not a single power move, but all of them—at the appropriate time. While the Dictator mandates a comfortably clear "Fire Phil," the Jedi Master suggests, "Who does Phil communicate best with on his team? What can they tell you about him? How can they inform a Nudge?" which leads you to my favorite superpower—the Debate. While it's not immediate, and the final Phil call is yours, it supports my core belief that an idea only gets better with more eyeballs.

Saying *No*

Somewhere in your third year of being a manager, the management pixies will appear in your office in a puff of sweet-smelling black smoke. There will be three of them, and one will be carrying a gorgeous black top hat.

"Are you LeRoy McManager?"

"I am."

The pixies laugh. "Congratulations, you have passed successfully through three years of management and we're here to reward you. But first, one question: Have you seen *Spider-Man?*"

"The first one or the sequel?"

"The first one."

"I have."

The pixies laugh again. "What do you think is the primary theme in *Spider-Man, LeRoy McManager?*"

"Um, hmmmm . . . Life's a bitch?"

Strangely, the pixies don't laugh. "No, try again. It's important."

"OK, well. Hmmmm . . . Peter's uncle said something they kept yammering about . . . *Oh, I know* . . . With great power comes great responsibility."

The pixies cheer and the one carrying the top hat flutters over to you and drops it in your lap. It's soft and strangely warm. The hat-bearing pixie looks up at you and grins, "You wear this hat when you want people to know who you are."

"And who am I?" You look down at the hat and notice massive white block letters on the front. It says:

I'M THE BOSS.

A slow grin stretches across your face, and you realize the hat has the vague smell of your mom's fresh baked bread. That smell has always given you a strange sense of confidence and you know that whenever you wear that hat, you'll be infused with that sense of confidence.

All three pixies leap into the air, giggling. "Good luck, LeRoy McManager, use your hat well!" More laughing. Another puff of black smoke and they're gone.

You lift the hat slowly in front of your face, staring at the white block letters, soaking in the sense of power the hat gives you, and you put it on.

You stride out of your office, never once wondering why the pixies were giggling so much because, well, you're the boss. The first person sees you walk by in your cloud of confidence, and once you walk around the corner, you don't hear them snicker because, again, you're the boss.

They're laughing because while they know you're the boss, they can see the other side of the hat. It reads:

... FOR NOW

Managers Lose It

I mean it. There are managers out there who are absolutely punch drunk with power, and if you're working for one of these folks, I'm really sorry. You're a resident of Crazy Town, and that means you never know what random crap is going to happen next, and that sucks.

Managers don't start crazy. It's a learned trait, and this chapter explores the single best tactic you can take with both your manager and yourself to avoid trips to Crazy Town. Let's tackle it first with a story about your manager.

You're merrily typing away at your keyboard, hard at work at the next great product, when your boss walks in and says, "Hey, can you work on a Gizzy Flibbet project?"

"Uh, aren't we supposed to be finishing Flubjam? We've barely even started it. It's going to take awhile."

"Oh yes yes, we're still doing Flubjam, but I need you to prototype the Gizzy Flibbet and I need it in two days for a meeting with the execs."

"Ooooooooo-K, you're the boss."

"That's right. I am the boss."

Two days pass and your team briefly pours its soul into the prototype project. Like all investigations, you discover each step of discovery takes three times as long as expected. The final prototype conveys the idea, but the process to create that result has left your team drained and pretty sure finishing the remaining work is going to take a really long time.

When your boss walks into your office, you summarize, "Here it is. It looks good, it'll take awhile to finish, and we're now very behind on our Flubjam work. Can we please get back to it?"

Squinting her eyes, she runs her fingertips along the front rim of her top hat. She nods and stares, "*OK, this is great.* Let's do this *and* Flubjam, *and* let's hit the same schedule! Go us!" She turns and leaves the room, leaving your office with the faint smell of bread.

I'll recap. Your boss has just picked the one scenario that involves the most work and has the least chance of succeeding. You're screwed, and while you might think your boss has lost it, you are a coconspirator in this disaster because you didn't do one simple thing: you didn't *say no.*

Losing It

Managers don't lose it simply because the pixies showed up with the top hat, they lose it because those they work with forget to look at the back of the hat. Remember:

Front: I'M THE BOSS.

Back: . . . FOR NOW.

Management is a myth, just like the top hat. We, as employees, believe it's there, so we treat these management types differently. We operate under the assumption that they are the ones who can make decisions. When the team is stuck on a hard problem, we gather in our manager's office, present our case, and then the manager nods and says, "Go that way!" More often than not, we're so happy to be past the hard problem, we don't even question whether it's the right decision or not. "He's got the top hat, so he must be right!"

No no no no. Also? No.

Managers lose it when they are no longer questioned in their decisions. When the team stops questioning authority, the manager slowly starts to believe that his decisions are always good, and while it feels great to be right all the time, it's statistically impossible. The most experienced managers in the world make horribly bad decisions all the time. The good ones have learned how to recover from their decisions with dignity, but more importantly, with help from the team.

Saying no forces an idea to defend itself with facts. It forces a manager under the influence of his top hat to stop and think. Yes, I know that top hat can be intimidating, and yeah, he's the guy who signs the checks, but each time you allow your manager to charge forward with unchecked blind enthusiasm, you only reinforce his perception that he's never wrong. That's a ticket straight to Crazy Town.

Recovering It

A good solid *no* can travel in any direction. Even when it's hard to do.

My team had just been clobbered by the executive team in the boardroom. We'd been flying high on the sales of the current product and thinking that we could do no wrong, so our presentation for the next version of the product was half-baked. We'd assumed that since the current version was doing so well the executives would ignore our hand-waving about the future, but they didn't.

The Q&A had started pleasantly, but three questions in, when it was clear we were making it up as we were going and there wasn't some master plan behind the flimsy presentation, they started firing the big guns. There is only one extraction technique from these types of beat-downs—you say, "Well, it looks like we need to schedule a follow-up meeting."

The team went into fire drill mode. We needed a product roadmap, we needed it in a week, and we need to rebuild the executive staff's confidence in the team. When the brainstorming began, everyone was rattled. We'd moved from the chosen team to the team who couldn't nail a roadmap presentation. Being shaken, the ideas bouncing around the room were timid. They were designed to appease the folks who had just yelled at us, and while my confidence was shaky, I knew it was time to say no again—to them and to the executive team that wanted a quick turnaround.

"No, we're not going for mediocre. No, no one wants us to do me-too design. And, no, we're not done with this roadmap until it's something that inspires everyone in the room."

Now, the difference between me standing up in my office and giving a speech on inspirational product roadmaps and a manager who's flirting with Crazy Town because of an executive beat-down is slim, but therein lies the art. Saying no is saying "stop," and in a valley full of people who thrive on endless movement, the ability to strategically choose when it's time to stop is the sign of a manager willing to defy convention.

Never Trust a Pixie

The top hat is not what it seems. Yes, the black velvety elegance is intended to give you confidence, but remember—on the back of that hat is a threat. It's not on the back because the pixies couldn't fit the entire message on the front. It's on the back because they don't want you to live in Crazy Town, but they also don't want you to be paralyzed by the reality that you're potentially one big, bad decision away from being out of a job. They want you to embrace the confidence that the top hat imparts because it will help you make great decisions for yourself, your team, and your product. Some of those great decisions will be the result of blind luck, and some will be because you know what you're doing. However, you will also make some bad decisions, which you will weather sometimes because they weren't that bad, and sometimes purely on your top hat moxie.

And then you're going to make a big, bad decision and you'll remember: "With great power comes great responsibility." As a manager, you are responsible for making great decisions and the best way to do that is to involve as much of the team as possible in every decision.

Your team is collectively smarter than you simply because there are more of them. More importantly, by including them in the decision process and creating a team where they feel they can say no, you're creating trust.

A team that trusts you is going to look out for you. They'll never sit back and watch as you merrily traipse into Crazy Town staring at the back of your hat thinking, "I wonder who gets the top hat next?"

The Process Is The Product

People screw up. Every single one of us. There are the anonymous screw-ups that no one but us recognizes, and then there are the public ones—the embarrassing disasters where you look up and all eyes on the team are on you. Whoops.

To prevent these screw-ups, the more organized members of the team create process. Their goal is to provide structure around the work we do and to eliminate guessing. These people are well intentioned, but they still annoy the folks who know, first, we're always going to screw up no matter how much process we have and, second, that screwing up often reveals more useful information than not screwing up.

Process creates a delectable, healthy tension between those who measure and those who create. In this tension, there are useless meetings, yelling in the hallways, and flame mails. I'd like to think the following chapters will help you avoid these conflicts, but you need them. Like a good screw-up, a healthy argument provides a different perspective, which, if everyone is paying attention, will help the process evolve. And love it or hate it, the process is how you build a product.

1.0

Max was a mess. We were on our third mojito at the Basin in Saratoga when it just came pouring out of him. The last 72 hours involved this:

- Two days in Los Angeles babysitting a customer's data center.

- Four hours of sleep.

- Two huge arguments with his wife on the cell phone.

- A marathon conference call with his boss, which resulted in a new trip to Chicago in two days.

The mojitos might've been talking, but it sounded like Max was sure that his wife was going to leave him; his company was about to crumble; and he was 12 hours and one plane flight from a nervous breakdown.

He said, "Shipping a 1.0 product isn't going to kill you, but it will try."

Understanding 1.0

In your career as a software developer, you're going to be screwed at some point. My advice is keep thinking, don't yell, treat those you work with decently, and you'll be fine. It's valuable experience, but it's nothing compared to 1.0.

1.0 is developing the first version of a new product. It's what all those startups are busily doing right now. They're working on some 1.0 idea that's good enough that a handful of bright people will forgo their lives in support of the chance of being right. See, we had a great idea. We're bazillionaires and we were right.

Most of those startups fail.

Before the Web site Fucked Company, failing was a quiet, somber thing. The dot-com explosion made colossal flameouts front-page news, and everyone discovered what most of us already knew.

Really. Most startups fail.

Why?

To understand the difficulty of 1.0, I need to give you a model for understanding how a 1.0 software product actually shows up. I've designed just such a model by heavily borrowing from a theory known as Maslow's Hierarchy of Needs, which is worth talking about all by its lonesome.

Maslow's theory contends that as humans meet their basic needs, they seek to satisfy successively higher needs that occupy a set hierarchy, as shown in Figure 19-1.

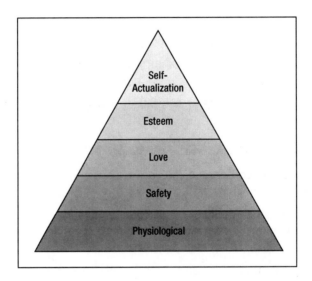

Figure 19-1. Maslow's Hierarchy of Needs

At the bottom of the pyramid is the biggest area of need: physiological needs. These are the basics: food, drink, air, sleep, etc. The idea is that you won't be able to focus on anything else in the hierarchy if these needs aren't met. Think of it like this: who cares about falling in love if you can't breathe?

Moving up the hierarchy, you have safety needs, love/belonging, esteem, and finally, the oddly named "self-actualization" tip of the pyramid, which is our instinctual need to make the most of our unique abilities. Translation: Writers write, singers sing.

There's a fine entry in Wikipedia regarding Maslow's hierarchy if I've piqued your interest (see http://en.wikipedia.org/wiki/Maslow's_hierarchy_of_needs). Personally, as a manager of humans, I stare at the hierarchy when dealing with folks on the edge. The hierarchy gives me insight into where exactly a person is stressing out. Are they in need of career advice? (Easy.) Or do they need marriage advice? (Harder.)

Rands 1.0 Hierarchy

In thinking about the difficulties of 1.0, I realized that Maslow's model applied to shipping the first version of a product. There's a hierarchy that defines what you need to build in order to ship 1.0, and it looks like Figure 19-2.

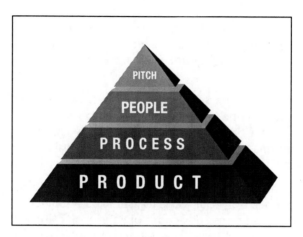

Figure 19-2. Rands 1.0 Hierarchy

Note regarding charts and graphs: Phillippe Kahn, the founder of Borland, told a great story about statistics that I think equally applies to charts and graphs. The story is, "Did you know it's a statistical fact that people with larger feet tend to be better spellers? [Insert awe.] It's because people with bigger feet are older."

Charts 'n' graphs paint the world in a clean, linear fashion that serves one purpose: supporting the message of the author. Do not trust charts 'n' graphs, but don't let that lack of trust blind you to the intent of the story.

Pitch

At the top of the hierarchy, there's Your Great Idea. I'm calling it "pitch" because I've got this alliteration thing going on. You can't get anywhere in building a product or a company without a phenomenal pitch. It doesn't matter if you're Mr. Charisma; you've got to have the idea because it defines the structure and constraints of everything below it. If you don't have the idea, you don't know who to hire, which is the second layer—people.

Before we talk about this second layer, let me first congratulate you. I'm tripping over myself happy that you've discovered the Next Big Thing, but there are some basic facts to pay attention to. The first is:

Fact #1: You're in a hurry. Don't forget it.

You're a fool if you think you have exclusive rights to your pitch. There are too many bright people staring at exactly the same infinite pile of evolving information to assume your innovation is original. The only thing that gives you this right is delivering 1.0, and first, you're going to need some people.

People

With your pitch in hand, you're going to find the people to build your idea. These are your founders. These are the folks who will not only build your 1.0, but more importantly, your engineering culture. Their arrival presents a challenge and a twist to the pyramid.

Your first few hires walk into a blank slate. Yes, they're believers in the pitch— otherwise they wouldn't be in the building—but now it's their pitch, which means they're going to ask the hard questions because they've got some skin in the game. These hard questions are going to help them start making decisions about the eventual products.

As the keeper of the pitch, you're going to try to stay involved, but you simply can't be there for every decision. Your job is to listen and watch incessantly so that you can detect how the decisions and actions of your people are slowly changing your pitch. This leads us to our twist. The Rands 1.0 Hierarchy is much scarier than Maslow's, because it really looks like Figure 19-3.

Figure 19-3. The Real Rands 1.0 Hierarchy

There's a good reason why folks don't build their pyramids like this—they fall over. The only way to keep them from falling over is to constantly push one side or the other. This is your startup. It's an impractical concept with your pitch sitting at the bottom defining everything above it. What will kill you about 1.0 will be how much time you're going to spend trying to keep this pyramid balanced, which brings us back to the topic at hand: people. Another basic fact:

Fact #2: No one is indispensable.

Now, I'm a people person. This entire book is devoted to figuring out how to make sure folks get along and get stuff done, but we're not talking about an established company here. We're talking about 1.0 and the rules are different because you are an unknown quantity and everyone is expecting you to fail.

Ever built a fire? What do you need? A match, some paper, and some kindling wood that catches fire easily. Your first three hires are your kindling. Their job is not to define the product roadmap, their job is to get things moving, and if things aren't moving, you need to get some more wood.

At my startup, I was brought in as the first engineering manager. The founders had brought on two free electrons with totally different temperaments (see Chapter 38for more on free electrons). One was burning the midnight oil on getting a working prototype done. He was fully aware we'd throw the whole thing away, but he knew that the ability to see the idea in code would change everyone's opinion of what we were doing. It would make the pitch real.

The other electron also loved the pitch, but he was working on infrastructure for future products. *He was what?* Yes, we had no product and one of our key hires was already investing in the future. When is investing in the future a bad idea? How about when the now is not defined? The second free electron was working under the assumption that 1.0 would be successful, and while I appreciated his enthusiasm, let's remember *Fact #0: Startups almost always fail.*

I spent some time with the second free electron and, as it often goes with very bright people on a mission, it was clear he wasn't going to be swayed, so I let him go. That day. One quick meeting with our VP and it was done.

As you'll learn in Chapter 38, you don't run into these types of stunning engineers often. Firing a free electron is pretty stupid for most companies because they have so much potential, but here's the deal: you aren't a company until 1.0 is done. A great way to topple your fledgling pyramid is to hire folks who are not getting the product done with a sense of urgency. Get 1.0 done and then worry what's next.

Process

There is no word that irks engineers more than *process*. Try it right now. Get everyone in your office and say something like, "I've defined a new process to assist our bug triage." Watch their faces sag. They hear "busywork." They think, "management is trying to justify itself."

This is not the word that defines the third level of the hierarchy. That word is *communication*.

Fact #3: Process defines communication.

Process is the means by which your team communicates. Whether this is via a wiki, e-mail, or the hallway, any team larger than one needs to define a means to share information. This is not an argument for specifications, documentation, or a whiteboard filled with dos and don'ts. You just need to agree how you're going to share information.

When your second engineer decides, "Yes, I'm going to capture my design decisions in a wiki," that's process. When your third engineer starts tracking bugs on that huge whiteboard in the meeting room, that's process. It doesn't have to be good, it doesn't even have to be universally agreed upon on, it just has to be stuck in a place where everyone can see it.

Microsoft's SourceSafe was the repository of choice when I landed at my first startup. Stop laughing. It did a fine job with a team of six engineers who had zero time to worry about source control. Sure, it was slow as hell and lost a day's work here and there because of various hiccups, but we were working on 1.0, and who had time to think about something more reliable?

Roland did.

Roland was a junior engineer and he was a Perforce fan. Roland did what any good employee of a startup would do. Over the course of a weekend, he set up a Perforce server, rewrote all of our build tools, and scheduled a 10 a.m. meeting on the following Monday, promising Krispy Kreme doughnuts. His message: "This is the way it is. Everything works better. Thank you and have a doughnut."

In a weekend, Roland fixed a major flaw in our process (crappy tools) and also demonstrated another fact of the hierarchy

Fact #4: Each layer shapes and moves those near it.

A sure sign of a healthy pyramid is that one layer invades another. Think of each change to people, process, and pitch as a shove in one direction. This movement requires compensation in the other layers, otherwise the whole thing falls over. Roland's decision to change the engineering process pissed off some folks. We lost some time to some source management edge cases that Roland hadn't thought of, but, within a week, we'd adjusted. Even the most vocal opponent of the change ended up in Roland's office arguing about how we could make it better.

If, in your organization, your pyramid is not constantly adjusting to keep itself upright, something's wrong. If the new folks aren't testing the pitch, they either don't buy it or they don't get it. If your engineers aren't arguing about the way they develop software *all the time,* they're becoming stagnant, and that trickles down to your pitch and trickles up to your product.

A great stagnation warning sign during 1.0 is when someone decides to create an organization chart defining "This is who does what." Now, investors and outside parties need this org chart to get a sense of whether you're real or not, but your

1.0 team does not. The whiteboard in the corner of the room, which lists who is doing what, is your org chart. The definition and hierarchy an org chart portrays is the first step in creating a culture of secrecy in your org. That might work for Apple, but you're not Apple, yet. You're hope and hard work.

Product

At some point, you're going to need to fake being done. You're going to need to release something that barely looks like your pitch because you don't have product until a neutral party stares at something.

Fact #5: You don't have a company until you have a product.

Product is not pitch. Pitch is the three-sentence idea that gave you the credibility to hire the people. The people argued about the pitch, they created process to refine and develop the pitch, and that changed it. The pyramid wobbled hither and fro during all of this. Maybe it fell completely over and you scrambled to stack those layers up again. Good job, there. You still don't have product.

The neutral parties, your customers, need to see what you've been building because all your people are completely insane. All that healthy shifting of the pyramid has been taxing them. Each shove forced them to adjust their perspective of the pitch, their relation to it, and adapting to change is fucking exhausting. Folks who say "I like change" are not currently working at a startup. Folks at a startup don't say much because they're busy adapting to the latest pyramid shift.

This state of constant change is the leading cause of startup burnout, and it's also the reason you've got to get that product out. The perspective of the neutral party is essential validation because you're nuts. Your pitch has been dissected and redefined so many times that it may no longer be something that is useful. A neutral party doesn't care about the pitch, your people, or any of the pyramid shoving you've been up to; they just care whether the product is useful.

Using the Pyramid

At no point will you ever draw this hierarchy on a whiteboard during an organizational crisis and say, "*Folks, pay attention to the pyramid—so says the Rands.*" The idea is to give you a tool that reminds you, "Hey, it's all connected!" The pitch guides the people. The people refine the pitch. People and pitch create process and product, and, yeah, it's all a big mess and that's why startups fail.

The pyramid gives you a hazy map to think about the problems your company might face. People will yell in the hallway and it might sound like they're arguing about product, but keep listening, maybe it's process. Even worse (better?), maybe it's pitch. Your one job as keeper of the pitch is figuring out which layer of the pyramid is being tested, and then figure out which way to shove the pyramid. This leads us to our last fact:

Fact #6: The lower the failure, the higher the cost.

A year into my startup, the founders were at a crossroads. We were doing an enterprise web application that was built for onsite deployment. Problem was, everyone was going loopy about hosted services. The pitch there was: "Look how much time and energy I'll save you by hosting this application in my data center, not yours." This idea flew in the face of years of Oracle, PeopleSoft, and IBM domination of that huge pile of business software and hardware sitting in your data center, but it was the Internet and the Internet was going to save the world.

The founders changed their pitch. "We'll just create copies of the software in our data center! We'll save money keeping our bits close to home!" No huge difference there? Wrong. This adjustment to our pitch changed the fundamental architecture of our product. Rather than have hundreds of customized versions of our software sitting in various data centers, we had to have one copy of our software that was configurable to each of our customers' needs, and that wasn't the product we designed.

It wasn't an instant disaster. We had piles of money to throw at this transformation, but the transition cost became so great that we stopped working on anything except getting the hosted application working and, right about then, the bubble burst.

Let's call "failure" a really bad decision. It's when you choose to change something and that change percolates up through the pyramid. If you make a bad decision regarding version control, well, you can probably adjust to that. You can fire a free electron and probably find another bright person who can channel the pitch better, but you're probably going to rattle more than you think. A failure of pitch is a structural failure that affects your entire company Everything in your company depends on the vision that you've presented and screwing that up can be fatal.

Building Culture

If you've actually got a pitch ready to go, again, that's terrific. This totally conceptual model I've thrown together doesn't cover some major topics that you need to understand. How are you going to fund this thing? Where do you find VCs? Where do you find great people? Your life will become an endless list of questions and decisions and you'll probably forget everything I just wrote in your frenetic sprint to keep your pitch alive, so I'll simplify. The hierarchy I describe is not a model for how to build a great product; it's a picture that describes the construction of the culture of your company. That's what you're really building in 1.0. A lasting, interesting culture that, if you're lucky, continues to produce great products.

Think of your five favorite companies and think about what made them successful. Yes, they probably had a great 1.0. Think about when you first saw a Mac. Think of the first time you saw Netscape. How about your first useful search on Google? Those products are the end result of people killing themselves to get the damned thing out the door, but these people weren't just creating that product. Their work defined the culture of the company, and that is what modeled their future success.

And that's why 1.0 is trying to kill you. 1.0 is expecting you to underestimate it. 1.0 wants you to think all you are building is a product, but the product is merely the outcome. A successful 1.0 is measured by the success of the product that ships, but it is built by a seemingly endless amount of decisions, arguments, failures, and successes that you can't plan for that will teach you everything you need to know, but are, inconveniently, trying to kill you.

How to Start

At the time of this writing, it's been almost seven years since I've updated the design for the Rands in Repose web site. In that time, I've done multiple designs, learned an entirely different publishing platform, and migrated the existing content over many times. What has always remained is an ever-growing list of details supplied by the act of starting.

The length of time since the last update isn't surprising. Since Rands was last updated, I've been busy. I've written over 200 articles and published 2 books. What's surprising is the amount of time I spend preparing to start via a vast array of impressive mental gymnastics on tasks *I want to do*. It's shocking. Case in point: since the major redesign of the site, my rough estimate is that for two solid months I've not actually been working on the site, but getting started. I'm not talking about actual measurable progress; I'm talking about the fussing, orienting, and random thinking surrounding getting started.

After the first three years of starting, I decided to get strategic. I decided to keep track. *Clearly, I have starting issues, so rather than obsess about them, I will enumerate and understand them. What, precisely, am I doing rather than working?*

A Critical Analysis of Beginning

Beginning is a three-phase commit: you're either fretting about starting, you're preparing to begin, or you've begun. It's the middle state of preparation I want to explore, because it is during this time that we unnecessarily torture ourselves. We lie to ourselves about wasting time and beat ourselves up with guilt-laden words such as *procrastination*, *slacker*, and *lazy*. But I believe we're actually getting important work done.

Specifically, I believe three things:

1. Your brain is smarter about thinking than you think.
   I believe the many states of preparation are your

brain cleverly and proactively trying to help you begin. Unfortunately, many of these states really do look like goofing off. This is why ...

2. Preparation, in its variety of forms, often gets a bad rap. You're under a deadline and your boss walks in to discover you reading about a satisfying walk to Central Park West.[1] He's going to ask, "What the hell does this have to do with the deadline?" You instinctively know this creative excursion is somehow helping, but your inability to explain on the spot does nothing to help your plight. What your boss has done is his favorite move—he's stressed you out—and ...

3. Stress is a creativity buzz kill. When you're stressed, you're in reaction and survival mode. Your mindset when you're stressed is, "How do I survive?" not "What is an elegant solution to this problem?" Survival—I'm a fan,[2] but whatever immense task is in front of you will not be conquered by the defensive strategies of survival. The elegant solution requires offense, and the lower the stress, the better the offense.

As I've watched myself stumble through the various states of starting, I've discovered there are two base mental states where I begin, and they are tightly coupled with the time of day. Specifically, the moves I need are entirely different depending on whether it's morning or evening.

Morning Stretch

The risk of morning is exuberance. Unbridled exuberance. Your body just spent a quiet night getting rid of all the mental and physical crap from the prior day and it's ready to go—in every way possible. The issue with morning isn't whether or not you start, it's wrangling what you start on. Most mornings I'm just as likely to write an article as I am to read about *every single Marvel movie* that will be produced in the next two years.

Rands, just start. You've got a big task. Just start it.

Quiet.

Those who do not understand creativity think it has a well-defined and measurable on/off switch, when in reality it's a walking dial with many labels. One label reads, for example, "Morose and apathetic," and another reads "Unexpectedly totally

---

[1] http://bobulate.com/post/3197597100/walking-versus-running
[2] www.randsinrepose.com/archives/2005/08/30/taking_time_to_think.html

cranking it out." This dial sports shy, mischievous feet—yes, feet—that allow it to simply walk away the moment you aren't paying attention. Each time it walks away, it finds a new place to hide.

I've spent a good portion of my life wondering where that damned dial is hiding.

For me, corralling and managing the creativity dial in the morning involves starting with *an unrelated creative excursion*. I have a bookmark group called Scrub, and contained within that group is a set of sites intended to focus the crazy enthusiasm into the creative. All it takes is a click and I'm looking at aggregated sets of words, images, and ideas. The idea of the unrelated creative excursion: creativity begets creativity. The act of experiencing the end result of others' creativity is the single best way for me to figure where the dial is hiding and conjure the demon I need to begin.[3]

The risk of creative divergence is still there, of course. These sites are not a surefire focusing lens, but I've chosen them carefully over time to be mentally delicious while not overly so. For example, articles in the *New Yorker* are full of creative inspiration, but they have no place in the Scrub group because it is too easy to lose myself in them.

The Scrub group might strike you as avoidance, but it's not; it's an alternative. There is something daunting about the task in front of you, and my suggestion is to admit that it's daunting. A frontal attack on daunting works for some, but creative solutions rarely involve straight lines. A random search for unrelated inspiration allows your brain to sidestep whatever weight you've built around the task. You get to sneak in a heretofore hidden side door that can only be discovered with the help of an unknown creative stranger.

My Scrub group is full of strangers. A current favorite is Hacker News.[4] Look, someone is describing how they did the effects for *TRON: Legacy*.[5] They really did go out of their way to make those Unix screens authentic. You know, I have an article about the beauty of the command line. I should write . . .

An Experienced Evening

The dial reads "Tired."

Whatever magical chemicals my body stockpiles during a night of sleep are gone in the evening. The day has occurred, and when I sit down at my desktop to look at my Scrub bookmark group, it feels as if gravity has increased and my mental wiring has been clogged with all the crap I've seen and heard during the day. I see words and images, but nothing gets through the heavy haze of the working day.

---

[3] www.ted.com/talks/elizabeth_gilbert_on_genius.html
[4] http://news.ycombinator.com/
[5] http://jtnimoy.net/workviewer.php?q=178

No . . . no work for me. How about some mindless World of Warcraft?

Mornings have the gift of optimism because nothing has screwed up your day, yet. Evenings are dark, repetitive reminders that no matter what you do, time is going to pass and you've likely wasted some of it. In this mental state, the creativity dial easily moves to the depressingly lowercase "uninspired and listless," and hides not just under your couch, but inside of it.

I discovered that I need to switch sides in my brain in my quest to find and adjust the dial in the evening. Rather than stimulating the creative side of my brain, I work the logical side. I give myself a task such as, What is *the smallest piece of research* I can do relative to the project? The new site needs footnotes. OK, I will find a single web page that describes the history of the footnote, I will take notes, and I will form a footnote opinion.

This exercise is not the creative wandering of the morning. This is using my structured research skills to understand and build a thing. It is a discernible to-do that, when complete, I can productively check off. It is a practical excursion in intellectual illumination geared to focus my tired brain so it can approach inspiration.

I have less success in evenings than mornings, but structure, logic, data, and facts—for me—are the best starting ingredients to invoke an evening of creative progress.

Happenstance

I need to disclose that I wrote a good portion of my last book in the evening after watching reruns of *Sex and the City*, and after weeks of thinking and writing about the act of starting. I cannot tell you why, but I can tell you why it's important.

Perhaps it was the show's complete dissimilarity from my day that reset my brain. Perhaps it was Carrie Bradshaw's Doogie Howser–like closing where she sums up the key lessons of the episode on her MacBook. Maybe seeing her write reminded me that "Hey, she can write, so maybe I can start, too."

My *Sex and the City* kick start wasn't a creative excursion or a piece of research; it was happenstance. I watched a few episodes two weeks back to see if I could repeat the effect—nothing. Thank god.

Whatever it is that you're not starting, I know it's hard to do, otherwise it'd already be done. Otherwise you wouldn't have spent weeks of time considering it rather than doing it.

We're addicted to quick fixes, top-ten lists, and four-hour work weeks, but the truth is that if it wasn't hard, everyone would be doing it, and a hard thing is never done by reading a list or a book or an article about doing it. A hard thing is done by figuring out how to start.

You've been spending a lot of time thinking the result is what matters. You have a bright-and-shiny goal in mind that is distracting you with its awesomeness. It is this allure of awesomeness that is the continued reason why you keep searching around your house looking for that mischievous walking creativity dial.

At this moment, the next major redesign for the Rands web site remains safely in limbo. The comfort of completion is a distant goal, but in the meantime, each weekend, I find something to start. A CSS tweak here, a new page there—the site may not be revolutionized, but it is certainly satisfying creative evolution.

My guarantee is that what is going to make this bright-and-shiny thing awesome isn't finishing. It's all the little, unexpected details you discover trying to start. It's all the small pieces of unexplainable execution that will not only make it yours, but also continue to teach you how you get things done. And when you're done, you'll discover that finishing, while cathartic, is just a good reason to go start something else.

21

Taking Time to Think

Lunch at Don Giovanni's with Phillip. He's amped. We haven't even seen our waiter and he's already cleared the table and is scribbling furiously on the white paper tablecloth.

"See, we needed to speed up our release cycle, which is, of course, insane, but we figured out a way! We call it train releases. We've got four releases going at the same time and a train leaves the station every month. If a feature is ready to go, it gets on the train, and if it's not, it waits for the next train. We've already released two trains in six weeks!"

I nod, watching the scribbles become increasingly incoherent. I'd buy Phillip a nice glass of Chianti to take the edge off, but he's a Mormon, so I try the truth.

"Phil, you're screwed twice. First, you're screwed because you're going to need twice the staff—at least—to qualify these ever-increasing releases, and you're a startup. You've got one QA guy, and if he hasn't blown a fuse yet, just wait a month. Second, and most important, you've got no downtime. You've got no time to design because everyone is going to be panicked about which train they're supposed to be riding.

"Phil, in order to create, you've got to think."

Reacting vs. Thinking

Why can't you think when you're busy?

Dumb question, right? Answer: "I can't think because I'm busy." Wrong. You can't think because when you're busy, you're not thinking, you're reacting.

Example: You walk into my office and start yelling, "Rands, it's two days from shipping and we've just found a bad bug, a showstopper. What do we do? Are we screwed?"

I will respond and my response might look like thinking, but I'm not doing anything creative because I've dealt with the showstopper-two-days-before-ship scenario *in every product I've ever built.* Survived it each time, too. Got some great stories. It's that experience I'm using when you walk into my office and tell me the sky is falling. I'm not actually doing anything new, I'm just telling you the story of how I propped the sky up last time.

Yes, you can argue that one can be exquisitely creative when one's hair is on fire. It's the "necessity is the mother of invention argument"; but, seriously, if your hair's on fire, are you going to take the time to seriously consider all hair-dousing techniques, or are you just going to stick your head in the nearest convenient bucket before it really hurts? Panic is the mother of the path of least resistance.

You won't be a successful manager without well-developed react instincts. A quiver full of experience gives you all sorts of arrows to shoot at problems, and the timing and accuracy of some of those shots will be brilliant, but your quiver will slowly empty unless you take the time to think.

For the sake of this chapter, let's partition your brain—one half is the creative brain. This is the part of your brain that is the source of inspiration. The other half of your brain is your reactive brain. This is the part of the brain that loves it when the sky is falling because it gets to move so gosh-darned quick.

Your reactive brain doesn't actually like to think because thinking is messy. Thinking involves slowing down and actually soaking in a problem, and your reactive brain thrives in the familiar. Your creative brain loves the unknown. It's a sponge and it's only happy when it's full of new ideas. This is part of the reason thinking is hard to pull off at work—it doesn't fit nicely into the daily course of business because it's full of mind-bending paradoxes and uncomfortable realities your mechanical manager is going to barf all over. Some examples:

- Thinking is not something you can constrain by time or a meeting. There is no beginning and there is no end—you never know when you're done.

- Doing more thinking always pays off, but time is money and you've got 27 other meetings this week.

- The more people you include in the thinking process, the more genuine ideas you'll find, but the process of finding those ideas will linearly slow down with each person who shows up.

- Everyone thinks differently.

The time to kick off your deep thinking is right after your last major release. It's when every single lesson of the prior release is forefront in the team's mind. They've just gone through the crunch where they had to stare at each poor design decision illuminated by repeated painful deferral of bugs. They're exhausted, but they have hope because they know they can fix it in the next release.

Getting Started

The first step is defining a time when the team can think. In the past, I was a fan of kicking things off with an offsite meeting. A good solid day of thinking somewhere other than corporate headquarters where folks can forget about their daily professional woes. The problem with this is that while everyone loves a field trip, the day is an illusion. Sure, the coffee tastes different and, yeah, everyone seems really excited about the next version, but tomorrow you're going back to headquarters, which is where you're going to do 95 percent of your actual thinking. You've got to create a thinking-conducive environment in your natural setting.

Start with two meetings a week. The first is a brainstorm meeting and the second is a prototype meeting. Both are, at least, an hour long.

Make sure there is time between the brainstorm and prototype meeting. Give everyone involved time to stew on the results of the brainstorm meeting. Conversely, you don't want to wait too long to see a prototype because you'll forget the context of the initial brainstorm. Once-a-week meetings are a study in futility because folks forget everything during the course of a weekend and meetings end up rehashing the same thoughts from the week before.

Players

When the meetings begin, you need a driver. Maybe it's you, maybe it's not. There's another paradox here. Structured thinking kills thinking, but unstructured thinking leads to useless chaos. Your meeting driver must be able to swerve the conversation back and forth between the two extremes, but generally keep it in the middle. Organics (see Chapter 36 for more on organics) tend to be best at this. More on this in a bit when we figure out if your meeting is actually working.

Whom to invite? This is the hard one. If you invite every single person on the team, you'll get nothing done . . . even with the world's best driver. You've got to start small and let the momentum build. This is where you might initially piss people off because everyone wants to sit in this meeting because everyone has an opinion. If you have an idea of what the initial topics will be, invite those you know have an educated opinion. If you have no clue where to start with topics, roll the dice . . . pick at random. You never know what you're going to find in the minds of engineers. The good news is that one of the best signs of a productive design process is that the players change. More on this in a moment.

One land mine you've got to be aware of in your attendee selection is obstructionists. These are folks who've fallen into a total react lifestyle. You can easily identify them by their tendency to map every new idea against previous experience and then declare the idea "unoriginal." The reasons for this attitude varies. Maybe they were early designers of the product and can't escape from the original design. Maybe it's the fear of the unknown. Whatever the cause, these folks are a creativity buzz kill and are not folks you want to invite to your initial brainstorm meetings.

Content

The goal for the first brainstorm meeting is to start reliving the pain of the last release. What bug did you hate to defer? What feature didn't get pulled off? Who hates this UI? Everyone? Yeah, I thought so. Hey, who is our customer anyway? You want to walk out of your first brainstorm meeting with five hot topics that folks want to address.

The second meeting is your prototype meeting. You want to see the results of the last brainstorm meeting in a prototype ... paper ... code ... wireframe ... bulleted list. It doesn't matter as long as there is documented evidence of what occurred in the prior meeting. Maybe you just had a list of customer types? How about a list of the five things the team hates about the product? Your goal here is documented continuity between meetings. This documentation will eventually turn into mock-ups or actual working prototypes, but out of the gate, keep the documentation focused on remembering what the hell happened last time.

When you do get to mock-ups or prototypes, keep them lightweight and devoid of detail. If it's week three and the team is arguing about which icons fit where, you're too deep. I'm a fan of wireframes when it comes to visually wiring an application together. They give all the geometry of a visual idea without suggesting a look or feel.

Is It Working?

OK, you're two weeks into the Rands Creativity Plan and it's going poorly. No one said anything during the first meeting because they've never been asked their opinion before. The meeting consisted of you in front of the whiteboard and a lot of nodding. This lack of brainstorming content led to a very dull prototype meeting, so you stuck with more brainstorming. Week two rolled around and folks started talking except, well, they were yelling because there's a fundamental disagreement about who the customer actually is. That's painful progress except when you roll into your second prototype meeting and everyone's silent again because who wants to be yelled at?

Good work. Really.

It's a big deal to mentally stumble about and bump into shit during your initial brainstorm meetings. This seeming lack of mental coordination is what finding innovation is all about ... but you still need to understand if you're making progress. Some things you can look for as the weeks pass:

- **Are decisions being made?** Is the group working well enough to make a decision? Yes? Good.

- **Are decisions being revisited?** Is the group limber enough to go backward to refine a previous decision? Even better.

- **Are decisions constantly being revisited?** OK, problem here. Your team has spun into creative nirvana. A good time to step back and apply a little structure to the process. Reviewing decisions to date is a good way to find structure and move forward. Oh, you weren't writing down the results of brainstorm meetings? Oops. Start now.

- **Are the players changing?** If you're four weeks in and the faces at the table haven't changed, you might have a problem. If you're working on a sizable project, there is no way you picked the right brainstorm team from the onset. The diversity of thought sitting outside of the room must be brought into the conversation. Time to start mixing it up.

- **Are basic truths about your design showing up?** These are the gems of brainstorm. These are decisions that are made that define the basic design of your problem. You'll know these when they show up, stand up to scrutiny, and eventually start virally wandering the hallways.

- **Is it therapy or work?** If you've just been through a brutal release, the team is going to spend the first brainstorming meetings venting. That's OK, they need it. If it's week three and you're still on the vent, it's time to make changes.

- **Are holy shit moments occurring?** Similar to the basic truth discovery, but louder and infrequent. *"Holy shit,* we're completely wrong." Holy shits are disruptive, but are a good sign of a limber creative process.

- **Is the to-do list growing or shrinking?** If you're early on in the design phase, it should be growing. If you're getting close to the end of your design phase, it better be getting smaller. I know engineers want to solve every problem in the product in any given major release, but *that never ever happens ever.* Better is the enemy of done, and if it's your project, you need to draw a line on what topics/ideas you intend to tackle and stick to it.

My rule of thumb is if you aren't staring at one hard decision per meeting . . . you might be wasting your time. You've got the wrong people and/or the wrong driver and while it sure is fun to have an hour to chat . . . that's all you're doing. Chatting.

When to Stop

If your meetings are healthy, the meetings will naturally move from one topic to another. Decisions are built, ideas are vetted, yelling occurs, and prototypes are reviewed. I've found that these meetings will slowly die off as you move from hard-core design into serious development. If they don't, then you're probably becoming addicted to thinking, and while that sounds appealing, you're not working for a university, you're working for your shareholders and they want to see new product yesterday. You can still fine-tune design during the depths of development, but the trend you want to see in your meetings is that questions are being answered, not created.

Fighting Stagnation

Google knows you've got to take time to think. It is rumored they ask their employees to spend one day a week working on their own projects. Do that math. Google is investing 20 percent of the engineering budget on thinking. I'm sure that nothing comes from a majority of those projects, but Google gets two wins out of the program. First, some of the projects create value for the company. It's probably one in five, but that's not the real value. Google is creating a culture of thinking by allowing their employees to wander about and bump into shit.

I don't know what you do and I don't know what you build. I am certain that if you don't demonstrate creative thinking in what you build, you're screwed because you, your team, and your product will stagnate. Kicking off brainstorming meetings are a tricky proposition. They are poorly defined, hard to run, and harder to measure. What comes out of these meetings might be brilliance or stupidity . . . the difference between the two is magnificently slim. Good luck.

The Value of the Soak

In 2006, I gave a presentation at the South by Southwest conference in Austin, Texas. My pitch was this: in creating a startup, you're going to be faced with a thousand seemingly inconsequential decisions. Tucked among those thousands of decisions are five decisions that actually matter. These decisions will change the face of your company. What I didn't say was that I believe it's next to impossible to figure out which decisions matter and which ones do not.

How depressing.

Here's the deal: you can spend a lot of energy deciding what the big decisions might be, but that's much less important than making the decision. There's a pile of thoughts on creating decision-friendly environments in Chapter 21, but that chapter focuses on the idea of thinking in a team scenario, and I want to talk about when you choose to take your thinking solo.

Let's start with the most infuriating e-mail you've ever received. I'm not talking about that jerk in tech support who is simply stupid, I'm talking about the e-mail from someone you trust ... a peer ... pissing you off in e-mail by commenting on a problem that needs to be solved and perhaps casting doubt on your ability to solve it. You're going to want to react to this e-mail in the same manner as if I came into your office and punched you in the face. It's your animal brain at work and it served you well when you were living in a cave doing the hunter-gathering thing because reacting slowly meant you were eaten or punched again.

Now. You have time to *soak*.

The soak is when you plant the seed of a thought in your brain and let it bump around in a rich stew of ideas, facts, and whatever other random crap that seems to relate. The soak is a protected activity that will rarely occur during your busy day because you're busy reacting to the familiar never-ending flood of things to do. The goal of the soak is simple: an original thought. Whatever the problem is that you're stewing on, you want to find a glimmer of inspiration that transforms your response from a predictable emotional flame-o-gram into a strategically considered thought and, ultimately, decision.

Emotion and Ignorance

At a prior gig, I was finally hitting my stride. After a two-year awkward getting-to-know-the-company phase, I was in the groove. I knew who was doing what, who was hungry, and who was coasting. I'd turned a small, bright idea of a product into a successful moneymaker, so my boss decided to saddle me with something completely different. An entirely new product built on technology I'd never used. It was a strategic-shift product for the company, which meant everyone would be watching. This visibility would amplify potential fuck-ups. This was the career-defining product for me.

Holy shit.

Having no clue where to start a new project and wanting to rip someone apart in e-mail share one important characteristic. The best move in both cases is to start with a good long soak.

I break soaking activities into two buckets: *active soaks* and *passive soaks*. The active soaks are activities that you can direct and usually involve gathering content, whereas passive soaks are activities when you just point your brain in a random direction and pray. Passive soaks are where the real work gets done—provided you laid the groundwork with an active soak. Let's start with that first.

Active Soaking

Ask dumb questions. Your first job when faced with ignorance is information acquisition, and, hopefully, there are folks out there who've already done some soaking. These folks have some facts, ideas, and opinions regarding whatever the problem might be, and you need to hear them all. The first five of these conversations can be awkward for managers because it'll be obvious after your first two questions ("What is it?" and "How does it work?") that you have absolutely no clue what's going on and you think it's a manager's job to appear knowledgeable.

Wrong. It's a manager's job to be clued in. You work in an industry populated with engineers, and these are folks who are paid a lot of money to care about the details, and that means they see right past feigned knowledge. Sure, they're not saying anything because you're the boss, but, um, you look stupid.

Soaking starts out uncomfortable, but with each ignorant question you ask, you're adding content to that managerial brain of yours. Asking dumb questions is the best way to start figuring out what is actually going on. Furthermore, asking any question of your team is a handy way to indirectly say, "I care about what we're doing enough to ask you what you think."

Pitch a stranger. Once you've asked enough dumb questions, a picture will start to form in your mind about what exactly you're doing. It's not a complete picture, it's more a rough sketch coupled with the mild relief that accompanies the sudden absence of ignorance. Now you've got to test your understanding with a qualified someone who is willing to listen to you ramble. Pitch this person on your picture and see what happens. Lots of nodding? Great, it's coming together. Blank stare? Oops, time for more dumb questions starting with the person you just pitched.

What I find when I pitch a stranger is that the words coming out of my mouth have very little to do with the picture that's in my head. The act of linearly mapping my thoughts into words and sentences exposes flaws or gaps in my thinking that I never find when the ideas are swirling around my head. This leads me to our next step.

Write it down, throw it away, write it down again. Once your stranger is no longer totally confused by your idea, it's time to write it down. This is the same process as pitching the stranger in that you're finding another medium to test your idea. The stranger gave you a chance to verbalize your pitch; writing it down routes your idea through a completely different part of your brain and then down through your fingers. Seeing the words on a piece of paper or flat panel monitor will, once again, expose gaps you can't see in the picture in your mind. Those gaps prove you've got more dumb questions, so go ask them, write it down again, and then throw it away. That's right, don't just close the document window; you need to get rid of everything you just wrote down. Toss it, empty the trash, and step away from the computer.

I know you're attached to some part of that document that you wrote—some witty thought that elegantly captured an angle on your problem—but remember what we're trying to solve here. This isn't whether or not you should get a blueberry-orange muffin on the way to work, this is a decision that matters, and solving it elegantly means you want to visit and revisit your response as many times as possible. Consigning your first written draft to the ether might forever lose a piece of wit, but if that wit shows up in the second draft, I guarantee that it belongs there and you'll never lose it again.

Passive Soaking

Once you've done all your active content acquisition, once you've pitched some strangers, once you've written it down a few times, you need to stop actively working on the problem. Remove that sticky from your screen, hide those second drafts on your desktop, and just stop working on it. Yes, you need to make a decision, you need to respond to whatever the problem is, and while I am saying you should remove all the physical artifacts of your active soak, you're not going to stop. You can't. Your brain won't let you.

Back to the original flame mail from your friend. You've received these before and you know the absolute wrong thing to do is immediately respond. Of course, your animal brain is dying to do so because _it feels so good to punch back_, but it's never the right move because your animal brain is defending itself, it's not resolving anything other than proving _boy, can I punch back or what?_ My advice regarding flame-o-grams and hard decisions is the same. Sleep on it.

A night's rest is one of the best ways to calm and alter your perspective on a problem. Ever gone to bed at night when the sky is falling and awoken to a blissfully simple way to easily prop the sky up? How'd that happen? The answer is, your brain never stops working. Better yet, it has the unique ability to subconsciously construct elegant solutions to hard problems when you least expect it. Call it inspiration, call it intuition, but don't stare at it too long because it's a shy ability. It does its best work when no one knows it's there.

Soaking Takes Time

Don't tell anyone I work with, but I earn a majority of my pay during the 40-minute drive to work in the morning. I get in the car with my cup of coffee, hit the road, and let my mind wander to whatever music is playing. Never do I think, "OK, Phil flamed me pretty hard yesterday . . . how am I going to deal with this?" My mind stumbles, it strikes out in random directions, and I never know where it'll end up. Still, if I've spent time actively soaking on the Phil problem the day before, my wandering often ends up somewhere Phil-like, and sometimes, the mental journey reveals a nugget of inspiration.

As practical advice goes, the soak is sometimes pretty thin. If your boss is waiting for you to weigh in on a critical decision, I am not advising you to say, "I have no clue what to do, I'm going to go ask dumb questions, pitch a stranger, write it down and then throw it away, and then forget everything I did." What I am saying is that any big decision, any big problem, deserves time and consideration. If you've got years of experience under your belt, you can probably wing it pretty well, but you're still going to be faced with situations where the right decision is to not decide, but think.

The soak is, hands down, the favorite part of my job. What I'm doing when I'm soaking on something is an act of creation. It's design work. It's strategy. It's removing the emotion and ignorance from a problem and then constructing an original solution that shows those I work with that I'm actively caring about what I do.

Managing Malcolm Events

The nerd frenzy around the original *Jurassic Park* was significant and led by the promise of lifelike computer animation. This was a win-win for engineers. Not only do we tap into our preadolescent dinosaur love, but we also get to watch the first movie where dinosaurs actually show up, and, by the way, using *the tools we wrote*. OK, so I was at Borland at the time, and we wrote programming languages and applications in the early 1990s, but *those ILM guys are just down the street. We're buds.*

Strangely, 18 years later, the memory that has stuck with me from the movie was a quote by Jeff Goldblum's character, Ian Malcolm. He was sitting in the Jurassic SUV, busily hitting on Laura Dern, trying to explain chaos theory to a paleobotanist, when he made a comment that burned itself into my brain.

He was demonstrating chaos theory by placing drops of water on the top of her raised hand and asking, "Which way is it going to fall?" (Smooth, really smooth, Jeff.) The drops fell in a different direction each time, and Malcolm attributed this to "the principle of tiny variations—the orientations of the hairs on your hand, the amount of blood distending in the skin, [they] never repeat, and vastly affect the outcome ..."

For you nerds out there who want to know more, go read about the butterfly effect. But for me, the quote encapsulates an essential part of practical software design. In the years since the movie, I've mutated the quote into this: "Seemingly insignificant events that are intent on screwing you in an unlikely way." These events are named after Ian Malcolm, as they are called *Malcolm events*.

We're in a Hurry

We're always in a hurry in the Silicon Valley. If we're not making new stuff, we're making stuff to help us make new stuff. Our stuff-building process varies from company to company but it usually follows a cycle that looks like this:

> **Design:** Brainstorm new stuff to make. Talk a lot. Throw a lot away. Talk some more.

> **Development:** Less talking, more doing. Engineers are heads-down and managers are wondering what they're supposed to do.

> **Deployment:** More talking, some yelling, managers are busily keeping everyone from killing each other, and then it's suddenly ... done.

We're in the design phase right now, you and I. I'm the manager, you're the senior engineer, and we're brainstorming our next release. We've each got a fuzzy picture of what we want to do in the next release, but it's not clear. There's nothing that defines the picture, so we're just throwing ideas against the wall to see what's going to stick.

Nothing appears to be sticking until you say something off the cuff; I take the idea, riff on it, write it on the whiteboard and *wham* ... that's the Feature. It's the piece of work, the design, that will define your release. We know it is because we both sit there staring at the whiteboard at the Feature knowing that this moment will define everything after it. Doesn't happen often; savor it.

This is not a Malcolm event. This moment is akin to a "holy shit" moment when you first understand a marvelous new technology. You must have these moments to have an inspired release, but you haven't been screwed by a Malcolm event, yet.

Let's keep moving.

Great, so we've got the Feature. Now the frenzy begins. We can't keep our paws off the whiteboard because we know that in the next 15 minutes, the rest of the features are just going to come pouring out. Now, during the frenzy, a whole pile of decisions are going to be made, and while we're valiantly going to try to capture them on our whiteboard, we're going to miss a few.

I want to pick one of these missed decisions. At first glance, it's not a big decision. In fact, in the creative frenzy that is the discovery of a release, it's a really small decision. When the meeting is over, we forget that it was made because we're digesting the mental high imparted by this discovery of the Feature.

Problem is, this decision does matter. What you don't know is that this decision clarifies the Feature in a critical way for those who weren't in the first meeting frenzy. By the way, *that's everyone.*

No one knows this yet, but this is your Malcolm event.

Understanding Malcolm Events

It's a month later, and development has begun and more folks are involved. Someone asks you a question about the Feature and the answer is the decision that was forgotten. No big deal, you answer the question and move on. A week later, you get asked the same question by a QA guy. Haven't you already answered this question? Yeah, you did. OK, no big deal. Here's the answer.

Another month passes and by your count, you've been asked the same clarifying question ten times and you're wondering, "Don't people get it? Isn't it obvious what the answer is?"

No, they don't. They weren't in the religious experience that was your original design meeting and, more bad news, these people who are asking the questions— they aren't the problem. It's the people who aren't asking. It's the ones who are assuming an answer to the question and not asking. They're thinking, "Well, if it was important, someone would've told me or written it down, right?"

A Malcolm event is when a seemingly insignificant event screws up your release in an unlikely way. In the case of this clarifying decision, it's a poor-communication tax. Everyone is wondering about this odd aspect of the Feature and in that confusion they are wasting time and they are wasting money.

The release might go swimmingly. The Malcolm event might just be an annoyance where, in every meeting, someone asks *the same lame question.* Or maybe you're not so lucky. Maybe the documentation folks never bother to ask a clarification question and your documentation describes your Feature poorly. Even worse, maybe the developer responsible for the Feature spends a month developing to his version of reality before you install a build and figure out that people can't read your mind.

There's a wide spectrum of cost for Malcolm events, so let's try to avoid them. Here's how.

Artifacts

Someone who has been reading this piece has had their hand up for most of the chapter. OK, what's your question?

"Rands, you're talking about specifications! Functional specifications! Interaction designs, visual designs, and wireframes! Who doesn't love wire—"

OK, hand down.

No, this is not a piece that is going to describe the many benefits of writing stuff down and, yes, there are many benefits, but this is a heavy-handed approach for avoiding Malcolm events.

Remember, we're talking about the little stuff here. I'm not talking about the broad strokes of a release, I'm talking about the seemingly inconsequential details that are intent on screwing you. A well-written specification will document all of your details, but do you have time to write and maintain specifications? I don't. I'm coming up on two decades of working at fairly successful companies, and I can count the number of useful specifications I've read on two hands. Really.

The issue isn't that specifications are a bad idea, it's that they are time-consuming. And remember, we're in a hurry. Still, something does need to be captured because the first thing we need to avoid a Malcolm event is an artifact.

An artifact captures an essential piece of knowledge. Yes, it can be a specification or a blurb or a picture or a priority or even an owner. The key is you've got to know it's essential to capture this artifact because you've been here before and you know that if this piece of knowledge is not well understood across the organization, you're screwed.

I learned this the hard way during the second release of our product at a startup. In an early brainstorming meeting, our VP of sales spent a good hour explaining the need for better performance. We all nodded knowing that a future release of the product would include a new application server that would improve our performance issues. The problem was, no one ever told the VP "no," and worse, when the product shipped, the performance was slightly worse. When the VP found out, he was in my office yelling for a solid 30 minutes.

In our next release, we correctly decided to hold off the application server for another six months, and every single feature list I wrote had the following line, in bold, at the top of the list: "No performance increases in this release."

Malcolm event detection is simply the hardest part of your job because it's the art of identifying the significantly insignificant, and I'd like to provide some great advice here, but my advice is simple and unfortunate. The only way you're going to learn to identify potential Malcolm events is by going through some horrible, horrible experiences.

Sorry.

Binders

Great, so using your past horrible experiences, you've captured an artifact. Let's say it's a semi-scribbled drawing of a brilliant UI design. Congratulations on your foresight to write something down. Now what? Where do you keep that drawing? In your Moleskine? Well, that's fashionable and useless. An artifact stuffed in your notebook is akin to not writing it down at all.

Successful artifact management is the key to avoiding Malcolm events, and the key to successful artifact management are the three As. These are:

Availability: Your artifact matters. You already know that, but does everyone else? It needs to be sitting somewhere where anyone who cares is going to trip over it. It's a wiki page, it's an e-mail sent to everyone, it's a presentation. I don't know what your organization communication patterns are, but you've got to stick your artifact in the middle of it. "Folks, this scribble is our future." This leads us to the next A.

Agreement: The reason you created your artifact is because you believe you've identified a critical piece of information, where critical could mean novel, controversial, or just important. By making your artifact available to the team, you're saying, "Pay attention to me," and this is a critical juncture. This is when you consign a Malcolm event to oblivion because you're making it common knowledge. It sounds like I'm just describing availability again, but I'm not. I'm talking about the hallway argument that goes down when Phil reads your weekly status reports and it reads, "We're not doing Phil's favorite feature."

So, you and Phil have it out. You debate pros and cons, he gives a little, you give a little, and suddenly, it's OK. We don't need to do Phil's feature because we're doing this other feature and Phil understands why.

Accuracy: This is the easiest part of the three As. As your artifact soaks through the organization, it's going to change. Folks are going to tweak the scribble, Phil is going to request a minor change, and your artifact is going to evolve. Take the time to revise the artifact as it evolves in the hallway because you never know what minor change might set off some random person who was fine with the first version of the artifact.

Availability, agreement, and accuracy. I call these nouns "binders" because they bind people to the Malcolm event. If they see, read it, and comment on it, it becomes bound to them. It's no longer an insignificant event, it's common knowledge.

Success Is Often Silence

Avoiding Malcolm events is completely unsatisfying and here's why: you know what failure sounds like, but success is silent. It's when the release goes well. It's when you don't have to release an immediate update to your major release. Avoiding a Malcolm event is when you managed to predict the future and no one is going to believe you when you tell them what you did because nothing happened.

Management is the care and feeding of the invisible. You're doing your best when it appears the least is happening. I love the thrill of the last month of a release as much as the next guy, but I suspect the reason we're yelling at each other, working weekends, and feeling the depressing weight of compromise is because we're surrounded by Malcolm events.

Capturing Context

Each organization in a company has its Favorite Application. It's not truly their favorite application; it's just the application they must use in their particular capacity in the organization. Stand up right now and walk into an unfamiliar part of your building and stalk your coworkers. If someone stops and asks you what you're doing, tell them, "Rands sent me," and vigorously nod your head. That always works.

As you walk the hallways of this strange new part of your organization, look at their screens. What's the consistent application sitting on their monitors? Is it Excel? Well, you're probably in some area of operations. Are you seeing a lot of Word? Maybe legal, possibly tech pubs. Is the cube empty? That's sales.

The most common application in engineering is an editor. Whether it's a terminal window or the world's fanciest integrated development environment, their Favorite Application is a code editor, but it's not their secret weapon. That would be version control.

The concept behind version control is simple. It's a central network repository for all the files of which a project is comprised. If I want to edit a file, I run a tool (which works alongside my editor) that makes a local read/write copy of that file on my system. I make my changes and then, using the same tool, I check in my file to the network. So, what's the big deal?

Usually, there is no deal. You merrily check in and check out your files with no fuss. The deal occurs when you realize that software projects are often massive collections of files that are edited by teams of people. A version control system solves the problem that occurs when two engineers have checked out and have changed the same file at the same time. Whoever checks in their changed file first has no deal. When the second one checks in, that engineer receives a message that warns,

"Hey, this file has changed while you had it checked out. Whaddayawannado?" The user then gets to figure out how to merge the two files into a consistent working whole.

That's version control as a traffic cop and that's cool because it prevents folks from bonking each other on the heads, but I haven't gotten to the major cool, and that's the other thing I do when I check in. I don't just check the file in; I also include information about what I changed:

"Rands added a new blingleforth function. It rocks."

The version control server then copies my new version of the file up, tags the new version with my name and my comments, and increments the version number associated with the file.

Let's ignore the useful fact that every single version of the file is stored in this system and focus on the comment I included with this change. This is the big deal. This is the secret weapon in engineering. We not only save every version of our work, we also capture the context of the change. Version control stores the thoughts that made our ideas bright.

If you're thinking, "My, what a quaint nerd custom," if you're not having a clouds-are-parting moment, think about two products: del.icio.us and Flickr. Both have built their feature sets around capturing context, and by context, I do mean tags. Each time someone adds a new link or photo to these services, they can add whatever tags they like. No rules. Just start typing words regarding what makes the link or photo relevant. That's context.

When you start stumbling around Flickr and del.icio.us, you realize the value that is created when people choose to capture and share the context of their content. At the South by Southwest Interactive conference in Austin, I was in awe of the folks who were taking the time not only to capture and upload their photos to Flickr, but also taking the time to carefully tag all their content. Thirty minutes after a presentation, there were dozens of tagged pictures sitting in Flickr for the presentation I just watched.

So What?

Think of the big project you're working on right now. For me, it's this chapter I'm merrily typing away and hitting the Save button every 12 seconds because I'm a twitchy saver. Comes from years of flaky Windows applications that liked to crash. *If you save a lot, you're not screwed.*

When should I capture context on this project? When should I stop and capture the thoughts about what I just wrote? Whenever I've created significance. I've been keeping track of these moments while I've been writing and so far. They are:

1. New intro down, borrowed from version control article I can never seem to finish.

2. Removed Wikipedia from example technology—Flickr 'n' del.icio.us are enough ... don't confuse them with wikis.

3. Keep moving disclosure paragraph around ... haven't found a home, yet. Might be wrongly in love with this paragraph.

Do these comments matter to you? No. Do they matter to me? Yes. Do I want my favorite editor to prompt me every time I hit the Save key for context? No. I want another verb, let's call it *wow*, and let's have it mean, "I've done something significant to my project and I want to capture the context of that change."

This is not an obvious activity for most people. In fact, huge passive-aggressive battles have been fought within my engineering teams over these change comments. It's a fight between those who are lazy and just want to check in their files and those who know that, while having the code safely in version control is good, understanding what is happening to the project on a day-to-day basis is even better. It's called a status report.

That's right; I finally found my technology angle on killing status reports. We need our tools to allow us to capture context at the moment we're being bright, not Friday at 4 p.m. when we're trying to get the hell out of work. How much easier would your status report process be if all you had to do on Friday afternoon was ask your favorite app, "Show me all the wow for the last week"? That report alone is enough incentive for me try to remember to record my wow among all my twitchy saving.

Nerd Disclosure

I'm serious a version control nerd. At Borland, I was the junior engineer, which means I was saddled with building the product duties. This means if the product did not build, someone yelled at me. This gave me a strong incentive to build an application that forced each engineer to make a comment, no matter how small, each time they checked into the project. *It's not me. It's him.* At Netscape, I watched in awe as CVS was merged with bug tracking and build systems via primal web applications. I still drool over Tinderbox. At my startup, I was the guy who took Microsoft SourceSafe out behind the building and kicked the shit out of it.

I live and breathe version control because I see the value. Each year, I learn more about more Favorite Applications. I learn how executives live and breathe presentation software. I learn about the magic that those folks in operations can coax out of Microsoft Excel. Everyone is hard at work creating stuff, and, with some minor tweaks to our Favorite Apps, we can wrestle version control from the nerds and help everyone index their brightness.

Trickle Theory

Buried.

Back at the startup, we were shifting gears. After six months of talking about shipping a product, we needed to ship a product, and nothing gets everyone's attention like a deadline. The good news was that QA had been doing its job, and there was a pile of work in our bug database. The bad news was that no one had looked at the database in months.

We had a rent-a-VP at the time, and as temporary executives go, he was sharp. He quickly deduced our goal—ship a quality beta—but he also quickly discerned that we had no idea about the quality of the product because of our pile of untriaged bugs.

He called a meeting with the QA manager, the tech support manager, and me. His advice: "Triage every single bug in this fashion and tell me how many bugs we've got to fix in order to ship this beta." And then he left.

Every single bug. 537 bugs. You gotta read the bug, possibly reproduce it, and then make an educated team decision. Let's assume an average of 5 minutes per, and you're talking about . . . crap . . . 45 hours of bug triage. It's an impossible task. I've got features to fix, people to manage, and I haven't seen the sun on a Saturday in two weeks.

Let's take a brief segue and talk about the huge value that exists in a bug database. In just about every company I've worked at, the only source of measurable truth regarding the product is the bug database. Marketing documents get stale. Test plans become decrepit. Test case databases slowly mutate into the unusable personal to-do list of QA. The bug database is the only source of data regarding your product.

I know this. I know that once I've effectively scrubbed the bug database, I've got the single most informed opinion regarding the product.

But.

537 unscrubbed bugs? 40-plus hours of bug drudgery?

Please. I've got a product to ship.

My normal approach when faced with an impossible task is analysis, because analysis gives you data, which in turn allows you to make a confident decision. So, I do what I did above: carefully estimate how long it will take to complete: 5 minutes X 537 = impossible. This fair estimate freezes me with fear. How in the world am I going to get my other five jobs done while scrubbing 40 hours of bugs? Once I'm good and lost in that fear, the impossible task, I'm no longer thinking about getting the task done, I'm thinking about the fear.

My advice is: Start.

"But Rands . . . I've got 300 tests to run and one day to . . ."

Stop. Go run one test. Now.

"Wait, wait, wait. Rands. Listen. They need this spec tomorrow at 9 a.m. . . ."

Shush. Quiet. Go write. Just a paragraph. Now.

Welcome to Trickle theory.

Our Villain

My traditional first move when managing impossible tasks is to put the task on a to-do list.

"There! It's on the list. Aaaaaaah . . . didn't that feel good? It's on the to-do list, which must mean it will be done at some point, right?" Wrong. Putting the task on the to-do list does one thing: it helps you avoids *the Critic.*

Every story needs a villain, and in this piece our villain is the Critic. This is your internal voice, which does careful and critical analysis of your life, and he's gained a powerful place in your head because he's saved your butt more than once.

He's the one who told you that offer from the startup smelled too good to be true. You remember that company, right? The one that simply vanished three months after you declined that stunning offer letter. It was the Critic who said, "How in the world can they afford to give anyone this type of offer when I don't even understand their business model?"

The Critic was the one who calmed you inner nerd and convinced you to not buy HDTV six years ago before it got really good, and he told you not to trust that fast-talking engineering manager who emphatically guaranteed his team would be done on schedule. The Critic said, "People who talk fast are moving quickly to cover up the gaps in their knowledge."

The Critic was right. The Critic gained credibility. The Critic can also amplify your fears at the worst possible moment. That's why, for this piece, he's still the villain.

I know it feels great to get that impossible task on the to-do list. I know it feels like you actually did something, but what you've done is avoid conflict. You know that if you start considering the impossible task, the Critic is going to chime in with his booming voice of practicality, *"Rands, what are you thinking? No one adds features two weeks before a ship date!"*

"OK, all right, you're right, but the boss wants it and when the boss gets something in his head it takes a lot of work to blah blah blah …" Now, you're justifying, you're worrying, and you're arguing with the Critic when what you should be doing is starting.

Nothing Happens Until You Start

Let's first break down *impossibleness*. For the sake of this chapter, there are two types of impossible tasks. First, there are impossibly dull tasks. This is work that requires no mental effort, but is vast in size. Bug scrubbing is a great example of this. At the other end of the spectrum are impossibly hard tasks. These are tasks like, "Hey Rands, we need a new product by Christmas. Yes, I know it's October. Ready? Go!"

Oddly, attacking both boring and hard tasks involve the same mental kung fu where your first move is starting.

Such silly, trivial advice . . . start. Still, take a moment and examine your mental to-do list or just look at your written one. How many terribly important tasks have been there more than a month? More than a year? Embarrassing, huh? It's not that they're not important; it's just that you didn't begin and you didn't begin because the moment you think about starting, the Critic weighs in, "How will you even start? You'll never finish! You don't even know where to start."

Begin. Go read the first bug. Don't think about how many are left. Go to the next one and watch what happens. In just a few minutes, you'll have made something resembling progress. Two more bugs, and it'll start to feel like momentum. Progress + momentum = confidence. The moment you see yourself tackle the smallest part of the impossible task, the quieter the Critic becomes, because you're slowly proving him wrong.

Iterate

The second piece of advice is simpler than the first, which is hard to imagine. Iterate. Once you've kicked yourself out of stop, iterate becomes a little easier, but if you're truly tackling an impossible task, the Critic simply isn't going to shut up.

"Wow, you've closed five bugs … Only 532 more to go, sport!" Iteration and repetition aren't going to silence the Critic. Progress will. A beautiful thing happens when you point your brain at an impossible task. Once you've begun and start chewing on whatever the task is, you'll start to see inefficiencies and begin to fine-tune your process. This is how an engineer who tells you, "It's going to take two weeks to write that code" comes back after the weekend and says, "It's done." He honestly believed that it was a two-week task, but as soon as he started chewing on the problem, he realized he'd written similar code a year ago, which, with a half a Saturday of tweaking, provided the same functionality.

The same applies to small, duller impossible tasks. Previously, when I estimated it'd take five minutes of triage for each bug, I didn't take into consideration that after about 50 bugs, I was going to be really good at scrubbing bugs. I'd start to identify people who generally wrote good bugs versus those who didn't have a clue. I'd learn the problematic areas of the product and learn where I could make snap judgments regarding bug viability. What was a 5-minute triage window for the first 50 bugs was 1 minute for the next 50, and that turned into an average of 15 seconds per bug for the second hundred when I really got rolling.

This means that my original estimate of needing 45 hours for bug scrubbage turned out to be roughly 7 hours. What I thought would take a week is actually going to take one solid day.

Do not believe that this gives you the authority to slice every single estimate by five. Turns out that impossible tasks, upon consideration, actually are terrifically hard. Believe this; an individual tends to be very bad at work estimates until they've begun the work.

Mix It Up

Crap. You've been saddled with an impossible task, and after a weekend of no sleep, you have confirmed, yes, the task is impossible. In fact, you've started, you've iterated, and you still have no clue how to actually complete the task. Story time.

This spring I had a crew come up to clear some brush on the property. Now, the property is a pleasant combination of oaks, bays, and redwoods, but much of it had become overgrown and inaccessible. My first thought when I moved in was, "Hell yes, I've got clearing mojo!" My thought after one weekend of clearing, when I was partially successful at clearing up 50 square feet of 5 *acres of forest* was, "Impossibly boring."

This attitude gave me a unique curiosity when the crew of three men showed up, chain-saws in hand, to clear the land. They had no issue starting and they clearly had the iteration thing down, but they also demonstrated the last and most important component to Trickle theory: mix it up.

It went like this: one guy would cut and drag brush into the fire, another would cut trees down, and the third would trim fallen trees. This went on for a while, and then they'd all switch. Now, drag guy was cut guy, cut guy was hauling wood guy, and trim guy was stack guy. During lunch, I sat down and asked, "When do you guys switch jobs?"

"When we're bored."

Beautiful, beautiful Trickle theory. How cool is this? If you're working on an impossibly hard or impossibly dull task and you find yourself mentally blocked by boredom or confusion, stop and do something else. The benefits of stopping are stunning.

First, stopping smacks the Critic squarely across the face. See, he's also the voice in your head saying, "Uh, if we don't work hard on this, we're screwed." And the longer you sit there grinding out the impossible task when you don't want to, the louder he gets.

Second, stopping to do something else is fun for you and your brain. It breaks the cycle of whatever tasks you're doing and points your gray matter at a whole new problem—and your brain loves new; it consumes new with vim and vigor, and that puts spring in your proverbial mental step.

Third, and most important, even though you are stopping, your brain is bright enough to keep background processing the impossible task. This is why we find so much inspiration in the shower; you're stopping and letting your brain wander, and your brain is smart. Your brain knows how important it is to rewrite that feature in two days and your brain is always working on that feature whether you know it or not.

"Wait, wait, wait. Rands, let me get this straight. Your suggestion when I've got a looming impossible deadline is to stop working on my deliverables?"

What I'm saying is, when you're facing an uphill mental battle with yourself regarding the impossible task, it's time to choose another battle ... that isn't a battle.

Entropy Always Wins

My life appears to be an endless series of tasks that are geared to slightly tidy up my world. Viewed as a whole, these tasks represent a lot of work. Viewed against the actual amount of entropy in play in my small part of the world, these tasks represent a futile effort.

Fact is, your world is changing faster than you'll ever be able to keep up with, and you can view that fact from two different perspectives:

- I believe I can control my world, and through an aggressive campaign of task management, personal goals, and a *can do* attitude, I will succeed in doing the impossible. Go me!

Or ...

- I know there is no controlling the world, but I will fluidly surf the entropy by constantly changing myself.

Surfing entropy takes confidence. This isn't Tony Robbins confidence; this is a personal confidence you earn by constantly adapting yourself to the impossible.

When the Sky Falls

A few years ago I wrote a piece that romanticized the state of the sky falling. The article is not about fixing disasters, it's about preventing them—but no matter how much you prepare, disasters happen.

The romance surrounding disasters is history speaking. When the disaster shows up and you see it, no one but you knows that you want to throw up. That's your brain releasing a complex chemical cocktail that is physically and emotionally preparing you for the most sensible course of action—making a fucking run for it.

But, strangely, you do not run.

Having watched, participated in, and created a bevy of sky-falling situations in my career, I take the process I use for managing these situations for granted. It feels like I'm working on pure and spontaneous instinct, but these are honed instincts that I've built and refined over a great many DEFCON 1 disasters—the world is about to end, or so the participants think—that I've had the unfortunate pleasure of attending.

This is my documentation of the process, and I sincerely hope you never have to deploy it, but I'm pretty sure you will. Before we start, here are a few assumptions and notes about this process:

- This is not a solo disaster. It's not just you; it involves a large group of people wrestling with a complex disaster, featuring different politics and motivations with an unknown root cause.

- No matter how much I sit here and EXPLAIN IN ALL CAPS THAT THIS PROCESS WORKS, you're going to skip at least one of the following four steps. That's cool. Each section includes a handy "This is what happens if you ignore this" section addendum so you clearly understand the magnitude of your omission.

- I'm going to describe this process simply and serially, but in reality these steps overlap and often run in parallel.

- Oh yeah, there's a good chance this disaster *is* your fault.

Let's begin.

Step 1: The Situation in the War Room

Your first job is to understand absolutely everything you need to know about the current state of the disaster—you are developing a mental model. Ideally, I want to be able to draw a complete picture for everyone about whatever the hell is currently happening. I need whiteboards—lots of them. I need a War Room.

The War Room is a base of operations. The requirements are simple: enough room to hold a quorum of people, a table, chairs, and lots and lots of whiteboards and markers. In this room, you are going to begin the immediate task of research, information gathering, and assessment. Every single person—everyone—who has any relevant knowledge about the situation is now going to parade through the War Room, and you're going to capture and triangulate all of their knowledge.

The intent of the War Room is to break everyone from their flow. The War Room includes a menagerie of people coming in and out, empty pizza boxes and Red Bull cans, and whiteboards full of indecipherable scribbles. It sends a clear message: the status quo is not presently working.

As the people start streaming in for the inquisition, remember that this first step is data collection, not problem solving and not judgment. The hardest part of this step is not jumping when you think you see a place where you can start moving. *That! That! That! We need to fix that!* It very well might be the right move to fix that, but you don't even know how much "that" there is, yet.

The initial goal during this step is information acquisition, not action. Each time you take action with incomplete data, you risk stoking rather than extinguishing the disaster fire. And, by the way, this type of lack-of-foresight, hyper-reactive mode is likely what got you here in the first place. The War Room is a place to focus on gathering a breadth of information first, then a depth, so you can answer the question, "Do we understand the situation?"

For me understanding comes in three forms:

1. The picture I begin to draw repeatedly on the whiteboard starts to represent a realistic picture of what has actually occurred.

2. A list of additional research, work, and potential next actions is developed, revised, and iteratively prioritized (but not yet acted on).

3. After much of numbers 1 and 2, I'm looking for a very precise moment. It always happens at a different time, but it is distinct. It is the moment I have the glimpse of a theory. *This ... is what we need to do.*

What happens if you ignore this

A surprising number of smart people skip this step. They believe that they can both assess and solve the problem at the same time. This is akin to saying, "I will solve a math equation that I can only half see." It's absurd, but it's precisely what someone does when they start making critical decisions with incomplete data.

Action feels like progress, but undirected action is not progress, nor is it a plan. You're going to barge into the office and start barking orders because that is what everyone expects, but if your orders are not shaped by what you're really attempting to do, you are just sending people scurrying around aimlessly. Yes, you may get lucky. Yes, everyone breathes a sigh of relief when you show up with your impressive sense of purpose. But in my experience, when my direction doesn't map to intent, I'm usually getting no closer to propping up the sky.

Step 2: The "Bet Your Car" Perspective

With your newfound confidence that you have fully described the problem in front of you and have a semblance of a fix, my timely buzz kill is this: I am 100 percent absolutely certain that you've missed something essential in your first pass. There are two ways to discover this: you can jump straight into the next step and discover this absence at the most inconvenient and credibility-destroying moment, or you can check your math. To do the latter, do two things.

The first thing you must do

Vet your model with at least three qualified others. These are people who were not directly involved in step 1 and who are people who don't need to understand the particulars of the disaster. But they can appreciate the broad strokes because they've been there and have no issue with telling you how screwed you are.

The joy that occurs at the end of step 1 is the discovery of a fix. This moment of illumination is gratifying because it's the first time you believe there is a chance the sky can be propped up. The bad news: Confidence is not a plan. This situation is very common with software developers who are fixing bugs. They look at the bug description, write a few lines of code, rebuild, and, voila, it's fixed, because when they reproduce the exact steps of the bug, the bug no longer occurs. They have no idea that this small change in the import-export code will also have unintended side effects on other file operations.

Having a solution where all the implications of the solution are not understood is not a fix. You must take the time to explore all the implications—and in my experience this takes *longer than it takes to come up with your plan.*

The second thing you must do

Once your qualified others have discovered those gaping holes and unintended consequences that are guaranteed to exist in your fix—your model—you need to throw the current version on the nearest whiteboard in the War Room with the folks who are responsible for the work that's going to go down over the next few days, and ask the same question: Does this picture, this list, make sense?

This is yet another error correction pass for gaping holes. It's also a pass on prioritization, but most importantly, it's an assignment of ownership.

One of the leading causes of sky-falling situations is distributed ownership, and as a strategy, distributed ownership seems very humane. We're going to put the right people on the right problems. *We're going to empower the most qualified people to make their own decisions regarding their local problems because they have local knowledge and can make the best decisions using this knowledge.* As a human being and a nerd who has an intense allergy to being told what to do, this model of distributed ownership appeals to me. I imagine small teams of bright people empowered because they feel they control their destiny.

A sky-falling situation exists not because of a single failure on one team. It's a collection of multiple large and small mistakes on many teams that snowballs into an unexpected worst-case scenario. Teams of people succeed and fail at scale. A likely major contribution to your current disaster is the fact that multiple well-meaning and fully informed people looked at an emergent disaster and thought, "Well, someone who is not me is going to handle this, right?"

Since you're the person who is racing to work while panicking about the sky falling, I'm going to call you what we called these folks during my tenure at Apple: the Directly Responsible Individual, or DRI. This name clearly describes the person who is directly responsible for whatever the situation might be, and it refers to a person. It's not the Directly Responsible Group of People with Good Intentions Who Are Attempting to Feel Good by Building Consensus but Who Are Mostly Wasting Everyone's Time. It's an individual who is owning the entire situation.

However, as the DRI, the person who is most likely to be yelled at, your job is to be accountable. Your job is not to own all of the work, which is why the last part of this step is to put a proper name next to each and every task, and, as much as possible, this name should not be yours. When you're done with this assignment, and someone in the War Room asks, "Hey, why isn't your name on the list?" Your answer is, "Because I'm the one making sure this whole thing is moving forward and I'm the one who gets fired if it doesn't."

What happens if you ignore this

There are a variety of skippable parts in step 2, but I'm not worried that you don't have an initial plan or that you're incapable of pulling trusted others in to distribute the load. The part that has screwed me the most is failing to understand all of the implications of my theory.

A former boss used to put this into clear perspective: "Do you understand all of the implications of your plan?" *Yes, I do.* "Give me your car keys." *Wait, what?* "Would you bet your car on the viability of your plan?" [Sound effect: shaking keys.] *Right, yeah, let me do one more pass.*

Step 3: Constant and Consistent Sky-Propping Pressure

When the sky is falling, everybody is watching. Everybody wants status an hour ago. Everybody is talking to everybody else about the state of your sky-falling situation, which means the Grapevine is actively working against you. The amount of fear, uncertainty, doubt, and outright lies generated about what's actually going on is impressive.

I'm assuming that you've got a credible plan that you've carefully vetted with others. I'm assuming you've assigned the work to competent folks who have a sense of ownership of their respective parts of the plan. I'm assuming the War Room is abuzz with the action defined by the plan. While all of this going on, your job is internal public relations.

As soon as I have something to report, I send the report to everyone who wants to know. If you walk by the War Room, poke your head in, and ask, "What's up, guys?" I add you to the distribution list. You're going to get every update until you beg to be removed. Anyone who mails me any random question—they're on the list. The game here isn't just overcommunication and Grapevine eradication; I'm still worried I missed something in the plan, and the status spamming is another means of vetting both the plan and the progress.

How often do I send status? It's a judgment call based on progress relative to the beginning of the disaster. The better the legitimate progress, the fewer the updates. It moves slowly from hourly updates to daily updates and ultimately to weekly ones, which is when I start thinking about tearing down the War Room.

What happens if you ignore this

It's hard to imagine someone not regularly broadcasting clear, demonstrative, measurable, and consistent progress. Maybe because you're still deep in research and don't yet have a theory, and you don't want to call attention to that fact? Maybe there hasn't been significant progress on anything since your last update? You still send status. The message you send by consistently keeping the folks who care up to date is not, "We've made unique progress" or "We have a theory." The message is, "We are applying constant and consistent pressure on propping up the sky."

The Elusive Step 0

I'm reading an early draft of this piece and it still feels like there's romanticism about this process. *Look at me, Captain of the War Room;* I'M GOING TO SAVE THE WORLD. There's nothing romantic about this situation. There's no glory in propping up the sky because, chances are, you and your team are partially responsible for this situation, and depending on the severity of the disaster, there's a good chance you could get fired. Even if you fix it.

There's a fourth step to this process that I've confusingly labeled as step 0. I've put the first step last because I believe it's the most important part of this process. I've put the first step last because if you're able to confidently answer the question it calls, you'll greatly increase the chances that you won't repeat this disaster in the future. The question is, What, precisely, are you trying to do?

It seems like a dumb and obvious question at this very moment, but right now you're chilling with your iPad in the coffee shop. You've just taken your third sip of that half-caf quad-shot latte and you don't have a care in the world. If the sky were actually falling, you'd be racing to work, breaking speeding laws, and frantically thinking, "How am I going to unfuck this situation?"

Unfucking this situation is a sensible and obvious outcome, and while you're driving 105 miles an hour down Highway 280 to the scene of the crime, I will repeat myself: *What, precisely, are you trying to do?*

It's a hard question to effectively answer when people are yelling, but phenomenal answers sound like this:

- We need to demonstrate to this customer that we are capable of exceeding their expectations.

- We need the people who depend on us to trust that their faith in us is not misplaced.

- We need the planet Earth to understand that we aren't evil.

You will notice that none of these answers read "unfuck the situation." When the sky is falling, as I've said before, immediate action feels like precisely the right course of action, because, HELLO, THE SKY IS FALLING. But there is a well-defined reason for this situation, and it's likely you won't know the reason for a while. It's agonizing, but my advice is to not make any decisions on a course of action until you have at least a credible answer to this question.

In the face of disaster, it's the wise person who does not act until they know. Unfucking the situation is a bandage. Understanding what you're truly trying to fix is a cure.

Hacking
Is Important

Back in the early 1990s, Borland International was the place to be an engineer. Coming off the purchase of Ashton-Tate, Borland was the third-largest software company, but, more importantly, it was a legitimate competitor of Microsoft. Philippe Kahn, the CEO at the time, was fond of motorcycles, saxophones, and brash statements at all-hands meetings: "We're barbarians, not bureaucrats!"

At the time, Kahn was not only navigating the integration of Ashton-Tate, he was in the midst of moving the product suite from DOS to Windows. All the products were complete object-oriented rewrites, and they were running late. Years late. At one all-hands, he explained how he wanted the company to think about itself. Recounted from a story in the *Los Angeles Times* from 1992:[1]

> *Kahn was reading a dense history of Central Asia a few years ago when it struck him that many of the nomadic tribes of the steppes were actually far more ethical and disciplined than the European "civilizations" they were confronting.*

> *They were austere and ambitious, eager for victory, but not given to celebrating it. They were organized around small, collaborative groups that were far more flexible and fast-moving than the entrenched societies of the time. They were outsiders and proud of it. They were barbarians.*

---

[1] Jonathan Weber, "Khan the Barbarian," *Los Angeles Times*, February 23, 1992 (http://articles.latimes.com/1992-02-23/business/fi-5118_1_borland-international-chairman-philippe-kahn).

Kahn's thinking regarding "barbarians" was prescient. It not only partially inspires agile and other lightweight software development methods, but it also reinforces a theme big companies are often unintentionally trying to forget: hacking is important.

"Hackers Believe Something Can Always Be Better"

Facebook doesn't want to be a big company. Like Google before it, Facebook took the time to carefully document the reasons it was not intending to become a traditional company in its S1 (corporate disclosure) filing,[2] and while this letter is positioned to the future legion of investors, it is a recipe for Facebook employees:

> *The Hacker Way is an approach to building that involves continuous improvement and iteration. Hackers believe that something can always be better, and that nothing is ever complete. They just have to go fix it—often in the face of people who say it's impossible or are content with the status quo.*

Facebook is worried about the growth paradox, which goes something like this: the end result of successful hacking is product, and that product needs to grow by building more things. The more you grow, the more things you have, and the more you need people whose job is simply to coordinate the increasingly interdependent building activities. These people, called managers, don't create product. They create process.

Hackers are allergic to process not because they don't understand the value; they're allergic to it because it violates their core values. These values are well documented in Zuckerberg's letter: "Done is better than perfect," "Code wins arguments," and "Hacker culture is extremely open and meritocratic." The folks who create process care about control, and they use politics to shape that control and to influence communications, and if there is ever a sentence that would cause a hacker to stand up and throw his or her keyboard at the screen, it's the first half of this one.

The growth paradox is that the chaotic means by which you found success might become distasteful to those you hire to maintain and build on that success. Once they've established themselves, they will point at the hacking and ask important-sounding questions such as, "What is it they are building?" or "How does this poorly defined thing fit into our overall strategy?" They will label these hackers "disruptors"—and they are 100 percent correct.

---

[2] http://blogs.wsj.com/deals/2012/02/01/mark-zuckerbergs-letter-from-the-facebook-filing/

Hacking is disruptive, and whether you code software, write books, or film movies, I believe bringing anything new into the world is a disruptive act. By being novel and compelling, the new is likely to replace something else, and that something else isn't being replaced without a fight.

Reasonable people are often scared by the new. This is because reasonable people are not barbarians, and they are not hackers. They appreciate the predictable, profitable, and knowable world that comes with a well-defined process, and I would like to thank each and every one of them because these people keep the trains running and on time. No one likes barbarians because the barbarian strategy is one at odds with civilization. By definition, a barbarian, a hacker, is building on a strategy that is at odds with the majority.

It's awesome.

Facebook's letter documents its core values: focus on impact, move fast, be bold, be open, and build social value. And as I read those bullets, I see two people at the table defining them: a high-impact, fast-moving and bold barbarian who couldn't care less about the biz dev guy who is arguing for being open and building social value.

Both people are essential to a business thriving, but only one of them knows that hacking is important.

Where's Dieter?

Apple solved the disruptive hacker problem by hiding it, and it starts with a question:

"Where's Dieter?"

"He moved to another project."

"Uh, he has 32 open radars and we've got two weeks until Feature Complete."

"He moved to another project."

"OK, what project?"

"I don't know."

It happens quietly, but the projects that could be the most disruptive to the company begin in silence. Someone, somewhere has a bright idea, and a handful of talented engineers are whisked off to a different building behind a locked door. Their status is "elsewhere" and their project is "need to know."

Having never sat with one of these projects, I can only infer how they work, but when you see the results, you know for certain—these guys and gals are hacking. Their projects are the definition of ambition, you've never heard their names, they're small and fast-moving, and they're outsiders in their own company. Sound familiar?

Now, I don't believe the secret projects are entirely about preventing disruption; there is a large marketing component. The return of Steve Jobs was the return of marketing, and a project being secret was less about secrecy and more about marketing. Steve wanted to be the first guy standing in front of the entire planet telling you the story: "You are not going to fucking believe what we've done."

Yes, there is internal jealousy about the teams performing the wizardry that resulted in products like the iPad, the iPhone, and AppleTV. There are people wondering, "Why wasn't I invited to the hacking?" Yes, this did create some elitism, but for better or worse, the secrecy kept this discussion out of the mainstream.

The secret projects at Apple are institutionalized hacking. They are places of "elsewhere" where the engineers don't have to worry about being barbarians because everyone there knows hacking is important.

Unintentionally Forgetting What It Took to Get You There

The story of every company begins with a clever hack. Pick any company and read its history, and I'm pretty sure there will be a well-documented origin story that will define its beginning and involves someone building something new and possibly of unexpected value. What isn't documented is the story of every moment before, when everyone surrounding the hacker asked, "Why the hell are doing you that?" or "Why would you take the risk with so little reward?" or "Why are you wasting your time?" What's not documented are the nine spectacular failures the hacker survived before they built one success.

The well-intentioned people who arrive after the initial success of the hack don't know of a world without it. They assume its existence and are tasked with growing the company around it. Don't for a moment think I don't value these people, because I happen to be one of them, but I am also intimately aware that the people who grow the company are not the same people who founded it.

A healthy product company is, confusingly, one at odds with itself. It has a healthy part that is attempting to normalize and to create predictability, but it needs another part that is tasked with building something new that is going to disrupt and eventually destroy that normality.

Failure to create some form of predictability will result in chaos. Failure to create some sort of well-maintained barbaric chaos inside the company guarantees that a fast-moving, ambitious, risk-taking, and ruthless someone else—someone outside the company—will invade, because they know what you forgot: hacking is important.

Versions Of You

Your team is populated by a unique set of individuals that are distinctly not you. Yes, you're on the same team and perhaps you share the same professional goals, but in the details each of you is different.

This section starts with what might the most important lesson regarding maintaining a healthy team: bored people quit. After that I go deep on the mindsets and habits of nerds, before, well, I start calling other people names, which is behavior I need to explain.

Most chapter titles come to me well before the piece is written. This is likely because much of my writing starts as part of a coffee-induced high driving to or from work, and there is no way I can completely remember my chain-of-consciousness, rambling thoughts from when I park the car to when I'm near a keyboard.

So I create a name.

And it needs to be a good descriptive name because I've got to remember 30 minutes of mental wandering just by thinking of it.

This last section is full of just these sorts of names. Inwards, outwards, organics, NADD, free electrons, bellwethers, incrementalists . . . I clearly have name-calling issues. But these names aren't just a handy memory device, they're the end result of years of sitting at a table and noticing and labeling the similarities among very different people.

These names are not intended to paint a complete picture of the people they describe. They merely give you a starting point for understanding where your particular person is coming from. In reality, your free electron is also an organic completionist. In reality, people are messy.

While I'm happy to provide you with a starting mental sketch for identifying the people on your team and in your company, your job isn't done there. Your job is not to figure out how to alienate people by calling them names, it's to figure out how to include them by taking time to understand what they need and doing your best to give it to them.

You need to remember that everyone is a slightly different version of you.

Finally, this section and this book finish a little selfishly. The final chapters walk you through a professional inevitability—how to prepare for your next job and how to be kind to the one you leave.

Bored People Quit

Much has been written about employee motivation and retention. It's written by folks who actively use words like *motivation* and *retention* and generally don't have a clue about the daily necessity of keeping your team professionally content, because they've either never done the work or have forgotten how it's done. These are the people who show up when your single best engineer casually and unexpectedly announces, "I'm quitting. I'm joining my good friend to found a start-up. This is my two-weeks' notice."

You call on the motivation and retention police because you believe they can perform the legendary "diving save." Whether it's HR or a well-intentioned manager with a distinguished title, these people scurry impressively. Meetings that go long into the evening are instantly scheduled with the disenfranchised employee.

It's an impressive show of force, and it sometimes works, but even if they stay, the damage has been done. They've quit, and when someone quits they are effectively saying, "I no longer believe in this company." What's worse is that what they were originally thinking was, "I'm bored."

Boredom is easier to fix than an absence of belief.

Detecting Boredom

There are many reasons other than boredom that someone will quit. Your company might suck or be headed toward suck. This person might randomly get an offer that fulfills their life's dream. There is a bevy of unpredictable reasons that someone will leave, but boredom is an aspect of their daily professional life you can not only easily assess, but also fix. More importantly, boredom is not initially catastrophic. Boredom shows up quietly and appears to pose no immediate threat. This makes it both easy to address and easy to ignore.

These are my three techniques for detecting boredom:

1. *You notice any change in daily routine:* A decrease in productivity is a great early sign that something's up, but what you are looking for is any change in the employee's routine. Increased snark? Unexpected vacations? Later arrivals? Earlier departures? Anything that strikes you as out of the ordinary for someone whose day you are familiar with is worth considering. The root cause of this change may have nothing to do with boredom, and the best way is figure that out is . . .

2. *You ask, "Are you bored?":* Even if you don't have a gut feeling, it's a good question to randomly ask your team. When I ask, I look you straight in the eyes, and if you can't stare me in the face and answer, I'm going to keep digging until you look me in the eye. Remember, the goal here is to discover boredom before they know it, and the act of a simple question might be just the mental impetus they need to see the early signs in themselves.

3. *They tell you. And you listen:* You'd think that someone walking into your office and stating that they're bored would set off all sorts of alarms in your head. The reality is that someone is going to tell you they're bored quietly and when you least expect it. They'll tell you halfway through your one-on-one, and they won't use the word *bored.* They'll say something innocuous like, ". . . and I really don't know what to do next," and you're going to blow right by the most important thing they've said in a while because you're worried about your next meeting.

As I've reflected on the regrettable departures of folks I've managed, hindsight allows me to point to the moment the person changed. Whether it was a detected subtle change or an outright declaration of their boredom, there was a clear sign that the work sitting in front of them was no longer interesting. And I ignored my observation. I assumed it was insignificant. *He's having a bad day.* I assumed things would just get better. In reality, the boredom was a seed. What was "I'm bored" grew roots and became "I'm bored and why isn't anyone doing anything about it?" and sprouted "I'm bored, I told my boss, and he . . . did nothing," and finally bloomed into "I don't want to work at a place where they don't care if I'm bored."

I think of boredom as a clock. Every second that someone on my team is bored, a second passes on this clock. After some aggregated amount of seconds, which varies for every person, they look at the time, throw up their arms, and quit.

A Boredom Plan of Action

Whether someone is bored or not, you always need to be able to answer two questions regarding each person on your team:

1. Where are they going?
2. What are you currently doing to get them there?

In your head, answers sound like this:

- Francis wants to be a senior engineer, and we're getting him there by giving him increasingly more responsibility.

- Ronald wants to build his own company, so I'm going out of my way to include him in meetings where he can learn how the sausage is really made.

- Brooke has no idea what she wants to do, so I'm throwing curveballs at her until she hits a home run.

Knowing the answers to these questions makes the rest easier, but if you don't have answers, you can start figuring them out by doing the following.

Keep an interesting problem squarely in front of them

Walk through your team right now and tell me the project they are working on that floats their boat. It doesn't need to always be their main project, but there must be a piece of work on their plate that makes their eyes light up when they talk about it. If their eyes aren't lighting up—if there is no project in mind that will get them rambling endlessly—then you ...

Let them experiment

Let them obsess. Let them scratch that itch. If there is no project on their plate that you know is engaging them, create time for them to explore whatever they want to obsess about. I absolutely guarantee there is an investigation somehow related to their work that they are dying to tinker with. The business justification for this wild-ass effort is likely not obvious, so I'll define it: the act of exploration is as valuable as the act of building.

Exploration is hard to justify because it's hard to measure. When exploration is complete, you often have nothing to hold up to your project manager to explain or justify the expenditure of time. Here's what you tell them: "My job isn't just building product; I also build people."

Remember they can only take one for the team for so long

There are legitimate and frequent situations where someone needs to suck it up and dig into crap work for longer than they'd like. This is an inevitable function of teams of people working together—work becomes stratified by perceived importance. There's no shit work when the work is all yours; there's just work you like to do and work you have to do.

Occasional stints on the latter are a good perspective-reset for everyone on the team, but being left too long on have-to work is a guarantee of eventual boredom. What isn't obvious is that there are folks who aren't going to complain, because they believe the right thing to do is take one for the team. They worry that that the act of complaining is tantamount to saying, "I don't believe I should do shit work," or they're simply wary of being accused of not being a team player.

We all get shit work, but it's the responsibility of the guy or gal in charge to dole this work out fairly and consistently. That means they're constantly aware of and communicating with the person who is currently taking one for them, and they know how long they've been taking it and when they're going to be done.

Protect their time

Embrace the ambiguity of their experiment. Agreeing to let them experiment and obsess about a fascinating project is only half the game. The business day is full of previously undiscovered things to do, and your knee-jerk response when you find new, urgent pieces of work is to saddle them on the guy who is working on . . . something. You don't know what it is, because he can barely describe it himself, *so please handle this urgent task. I swear when you're done you can get back to . . . whatever it is you're doing.*

A terrific way to accelerate the boredom clock is to promise productive and creative time that is then taken away. In the heat of the moment, the ambiguous nature of their experiment makes the decision easy: *get this urgent, unplanned task done, or make progress on the unmeasurable?* The only thing this decision teaches your team is how little you value the cultivation of your people.

Aggressively remove noise

In addition to previously undiscovered work, a daily set of distractions courtesy of exhausting people will pull your engineer away from their work. Random meetings, phone calls, interviews. These 30- to 60-minute tasks feel transactional and brief, and there is no way you can fully remove a team member from them, but you manage them. Similar to crap work, it's your job to evenly spread the load of daily noise across the team. More importantly, it's your job to remember that productivity costs surrounding these microtasks don't just involve the 30 minutes necessary to get them done, they include the context-switching tax involved in stopping their work, preparing for the task, doing the task, and then rebuilding the context regarding the work that floats their boat.

There are two aspects of interesting work that equally fire up the nerd brain: the identification of interesting work and making progress on that work. And progress is not measured in interrupt-driven minutes; it's blocks of delicious, uninterrupted hours.

Tell them what the hell is going on

Much of the above activity implies that you're paying attention, but your attention is only half the solution. The other half is regularly keeping folks in the loop regarding your thoughts. In terms of a low-cost means of keeping your team content, the simple act of saying, "I know where you want to be and I'm thinking about how to get you there" is a way to demonstrate you care about the growth of your team.

Don't Forget What It's Like to Build a Thing

This piece might read like I believe that engineering is some privileged artisan class and that I'm overly protective, and *that is exactly what I believe*. My gig is the care and feeding of engineers, and their productivity is my productivity. If they all leave, I have exactly no job.

Part of your credibility as a leader is your public and repeated declaration that it's your job to help your team succeed, but you have another task: you need to keep building stuff.

I've gone back and forth on whether managers should code, and my opinion is: *don't stop coding*. Each week that passes where you don't share the joy, despair, and discovery of software development is a week when you slowly forget what it means to be a software developer. Over time it means you'll have a harder time talking to engineers because you'll forget how they think and how they become bored.

Bellwethers

Let's start by not deluding ourselves. Hiring anyone is a risk. Google is famous for the intense and lengthy scrutiny they put their candidates under. The Google interview might be intense, but when they decide to hire, they're rolling the dice.

You're not going to know whom you hired for months.

This doesn't mean you can't improve your odds.

For me, success in an interview is extracting as much information as possible from the candidate. This doesn't happen because you've got a compelling set of interview questions; it comes from throwing a wildly different set of interviewers at your candidate. What these people find, through their diversity of perspective, is the best information you can have to make a hiring decision.

The Core Interview Team

There are two key groups that need to be paraded by your candidate, and the first one should be obvious, but it's often screwed up. Everyone on the team needs to interview every candidate. I'm going to repeat myself since Dave the Curmudgeon Engineer keeps telling you that he's not interested in interviewing, but he's got to be on the list. Every time.

Interviewing is a team sport and failing to get everyone's perspective regarding a candidate is not only a lost opportunity in terms of gathering some random piece of perspective, but it also sends an implied message to the team when Dave gets excused. The message is, "Dave's opinion doesn't matter." Now combine that message with the question you should be asking yourself, "Why doesn't Dave care about the people he might be working with?" and you've got more than enough reason to insist that everyone on the team interviews candidates.

The other key interview group is trickier. This is your go-to set of interviewers that you trust. They are your *bellwethers*, and when they give a candidate a thumbs down, it's over.

Your bellwether team is where you gather the most perspective. The coworker interviews are going to find some informational gems, and their opinions will greatly affect your decision to hire, but bellwethers are your constant. When they tell you, "This guy is going to change the face of your team," you believe them because they are rarely wrong.

There are three key bellwethers I have for each interview.

Technical

In software development, this is the most obvious skill that needs to be assessed, but it's also the one that is done the worst. Engineers are great at being technical, but they aren't great at being social. This means that there's a good chance the best engineer on the team might be the worst technical interviewer because he's uncomfortable dealing with human beings. This means that when you send him in to figure out whether your candidate knows anything about database normalization, he's going to be more nervous than the candidate about asking a hard technical question.

Find a technical bully.

Yes, there are lots of valuable things to learn about communication style, vision, and personality, but if you're an engineering manager and you can't assess technical ability, you're screwed. You're going to be hiring smooth-talking QA guys who don't know how to code. Whoops.

Finding your technical bellwether is easy. Who technically scared the hell out of you when you interviewed? If you're a manager and didn't get asked technical questions, go wandering around other engineering groups and find the bully. He's there. He knows his stuff and has no issue with figuring out whether your candidate does as well.

Cultural

Your second bellwether is cultural. They've got two aspects of the candidate that they need to assess. First, cultural fit within the team, and second, cultural fit within the company. This gets into the fuzzy world of understanding personalities and that means it's going to be easier to find your technical bellwether than your cultural one because technical ability is quantifiable. "Yes, this guy is a C++ god." The next question is, "OK, so he's a god; is he going to piss off the rest of the team by being godlike?"

A cultural fit is a team fit. Ideally, your team is a functioning unit right now and your next hire should support that function rather than detract from it.

Your cultural bellwether is the person on the team who is going to tell you, "This guy is going to add, not detract." Who you're looking for in your bellwether is the person who best represents the soul of the team. This is the person who can figure out your candidate.

Vision (Strategic or Tactical?)

Your last bellwether vets vision. Their job is to figure out the trajectory of the candidate. Are they up and coming? Do they want to change the world? Have they carved out a safe little corner of technology that is all theirs? I don't know who you need on your team, but you do, and you need to know whether the person you're hiring is strategic or tactical.

A strategic hire is someone who is going to push their agenda, their opinion. They are actively engaged in what they are doing, networking with others who do it, and they'll tell anyone, at length, about how they're going to do it. Strategic hires are going to piss people off because of the annoying intensity of their agenda.

A tactical hire is a person who is filling a well-defined need. "We need a database guy." Like strategics, tacticals know their stuff, but that's all that they know. Also, they're not that interested in pushing an agenda. They just want to get their work done in relative silence.

I'm making no judgment regarding whether strategic or tactical is a better hire for you because I don't have a clue who you're hiring. What's important is to understand what type of vision you need for your hire, and, more importantly, who the right person is to interview for this ability. My preference is that the manager is the person who is the bellwether for vision because that's their job for the group. It's not just that you know what the team needs, it's that vision defines career path and you need to know, as early as possible, what it's going to take to keep a future hire engaged. A strategic isn't going to be with your team long because you simply don't move fast enough, whereas a tactical is going to be happy as long as you keep the work relevant and constant.

Team Consensus

Once the team and the bellwethers have interviewed your candidate, it's time to gather everyone together and hear what they think. This is another time when eager managers try to save time by having the interviewers send their feedback via mail or grab an opinion in the hallway.

Wrong. You always have an interview feedback meeting. The ultimate choice to hire is the hiring manager's, but everyone who takes the time to interview the candidate has a vote, and while they walk out of the interview with an opinion, they haven't really voted until they've heard everyone's feedback. Watch what happens. Gather everyone together and go around the table. For each person who gives their feedback, take notes and notice, as each person talks, how folks who already talked continue to add more information, and, sometimes, even change their opinion. What you're seeing happen in this meeting is consensus building. Opinions are being shaped by information, but the group is also coming to a collective decision. This is why every team member needs to be on the interview schedule. While it's your decision to hire, you'd be a fool not to follow the lead set by the team.

Be a Fool

There are times when you need to be a fool, and this is when the right hire intentionally isn't a fit for the team. This is another area where your bellwethers may prove more useful than the team's opinion. At my prior gig, we had a curmudgeon architect who, while talented, was creating an aura of negativity in the group. It was the curmudgeon's opinion spilling over on the rest of team, and after two years, it needed an adjustment.

Looking for fresh blood and new perspective, I began recruiting from local universities. My cultural bellwether was one of the first engineers I'd hired, but for this position I went to another engineering manager I admired and asked, "Who is the best person to interview for the culture of your team?"

"That'd be Frank."

Frank became my cultural bellwether because I wanted to change the culture of the team. As we brought college hires through the interview process, the feedback meetings weren't surprising. "He's too young! He doesn't know about this technology! We've got too much to do to bring this green person up to speed." This was the existing engineering team taking its content and cultural cues from the senior curmudgeon, and it wasn't surprising that Frank's feedback consistently contradicted the rest of the team. "He's bright. Good fit for the culture and I want to work with this kid."

You're thinking that contradicting the team's consensus opinion on a hiring decision is a downside to the group feedback meeting. It's not. While you need to take special care to explain your decision to each person on the team, you can use the team's consistent negative feedback as part of your reasoning and part of your explanation.

"You remember that feedback? You remember the yelling? Yeah, I'm tired of the yelling, aren't you?"

Still Delusional

We're still deluding ourselves. Even with three of the best bellwethers you can find, hiring anyone is a huge risk. The idea that you can successfully profile a candidate in a phone screen and two rounds of interviews is absurd. All you are getting is a taste. I know you asked them, "How do you deal with stressful situations?" but the fact is you won't actually know who they are until some real stress shows up.

You need to hire. You need to be able to grow your team and that means taking a risk on these people who are a little more than a résumé and some good conversation. While I believe a solid set of bellwether and team interviews is the best means of gathering in-person data about a candidate, don't stop there. Go read their weblog. Find out if they've contributed to open source. Read their posts to mailing lists. In-person interviews are going to give you a glimpse of a person, but anything you can do to complete the picture won't only give you a better perspective, it will reduce the risk that you're hiring a stranger.

The Ninety-Day Interview

When you accept a new job, you don't know who you are going to work with, what you are going to be doing, and how much (or little) you're going to like it. Call everyone you want. Ask their opinions. Trust the fact that a good friend referred you for the gig. Revel in the idea that the company has a good pedigree, but don't delude yourself that in a smattering of interview hours you're going to have anything more than a vague hint of your new life.

Try this. Tell me about your best friend. Give me a bulleted list of five noteworthy things you think I should know about your best friend. Got it? Read it out loud. Does this do justice to your best friend? I hear you when you say, "He'd do anything for me," but why is that? Why is he protective of you? What's the story behind the bullet? That's what I want to know.

Each person in your new team has a story they want to tell you and it's never a bulleted list. Some are going to freely give this story whereas others will carefully protect the fact they even have a story, but until each person you need to work with has shared this story with you (and vice versa), the interview isn't over. The jury is out and you won't know if this new job that you've begun is actually your job.

Deliberation

Your first job is to relax. Like the first day of school, you're going to overcompensate in your first day, your first week. Most people do not lay their clothes out the night before they go to work. You're doing this to calm yourself. Those clothes neatly laid out at the end of your bed are a visual reminder that you have control over this thing that you can't control.

Relax. There's an industry standard regarding the amount of time it takes to make a hire, and it's 90 days. New managers hate when I tell them this because they're so giddy they've got a new requisition and, *boy, watch how fast I can hire.* Yes, yes. I appreciate your velocity, but I'm not going to worry about your hire for 90 days.

This chunk of time applies to your new job as well. You've got 90 days—3 months— to finish your job interview. Draw an X on a calendar 90 days from now. Make it a physical act that reminds you to relax and to listen rather than fret about what you don't know. The new team isn't going to trust you until you stop laying out your clothes, until you stop being deliberate.

I know you've done this before: you've had five other jobs and you have well-refined people-assessment instincts. Except, well, they're biased. These instincts are based on where you've been and you have never been here before. My suggestion is that the less you trust your instincts, the more you'll learn about your new job, and that's why I wrote you a 90-days list . . .

1. Stay Late, Show Up Early

You need a map of the people you work with, and I find the best way to start scribbling this map is to understand people and their relation to the day. When do they get there? How long until they engage in what they do? Coffee run? Wait, no. Late arriver. Doesn't leave until he gets something done. Makes his coffee run at 4:30 p.m. Doesn't drink coffee? Really? Why? These long days of watching give you insight, and they give you tools for understanding what each of your team members wants.

2. Accept Every Lunch Invitation You Get

People are stretching themselves for you the first few weeks you show up. They're going to go out of their way to include you, and no matter who they are, you've got to take the time to reciprocate. The lunch invite from that guy in the group you're pretty sure you'll never interact with will result in stories, and you have a stunning lack of stories right now.

3. Always Ask About Acronyms

It's great that we're all speaking English, but why is it that you're sitting in your first staff meeting and not understanding a word? It's because every team develops acronyms, metaphors, and clever ways to describe their uniqueness, which you must understand. Cracking the language nut is absolutely essential to assessing the hand you've been dealt, and you're going to need to ask a couple of times.

4. Say Something Really Stupid

Good news, you're going to do this whether it's on this list or not. I'm saying it's OK. This stupid thing that you're going to say is going to demonstrate your nascent engagement in your job and when they stop giggling, the team is going to know you're desperately trying to figure it all out.

5. Have a Drink

Similar to the lunch task, but more valuable. No barrier is crossed when someone invites you to lunch, but when you get the drink invite, someone is saying, "C'mon. Let's go try a different version of honesty." Stories are revealed over drinks, not lunch.

> **WARNING** *The next three on the list are at the bottom for a reason. These are advanced moves that you don't want to attempt until you've built some confidence that if they go horribly wrong, you have some assurance that you won't permanently damage your still-developing reputation. Read on.*

6. Tell Someone What to Do

Everything I've talked about so far involves listening and asking questions. This task involves you saying something. More importantly, it involves you telling someone what to do. I don't know who you're telling or what you're saying, but the goal is to exert your influence, to test your influence. More importantly, to test your knowledge of the organization and see if this thing you have to say is true. Telling is the sound of your instincts aligning to this particular organization and this thing you are saying is your first bit of inspiration. Trust it. Tell the right person and realize that everyone was waiting for you to say it.

7. Have an Argument

This is the riskiest item on the list, but potentially the most revealing. There's a good chance when you pull a number 6 that this is going to happen anyway. Again, what you are willing to argue about and who is going to be on the other side of the argument is a function of your situation. What you want to understand is, how does the organization value conflict? Is it OK that you're digging your heels in? Do others engage in the argument? Who swoops in to save the day? Can these people argue without losing their shit? Does this team argue out in the open or do they use devious passive-aggressive subtlety?

You're going to learn two valuable things during this professional battle. First, how does this group of people make a decision? Second, you're going to have a better taste of their passion and their velocity.

8. Find Your Inner Circle

In your arguments, lunches, drinks, and late nights, you're going to find kindred spirits. This is the short list of people who share your instincts. These are the ones who complete your sentences and they know your stories. These are the ones who welcome the argument because they know great decisions are made by many. Your inner circle is not exclusive because you'll go nowhere drawing relationship boundaries among the team. This is the list of people with whom you share your raw inspiration and your stories because you know they'll gleefully help refine them.

The discovery of your inner circle won't happen until time has passed. You'll instinctively be attracted to people who feel comfortable, who feel right, but they can't be in the inner circle until they've passed the test of time. They've got to pass through the 90-day list a few times before you've heard enough stories to let them in.

Finishing the Interview

It's not just that you forgot to ask key questions during your initial interview process; it's that the person you were walking into that interview as isn't who you are. You're a résumé, you're a referral, and you're a reputation.

Your job interview isn't over until you've asked all the questions and heard all the stories.

Your job interview isn't over until you understand the unique structure that has formed around this particular group of people. It's not just the organizational chart, it's the intricate personalities that have settled into a comfortable, complex communication structure.

Your job interview isn't over until you have a framework for how you are going to interact with these people, and that means understanding not only their goals, but also their invaluable personal quirks. What they tell you the first week has more to do with the fact that you're new than what they actually feel. What they tell you after 90 days is the truth.

Your job interview isn't over until you've changed to become part of a new team.

Managing Nerds

Over a decade ago, the world was collectively freaked out by the Y2K bug.[1] The idea was that when innumerable software-driven clocks flipped at midnight from 1999 to 2000, the digital shit was going to hit the fan. I blame the origin of the worldwide freak-out on the nerds.

Y2K collectively freaked out the nerds, because every single software engineer has been bitten by reports of edge cases that we previously believed to be impossible. We've been shocked how often a demo has become a product and remained in production for years. We know that it is an inherent property of complex systems that they will contain both our best work and our worst guesses.

I call this state of mind the Nerd Burden. It's a curse put upon nerds who know how a system works, and, more importantly, what it took to build. Understanding the Nerd Burden is a good way to get into the nerd mind and start to figure out how to manage nerds.

A Worst-Case Scenario

This is a chapter on nerd management. The usual requirement is that in order to manage nerds, you need to be one. For the sake of this chapter, I'm assuming a worst-case scenario—you are not a nerd, but your job involves daily nerd management. My condolences; these guys and gals can eat you alive.

A good place to get mentally limber regarding nerds is with the Nerd Handbook.[2] This is intended for the significant others of nerds and geeks, and it's a good place to start understanding the nerd mindset. However, where the handbook explains the care and feeding of nerds in the home, this piece is concerned with nerds at work.

---

[1] http://en.wikipedia.org/wiki/Year_2000_problem
[2] http://randsinrepose.com/archives/2007/11/11/the_nerd_handbook.html

Multiple generations of nerds are in the workforce now, so your preconceived notions of nerdery are not as useful as you thought. Discard the nerd extremes: the curmudgeonly pocket protector set is retired or retiring, and there's a good chance that the slick, brown-haired guy sitting across the bar wearing the $300 Ted Baker shirt is a fucking Python wizard.

Fortunately, a career as a nerd in software engineering still requires a well-defined mental skill set, not any particular sartorial flair, and successfully acquiring and refining that skill set has tweaked the nerd's brain in a unique way that will start to define your nerd management strategy.

▨ **Disclaimer**   As with all of my writing, I usually use *he* as a convenience. There are plenty of female nerds out there, and they display much of the same behavior.

A Problem

In front of you is the Problem. While I don't know what the Problem is, I do know that you have a bright team of talented nerds working for you, and I know that you don't have a clue how to tackle the Problem. You need the nerds and you don't know where to start. The Problem is unique in that your normal leadership moves aren't going to work. You can already predict the collective nerd reaction, and it's the opposite of what you need to happen.

Rather than attacking this Problem directly, let's turn it around and explore the inner workings of your nerd's mental landscape for inspired next steps.

The nerd as system thinker is a point I've been making since I wrote the Nerd Handbook, and one I explore further in *Being Geek* (O'Reilly, 2010).[3] Briefly, a nerd is motivated to understand how a thing works—how it fits together. This drive comes from the nerd's favorite tool, the computer, which is a blissful construction of logical knowability. Years of mastering the computer have created a strong belief in the illusory, predictable calm that emerges from the chaos as you consistently follow the rules that define a system.

If I had to give you a single piece of managerial advice, I would say, "Your job with your nerd is to bring calm to their chaos." Let's begin.

Your nerd treasures consistency. Your staff meeting is an entertaining affair. You keep it light, you relay developing corporate shenanigans, and you crush rumors as best you can. Occasionally, you need to make a decision on the spot—random policy enforcement: should Kate get that sweet office with the window?

---

[3] www.beinggeek.com/

You: "Sure, Kate deserves it . . . she's doing great work."

Suddenly, a normally chatty staff meeting is full of silence. What happened?

First, you nonchalantly barged your way though one of the three guaranteed topics that will cause anyone, not just nerds, to lose their goddamned minds: space, compensation, and titles. Second, your off-the-cuff decision regarding Kate is somehow inconsistent with your team. Remember, you are sitting in a room full of nerds who—just for intellectual sport—are parsing every decision you make, analyzing it, and comparing that analysis against *every single decision you've ever made in their presence*. That silence? That's the silent nerd rage that arrives when they discover meaningful inconsistency.

The rules regarding who gets a window have never been written down, but they are known: you are either a manager who needs to have one-on-ones or you've been with the group for multiple years and you have *senior* in your title. Kate has neither, and while her great work might be cause for awarding her the office, by not explicitly stating that there is an addendum to the unspoken rules regarding office windows, you are in consistency violation. You are less predictable because you are no longer following the rules of the system.

A predictable world is a comforting world to your nerd. Your inconsistency on the office ruling now has them wondering, "What the hell other random crap is coming down the line? How the hell am I supposed to get my work done when my boss engages in fits of randomness?" According to your nerd, a predictable world is a world where we know what is going to happen next. See . . .

Your nerd also treasures efficiency. When a nerd is mentally noting every single decision that you make, he is not doing so because he wants to catch you in a lie or an inconsistency. What the nerd is doing is what he always does—sifting though impressive piles of information and discovering rules so he can discover the optimal system that governs everything. Grand Unification Theory? Yeah, a nerd invented that so he could sleep at night.

With an understanding of the rules, your nerd can choose a course of action that requires the least amount of energy. This isn't laziness; this is the joy that in a world full of chaotic and political people with obscure agendas and erratic behavior, your nerd can conquer the chaos with logical, efficient predictability. Your nerd has a deliberate goal in mind that you need to support. Your nerd is . . .

Chasing the Two Highs

In the Nerd Handbook, I called this the High, but there are two Highs:

The First High: When nerds see a knot, they want to unravel it. After each Christmas, someone screws up the Christmas tree lights. They remove the lights from the tree and carefully fold the lights as they lay them in the box. Mysteriously, somewhere between last year's folding and this year's joy of finding the lights, these lights become a knotted mess.

The process of unknotting the lights is a seemingly haphazard one—you sit on the floor swearing and slowly pulling a single green cable through a mess of wires and lights and feeling like you're making no progress—until you do. There's a magical moment when the knot feels solved. There's still a knot in front of you, but it's collapsing on itself and unencumbered wire is just spilling out of it.

This mental achievement is the first nerd high. It's the liberating moment when we suddenly understand the problem, but right behind that, the solution is something greater. It's . . .

The Second High: Complete knot domination. The world is full of knots, and untying each has its own unique high. Your nerd spends a good portion of her day busily untying these knots, whether it's that subtle tweak to a mail filter that allows her to parse her mail faster, or the 30 seconds she spends tweaking the font size in her favorite editor to achieve perfect readability. This constant removal of friction is satisfying, but eventually she'll ask, "What's with all the fucking knots?" and attack.

A switch flips when your nerd drops into this mode. She's no longer trying to unravel the knot; she wants to understand why all knots exist. Nerds have a razor focus on a complete understanding of the system that is currently pissing them off, and they use this understanding to build a completely knot-free product. This is the Second High.

Chasing the Second High is where nerds earn their salary. If the First High is the joy of understanding, the Second High is the act of creation. If you want your nerd to rock your world by building something revolutionary, you want them chasing the Second High. This is why . . .

You obsessively protect both your nerd's time and space. Until you've experienced the solving of a seemingly impossible problem, it's hard to understand how far a nerd will go to protect his problem-solving focus. (See Chapter 33.) The road to either High is a mental state traditionally called the Zone. There are three things to know about the Zone:

1. The almost-constant quest of the nerd is managing all the crap that is preventing him from entering the Zone as he searches for the Highs. Meetings, casual useless fly-bys, biological nuisances, that mysterious knock-knock-knocking that comes from the ceiling tiles whenever the AC kicks in—what the nerd is doing in the first 15 minutes of getting in the Zone is building focus, and it's a Jenga-like construction that small distractions can topple.

2. Every single second you allow a nerd to remain in the Zone is a second where something fucking miraculous can occur.

3. As explained in "A Nerd in a Cave," Chapter 33, your
    nerd has built himself a cave. It might not actually
    look like a cave, or maybe it does. The goal around its
    construction is simple: protect the Zone so we can
    chase the Highs. Stand up right now and walk to each
    of your nerds' offices and spelunk the caves. Ask the
    question, "How are they protecting their focus?" Back to
    the door? Headphones? Massive screen real estate? To
    understand what your nerd does to protect his cave, you
    need to ask . . .

What is your nerd's hoodie? I write better when I'm wearing a hoodie. There's something warm and cavelike about having my head surrounded—it gives me permission to ignore the world. Over time, those around me know that interrupting hoodie-writing is a capital offense. They know when I reach to pull the hoodie over my head that I've successfully discarded all distractions on the planet Earth and am currently communing with the pure essence of whatever I'm working on.

It's irrational and it's delicious.

Your nerd has a hoodie. It's a visual cue to stay away as she chases her Highs, and your job is both identification and enforcement. I don't know your nerds, so I don't know what you'll discover, but I am confident that these hoodie-like obsessions will often make no sense to you—even if you ask. *Yes, there will always be Mountain Dew nearby. Of course, we will never be without square pink Post-it notes.*

Don't sweat it. Support it. Also, understand the interesting potentially negative by-products of all this nerdery, such as . . .

> *Not-invented-here syndrome:* When you ask your nerd to
> build something significant, your nerd is predisposed to
> build it himself rather than borrowing from someone else.
> Strike that: your nerd's default opening position when
> asked to build a thing is, "We can build it better than
> anyone else."
>
> First, they probably can, but it's an expensive proposition.
> Second, understanding why this is their opening position
> is important. The ideal mental state of the nerd with
> regard to the Problem is the First High—a completely
> understood model of the problem. The issue is that each
> nerd's strategic approach for this high is different.
>
> Unfortunately, code is often the only documentation
> of our inspiration, and your nerd would rather design
> his own inspiration than adapt someone else's. When a
> nerd says, "We can build it better," he's saying, "I have not
> devoted the necessary time to understand the existing

solution, and it's more fun to build than to investigate someone else's crap."

If your nerd is bent on building it instead of buying it, fine, ask him to prove it. Make the Problem the explanation of why building new is a more logical and strategic approach than pulling a working solution off the shelf.

The bitter nerd: Another default opening position for the nerd is bitterness—the curmudgeon. Your triage: _Why can't he be a team player?_ There are chronically negative nerds out there, but in my experience with nerd management, it's more often the case that the nerd is bitter because they've seen this situation before four times, and it has played out exactly the same way. Each time: _Whenever management feels they're out of touch, we all get shuttled off to an off-site where we spend two days talking too much and not acting enough._

Nerds aren't typically bitter; they're just well informed. Snark from nerds is a leading indicator that I'm wasting their time, and when I find it, I ask questions until I understand the inefficiency so I can change it or explain it.

The disinterested or drifting nerd: Your nerd won't engage. It's been a week and a half, and as far as you can tell, all she's done is create and endlessly edit a to-do list on her whiteboard. Whether she's disinterested or drifting, your nerd is stuck. There are two likely situations here: she doesn't want to engage or she can't.

Triage here is similar to the not-invented-here syndrome—is the problem shiny? Meaning, is there something unique that will allow for the possibility of original work? OK, it's shiny. But is it too shiny? Is your nerd outside of the comfort zone of his ability? My favorite move when a nerd appears stuck is pairing him with a credible technical peer—not a competitor, but a cohort.

Once you've discovered the productivity of the Highs, you're going to attempt to invoke them. Bad news. The invocation process is entirely owned by and unique to your nerd. You can protect the cave and honor the hoodie, but your nerd will choose when to go deep. The amount of pressure you put on your nerd to engage is directly proportionate to the amount of resistance you'll encounter.

Find a cohort—someone who will be receptive to the perceived lack of shininess or someone who will say the one thing necessary to get your nerd chasing the Highs.

The Nerd Burden

I've spent a lot of time painting nerds as obsessive control freaks bent on controlling the universe. Fact is, your nerd understands how the system works. She knows what you know—chaos is a guarantee. It's neither efficient nor predictable, but it's going to happen.

You and your nerd are surprisingly goal aligned with regard to the chaos. You want her to build a thing and you want her to build it well. You want it to perform reliably in bizarre situations that no one can predict. You want it to scale when you least expect it. And you want to be amazed.

Amaze your nerd. Build calm and dark places where invoking the Zone is trivial. Perform consistently and efficiently around your nerds so they can spend their energy on what they build and not worry about that which they can't control. Help them scale by knowing when they're stuck or simply bored. And let them chase those Highs, because then they can amaze everyone.

NADD

The gist of the book *Guns of the South* is straightforward, yet odd. What if, during the Civil War, the South became equipped with a lot of AK-47s? Long story very short, they would have won. Handily. The author, Harry Turtledove, chose not to focus on time travel or other delectable science fiction tidbits; he spends the time on, "Yay! The South won! So, uh, what are they going to do about that whole slavery thing?"

While I'm certain Civil War enthusiasts would enjoy this book, it is not geared for someone with my particular disability: *nerd attention deficiency disorder*, or NADD. While I read this book, this innocuous condition reared its head when it became clear that it was an in-depth exploration of the lifestyles and morality during an alternative post-Civil War period . . . *ZzZzZzzZZzz*.

Now, *Guns* is a fine read, but more than once I was flipping ahead through the pages wondering, "OK, how long is this chapter?" When I neared the end of the book and it became clear that some time traveler from the future wasn't going to appear and, using some whizbang futuristic device, join the North and South together, well, I was disappointed. Sure, I'm happy that President Lee learned his lesson and started abolishing slavery on his own, but . . . no lasers? Please.

Folks, I'm a nerd. I need rapid-fire content delivered in short, clever, punchy phrases. Give me Coupland, give me Calvin and Hobbes, give me Asimov, give me the Watchmen. I need this type of content because I'm horribly afflicted with NADD.

If you're still with me, it might mean you also suffer from some type of NADD-related disorder. Let's find out.

Stop reading this book right now and walk over to your desktop. How many things were you doing when you were last there? Me, I've got a terminal window session open to a chat room, I'm listening to music, I've got Safari open with three tabs where I'm watching stocks on E*TRADE, I'm tinkering with a web site, and I'm looking at weekend movie returns. Not done yet. I've got iChat open, ESPN.com is downloading sports trailers in the background, and I've got two notepads open where I'm capturing random thoughts for later integration into various to-do lists. Oh yeah, I'm rewriting this chapter as well.

Folks, this isn't multitasking. This is an advanced case of nerd attention deficiency disorder. I am unable to function at my desktop unless I've got, at least, five tasks going on at the same time. If your count comes close, you're probably afflicted as well. Most excellent.

A Nerd Diagnosis

My mother first helped diagnose me with NADD. It was the late 1980s and she was bringing me dinner in my bedroom (nerd). I was merrily typing away to my friends in some primitive chat room on my IBM XT (super nerd), listening to music (probably Flock of Seagulls—nerd++), and watching *Back to the Future* with the sound off (nerrrrrrrrrrd). She commented, "How can you focus on anything with all this stuff going on?" I responded, "Mom, I can't focus without all this noise."

The existence of NADD in your life is directly related to how you've chosen to deal with the media deluge that has accompanied our insatiable thirst for new technology. You've likely gone one of three ways:

1. You've checked out. You don't own a TV and it's unlikely you're even reading this chapter.

2. You enjoy your content in moderation. When I asked you to count the windows on your desktop, you either said, "One, my mail client, to read my incoming e-mail," or you made yourself a note to check this *after* reading this chapter. You probably own a day planner, which you can touch from where you are sitting right now.

3. You surf the content fire hose. Give me tabbed browsing, tabbed instant messaging, music all the time, and TiVO TiVO TiVO. Welcome to NADD.

The presence of NADD in your friends is equally easily detectable. Here's a simple test: Ask to sit down at their computer and start mucking with stuff on their desktop. Move an icon here, adjust a window there. If your friend calmly watches as you tinker away, they're probably NADD-free. However, if your friend is anxiously rubbing their forehead and climbing out of their skin when you move that icon *12 pixels to the right*, there's NADD in the house. *Back away from the computer.*

The Context Switch

You may think the core competency behind NADD is multitasking, and it's true, NADD sufferers are amazing multitaskers, but it isn't their fundamental skill. It's the context switch.

The idea of the context switch is key to understanding NADD and it's a simple concept. In order to focus on something, you need to spend time and energy to get your brain in the right mental state. Think about your Sunday morning reading of the *New York Times*. You've got your coffee, your comfortable pajamas, your couch, and you've got whatever story it is that you're reading. All of this is your context.

Now, halfway through your current story, I'm going to rip the paper from your hands and turn on CNN, which happens to be running exactly the same story that you were just reading.

What. The hell. Just happened?

You just experienced a context switch. It's not a horrible one, since you're luckily experiencing the same story; it's just in a different medium—TV Talking heads with that annoying scrolling news bar at the bottom of the screen.

Still, it's jarring, right? Forget about why I'm yanking the paper from your hands, I'm talking about the mental shift from reading a story to watching it. It takes time to switch. For you. A healthy NADD sufferer would barely notice the switch. In fact, chances are, they're already digesting their news via random different media right this second.

What separates a NADD sufferer from everyone else is that the context switch is transparent. The mental muscle that drives the context switch is well developed because it's spent a lifetime switching between random streams of data, trying to make sense of a colossal amount of noise to hear what is relevant.

Anyone can multitask. NADD sufferers multitask with deft purpose. They're on a quest of high-speed information acquisition and processing.

Leveraging NADD

I'm making NADD sound like a trait of information-obsessive power freaks, and, well, it is. How else can you deal with a world where media is forced on you at you at every turn? You become very adept at controlling it. There's more good news.

Folks who are not afflicted with NADD think those who are can't focus because— look at us—we're all over the place. *Please stop clicking on things—you are giving me a headache.* Wrong. Those with NADD have an amazing ability to focus when they choose to. Granted, it's not our natural state, and yes, it can take us longer than some to get in the zone (see Chapter 33 for more about the zone), but when we're there—*boy howdy.*

The web is designed with NADD in mind. Whether it's the short burst of information that comprises a weblog or the RSS behind it, which allows me to read *every weblog ever,* the Web knows about NADD. It knows that any good web page is not designed to answer the question "Do you want to learn?" it's "How long do I have your attention?"

NADD can advance your career, if you're in the right career. Ever worked at a startup? Ever shipped software? What are the last few weeks like? We call it a fire drill because everyone is running around like a crazy person doing random, unexpected shit. NADD is the perfect affliction for managing this situation because it's an affliction that reduces the cost of the context switch.

If the building you are currently in is burning to the ground, go find the person with NADD on your floor. Not only will they know where the fire escape is, they'll probably have some helpful tips about how to avoid smoke inhalation, as well as a vast array of likely probabilities regarding survival rates in multistory building fires. How is it this junior software engineer knows all this? Who knows, maybe he read it on a weblog two years ago. Perhaps a close virtual friend of his in New York is a firefighter. Does it matter? He may save your life, or more likely, keep you well informed with useless facts before you are burned to a crisp.

Downsides

I'm making NADD sound like a rosy affliction. There are downsides.

First, it's a lot of work to figure out your personal regimen of digesting the world, and sorry, you are going to miss things. This will annoy you, but it will also drive you incessantly to look for *the next big thing.*

Second, you're going to sound like a know-it-all. Try not to. Most people don't actually know that much random trivia, useless info, obscure facts, assorted news, current events, and complex mathematical formulas. These people are happy without it and simply because you're brimming with the latest and greatest information doesn't mean that everyone is going to want to hear about it.

You're not going to have much patience with those who have not chosen a NADD-like life. Occasionally, you'll attempt to impart your fractured wisdom, only to throw your hands up four minutes later when it's clear, "Crap, they just don't get it." Chances are, they might've gotten it, and you're just afflicted with a disease where your attention span is that of a second grader.

Whether you're afflicted with NADD or not, you need to understand one thing. It's not going away. The generation that invented NADD in the 1980s and 1990s has been replaced by the generation that never knew a world without it, and they're going to be annoying in their own unique way.

33

A Nerd in a Cave

The first few days of any significant overseas trip, I'm a jerk. It's not just the jetlag that's poisoning my attitude; it's the lack of context. I get twitchy when I don't know where my stuff is. Combine that with the fact that no one is speaking English, there are two toilets in the bathroom, and I have no idea what time it is, and you can begin to understand why I'm in such a foul mood.

Three days in, I'm sleeping, I know it's called a bidet, and I'm working hard on my Italian "R" and "U" sounds. I'm having fun, but I'm still thinking about my lack of context. I'm thinking about the familiar place I've built so that I can work.

The Cave

I have a cave. It came as part of the house. I didn't paint the walls blood red; they came that way. Most folks who get the tour walk into the cave and gasp at the walls. "They're so dark. How can you think surrounded by this ominous redness?" I nod and grin slightly and shuffle them off to the next room. See, I love my cave. The thick, blood-red walls wrap me in comfort, and that is what a cave does.

My cave is my intellectual home. My kitchen is where I eat, my bed is where I sleep, and my cave is where I think. Everyone has some sort of cave; just follow them around their house. It might be a garage full of tools or a kitchen full of cookware, but there is a cave stashed somewhere in the house.

The nerd cave has some specific traits:

> *A computer on a desk with ready access to the Internet:* The
> fact that a computer without an Internet connection
> is essentially a very expensive DVD player is a recent
> development, but the fact is, when I sit down at my
> MacBook and there is no wireless, I think, "Well, I could

play Bejeweled, right?" In the cave, the Internet is the lifeblood. It connects this dark place with the rest of the world.

World-canceling features such as a door or noise-reducing headphones: These features are a nuisance to significant others interested in communication, but I'll get to that in a moment.

A random collection of comforting nerd knickknacks: This varies wildly from nerd to nerd, but there is always at least one object or talisman of nerddom sitting in the cave. I have this white, carved stone polar bear staring at me right now. I think I got it for Christmas. It's been staring at me for ten years now, and each time I sit down in the cave I worry that if the polar bear weren't there ... I wouldn't be able to write.

Something to drink: This may be my thing, but I can't really settle into the cave without something liquid. Right now, it's a cup of homebrew by Peet's. In the afternoon, it's a glass of water. In the evening, it might be wine or a beer. For me, the drink is a mental pause where I intensely scrutinize the last 30 seconds. What did I just write? What am I trying to say? [Sip] OK, back to work.

A well-defined layout: This ties into my NADD (see Chapter 32), but I have deep knowledge of the layout of my cave. Each month, the housecleaners come for a tidying of the house, and each month I walk into my office when they are done and spend 30 minutes adjusting my monitors, relocating my pens, and re-piling my papers. I think it's great that someone is coming to clean the house, but I wish they'd *stop touching my stuff.*

A view: Like the drink, the view is a mental break, an escape to somewhere else that provides a brief alteration of perspective. This is why everyone in the office wants a window. It's not a status symbol, it's an escape. I've seen nerds without a view go to great lengths to create one. My manager at UCSC built a window frame in his subterranean office and put posters from around the world behind it. When I left UCSC, he had a poster of Audrey Hepburn from *Breakfast at Tiffany's.*

It's an ominous name: the cave. It alludes to a dark, damp place where you are likely to be eaten by a grue. The irony is that the purpose of a cave is not to insulate, its purpose is to germinate. I'll explain.

The Zone

Each weekend morning, my process is this: I wake up, walk upstairs, sit down at the computer, and figure out what is happening on the planet. Once I'm comfortable that the sky is not falling, I walk to the kitchen, grind my coffee beans, and begin to boil water. While the water is heating up, I return to my computer and follow up on whatever tidbits tickled my fancy from my first pass. This morning, it was some font research, followed by looking into options for wireless headphones. Turns out, Sony sucks. Go figure. Water's boiling! Back to the kitchen, where I pour hot water into my French press and dig up my favorite ceramic cup. The coffee needs to sit for three minutes, which means back to the computer! OK, so why do Sony headphones suck? Poor sound quality? Bad design? Bit of both, really. Coffee's ready, so one more trip to the kitchen, where I pour the steaming brew into my favorite cup and travel, once more, back to my cave.

It looks like a lot of work, but I do it instinctively. It's a routine designed to do one thing—get me into *the zone*. Much has been written elsewhere about the mental state that is the zone, but I will say this: it is a deeply creative space where inspiration is built. Anything that you perceive as beautiful, useful, or fun came from someone stumbling through the zone.

Once I've successfully traversed my morning routine and have entered the zone, I am *off limits*. I mean it. Intruding into the cave and disrupting the zone is no different than standing up in the middle of the first-ever showing of *The Empire Strikes Back,* jumping up and down, and yelling, *"Darth Vader is Luke's father! Darth Vader is Luke's father!"* Not only are you ruining the mood, you're killing a major creative work.

No, I'm not going to answer the phone. In fact, it's a sure sign of compromised cave design if I can even hear the phone ring. And no, I don't hear you when you walk in and ask if we should go to the park tomorrow. I don't hear you the second time, either. I don't mean I'm ignoring you, because that'd involve using precious brain cycles I need for the zone . . . I really *can't* hear you. That's how deep I am in the zone.

No, I have no idea that it's been four hours since I closed the door and began furiously typing. Really, the only things I know are (a) when my coffee cup is empty, and (b) when I need to head to the bathroom.

Yes. When you successfully penetrate the zone, there is a chance I'll be an asshole. In fact, I might snap.

The Snap

This is where I apologize.

No one deserves to be on the receiving end *of the snap.* All you were really doing was coming in to see when I was done because we agreed we'd go surfing this afternoon. Still, I got in the zone and I'm writing this wicked article and *who are you and what do you want?* The snap is a glare, a raised voice ... something designed to indicate you are *pissing me off* with your presence.

It's not fair, I realize that, but think of it like this: if you walk up to me and slap me across the face, I'm not going to think, "Why'd you do that?" I'm not going to take the time to dissect the situation. My instinct is going to be pure, primal, and immediate. I'm going to slap you back.

The reason for this irrational reaction is antiquated brain wiring. Four million years ago it was to my evolutionary advantage to respond to slaps as quickly as possible because they were often precursors to being eaten. Rather than piping my slap response through the "What is a reasonable response?" portion of my brain, it's wired straight into my "React immediately or else" area. Somehow, the snap response has the same wiring. Invasion of the zone is akin to some primal activity that required the brain to wire itself for immediate, irrational response.

It's not right, it's not socially acceptable, and I regret my actions 30 seconds later, but in 20 years of nerdery, the quest hasn't been to kill the snap, but figure out how to manage it.

The Place

Try as I might, I don't always make it to the zone. I'll go through all my odd little pre-zone activities of drink and music selection. I'll slightly adjust the five essential objects on my desk and I'll begin ... playing World of Warcraft.

This is not the zone ... this is *the place*. It is very similar to the zone in appearance, but mentally, it's a different muscle that I'm exercising. If the zone is akin to playing power forward in a championship hockey game, the place is the six hours spent in the weight room the day before. Yes, I'm working out my mental muscles, but I'm not really doing anything.

The rule is this: your significant other can interrupt the place with impunity. I might snap, but if you let me linger in the place like you should let me work in the zone, you'll never see me. If you walk into my office to ask me something and see a half-naked night elf dancing on my screen, you are hereby authorized to invade. Mistakes will happen and you'll invade the zone thinking that it's the place, but after I've cooled down, it's my responsibility to explain why what looks like the place is actually the zone.

Other Places

Nerds are rewarded for structure. We get big bucks for reliably generating useful technology that works. Sure, we're artists, but it's an art of patterns, repetition, structure, and efficiency (I swear, it's sexy). This makes it not surprising that the places we create in our homes and in our minds are designed in the same fashion.

The risk with these places is the same risk with all comfortable places. In the comfort, we forget that some of the most interesting stuff happens elsewhere.

34

Meeting
Creatures

Worst meeting ever.

It's not that the attendee list is wrong. All the right people are there and they're bright and they're the decision makers. It's not that the topic is boring or poorly defined. It's a big deal. The problem with this meeting is that it's never going to end.

See, about a year ago, one of our senior engineers was reading our contract with our application server. He read, "Support ends in two years. We're done. You're on your own." He freaked out, called a meeting, and freaked out again in the meeting to make sure we knew it was a big deal, so we agreed it was a big deal. To-do lists were generated, follow-up meetings were scheduled . . . it all had a pleasant "look what we can do when the sky is falling" vibe. Love it when folks scurry with purpose.

Present day. It's *a year* later and we haven't made the switch. The senior engineer who raised the red flag a year ago is, surprisingly, actually in this version of the meeting, although he is a shell of the engineer he was a year ago. I guarantee he's not going to say a thing because he knows what I know . . .

. . . this is the worst meeting ever.

We knew nine months ago what we needed to do to make the transition to the new server application, but the problem is, it's really fucking scary. It's one of those "We're not going to know half of what we need to do until we start" scenarios, and starting means betting the company. Once we begin the transition, there is no going back and this scares the hell out of everyone, including the VP who will not make a decision.

Each month for the past 12 months, we have had the same meeting. This is the problem, these are the risks, this is what we know, this is what we don't know. All that preliminary crap takes 30 minutes, and since it's been a month since we last heard it, everyone needs to be reminded of all the intricacies. Heads nod while I slowly dig my nails into the conference room table. We then begin the chasing-our-tail portion of the meeting, where all the same questions are asked and answered again. This is why the senior engineer is no longer engaged. He's tired of repeating himself.

Meetings are composed of people, but more interesting, meetings are composed of creatures. These are the roles, traits, and quirks of the people who show up in your meetings, and after you've sat through a couple thousand, you'll see the same creatures keep showing up. Knowing who they are can help you understand your meeting. Knowing what they do can save you time.

The Anchor

Slogan: "It's all about me."

The *anchor* is the big cheese. This is the person that everyone is talking to and this is the person who will decide on whatever needs deciding. When this person talks, everyone in the meeting is listening.

Meetings are power struggles between those who want something and those who don't want to give it to them. If you're walking into a meeting and you need something, your first job is to identify this person. This person is the reason the meeting is happening, and if you don't know who they are, you're missing essential subtext. It's actually pretty easy. Just wait for someone to say something controversial and see who everyone looks at.

There are two major things to be wary of with your anchor. First, make sure they know their job. For standing meetings with the usual suspects, the role is obvious, but for one-time meetings, you can't assume the anchor knows it's all about them. A clear agenda that anoints the anchor right out of the gate is the best way to make sure everyone knows who the decision maker is.

Second, you've got to know what to do when there is no anchor present. You're 15 minutes in and you know the senior VP who is actually going to help here is not present. Sure, there are eight other people here that like to talk, but the best move is a reschedule. You're wasting time.

Laptop Larry

Slogan: "Pardon me, what?"

Larry is easy to identify. He's got his MacBook in front of him. That's him right there. If the MacBook somehow isn't enough, just look for lots of intense nodding from Larry . . . that's him not listening.

Larry pisses me off. He goes to regularly scheduled meetings that he knows are going to be 75 percent irrelevant to him, so he brings his computer so he can work. Turns out he doesn't work because he's spending half his time half-listening to the meeting proceedings. Go read that last sentence again. He's not working and he's not really listening which means he is actually a net negative when it comes to productivity.

Ask Larry to put his computer away. I mean it. If you can't vivaciously participate in a meeting you were invited to, you should not be there. "Rands Rands Rands . . . I take notes on my computer." No, you don't. You take notes and when I use some proper noun you don't recognize, you surf Wikipedia. If notes must be taken, designate one person to do it; I want you asking me what the proper noun is . . . not consulting Wikipedia.

A useful meeting is not a speech; it's a debate. If I'm up there flapping my lips and you disagree or don't understand, I don't want you to nod, I want you to yell at me.

Mr. Irrelevant

Slogan: "I'm just happy to be here."

Why is Mr. Irrelevant here? He doesn't have anything to add, he's just all smiles because someone took the time to include him in what must be a very important meeting. He is mostly harmless.

The problem that needs solving with regard to Mr. Irrelevant is figuring out who invited this guy to the meeting. What were they trying to do? Why is it that you're paying Mr. Irrelevant to sit in this meeting, nod a lot, and take notes? If you uninvited him, he's not going to be pissed, but the question is, who is going to be pissed? Why did they invite Mr. Irrelevant? Is he a mole? Is someone gathering essential information because they can't be there?

There is a reason Mr. Irrelevant is in your meeting and you need to understand that reason before you punt him.

Chatty Patty

Slogan: "I don't shut up."

Another easy identification. This one never shuts up. Ever.

Your main issue here is time. Chatty Patty is incapable of conveying thoughts in a concise manner, which means every time she opens her mouth, everyone else is checking out.

Your first job is to figure out whether Chatty Patty is actually Ms. Irrelevant. Fortunately, getting her talking is no issue. Your job is to figure out whether the signal-to-noise ratio is acceptable. Once you've determined if she actually needs to be there, you next job is containment and, to do that, you've got to play her game.

Containing Patty is a simple process of asking questions in a manner that she wants to hear, meaning with lots and lots of words. Questions for Chatty Patty must be precise so she can't verbally wander. Rather than ask, "How is QA?" you ask, "Patty, I've read your test plan, your current test results, and I understand you have a brief assessment for us regarding the quality of the product. Could you please give us a brief assessment?"

You're going to feel silly constructing these lengthy, repetitive requests, but not only are you giving Patty a well-defined space to wander in, you're also saving time for everyone in the meeting.

Warning: Don't ever, ever argue with Chatty Patty in a meeting setting. Combining Patty's natural loquaciousness with emotion is a recipe for disaster. Remember, she already doesn't know how to end a thought. Throw some emotional in there and she might never stop.

Translator Tim

Slogan: "I know every acronym ever. FTW!"

Tim is the first of two utility creatures. His role is simple: he speaks the language of everyone in the room. When hardware and software get together to talk about the issue, Tim is the guy who translates software acronyms into hardware acronyms. Tim is essential when you've got groups of folks who come from very different parts of the organization.

You need to be wary if Tim isn't neutral with regard to the topic that he's translating. If he's biased, he's translating in his favor, which means if Tim is on your team, you're in a good shape. If he's not, you might want to go find your own Tim.

Sally Synthesizer

Slogan: "What he's saying is . . ."

I love Sally because Sally's job is to end meetings. As our second utility creature, Sally grabs the conversation, no matter how messy it might be, and derives the basic truth of what was just discussed.

In large group meetings with a diverse set of personalities, you must have a Sally in the room because she's not missing a thing that's being said and, more importantly, she's aware of the relative significance not only of what is being said, but also who is saying it. She knows who the anchor is, she knows how to shut Patty up, and while it might appear that she's just stating the obvious, she's providing essential forward momentum to the meeting.

Like Tim, if Sally is biased in a meeting, she's synthesizing in her favor. Also, Sally can get drunk with power because her skill is invaluable. When she starts to think she's an anchor, you've got a problem.

Curveball Kurt

Slogan: "The sky is pancakes."

Kurt is easy to identify. You have no clue what he's talking about.

The first order of business once you've identified Kurt is figuring out if he's Mr. Irrelevant. This can be tricky since whenever you ask him a question, you see his lips move, he's clearly speaking English, but you have no idea what he's trying to say. Hopefully, Translator Tim or Sally Synthesizer is in the room to help out here.

Your absolute worst situation is when your anchor is a Curveball. It happens more than you'd think. The most likely case is combining groups on vastly different parts of the organization chart. Think of executives brainstorming with engineers. Every executive wants to think they can chum it up with anyone in the organization, but when it comes to their day-to-day job, they literally speak a different language. This means you've got Curveball Kurt on both sides of the table. This is an impossible meeting without some type of translator and synthesizer in the room.

The Snake

Slogan: "I'm actually the anchor. Sssssssh!"

Some anchors like to hide. It goes like this:

Big meeting with the executives. Sally gets up, sets the agenda, asks Larry to please, for the last time, put the laptop away, and then the meeting begins. Curveball Kurt gets up and says something unintelligible. Translator Tim jumps in and translates for Kurt, but he translates to the executive in the *right* corner. Aha! There's your anchor. Pay attention to the *right* corner.

The meeting proceeds. Mr. Irrelevant says something funny, everyone laughs and then wonders when someone will remove this boob from the meeting. Finally, we reach the crescendo of the meeting and the decision needs to be made and all heads turn to the anchor. We wait for a second and he says, "Snake? Your thoughts?"

The *snake* is the anchor in hiding and he's in the *left* corner. For some reason, he's got the fake anchor out there taking the heat while he sits there taking it all in. Maybe he doesn't like the spotlight. Maybe there is some strategic advantage to the room not knowing he's the man, but he is. Fortunately for everyone, the snake move only works a few times within a company before word gets out who the real anchor is.

Back to the worst meeting ever. It's the last one on the server issue I ever attended because when I walked in, I knew what the problem was. We all thought we had an anchor in our VP of engineering, but, the problem is, he wasn't willing to assume the anchor role. Since we had a bet-the-company decision on the table, we should've grabbed the CEO the moment it was clear the VP couldn't anchor the meeting.

You might think we were also missing Sally Synthesizer—someone to capture the essence of what happened—but that was me. I was trying to move the meeting forward by capturing the major thoughts, repeating them for everyone to hear, but it was a useless task since the anchor didn't want his job.

Forty-five minutes after the meeting began, I did something I'd never ever done before. I walked out of a meeting where I was a key player because I simply couldn't waste any more time on this uselessness. Stood up, walked out, and slammed the door. Yes, it's an emotional move that is almost always a bad move in business, but near the top of my list of professional pet peeves is the following:

Do not waste my time.

Incrementalists and Completionists

I recently got into a war of words with a coworker regarding the proper solution to a problem with one of our products. As an aside, let me say that e-mail is never ever ever never ever the right way to resolve controversy. Too much subtlety is lost when you're YELLING IN ALL CAPS at your program manager. Don't waste your time solving problems in e-mail. Stand up. Walk down the hall. And look the person in the eye. You'll live longer.

Anyhow.

What was intriguing about my e-mail exchange with the coworker was that we weren't disagreeing about whether or not we should do something about the problem. We were arguing about how much we should do. The disagreement reminded me that there are two distinct personalities when it comes to devising solutions to problems: incrementalists and completionists.

Incrementalists are realists. They have a pretty good idea of what is achievable given a problem to solve, a product to ship. They're intimately aware of how many resources are available and the shape of the political landscape with regard to the problem, and they know who knows what. They tend to know all the secrets and they like to be recognized for that fact.

Completionists are dreamers. They have a very good idea how to solve a given problem, and that answer is to solve it right. Their mantra is, "If you're going to spend the time to solve a problem, solve it in a manner so that you aren't going to be solving it again in three months." I used to think that architects were the only real completionists in an organization, but I was wrong. Architects are the only recognized completionists, but the personality is hiding all over the place.

Rewind to my situation. The actual problem is irrelevant, but here's the background. The coworker discovered a problem in our product and reported it. I responded and suggested a minor improvement that didn't solve the core problem but was achievable given our schedule. The coworker responded with, "Why do this if we don't solve the problem?" I responded, "We don't have time to solve it and something is better than nothing." Coworker: "This is less than nothing!" Insert stunned silence.

Remember, the coworker identified (correctly) the original problem. So, why in the world don't they see the value of my solution? The reason is that this is an incrementalist doing battle with a completionist. This isn't a battle of wrong versus right; it's the battle of right versus right. Bizarre.

How does anything get done with incrementalists and completionists arguing about degrees of rightness? Here's the trick. You want them to argue, you just don't want them to kill each other. This is where you, the manager, come in.

Somewhere in the Middle

First, we're going to ignore the problem that has your incrementalist and completionist at each other's throats. It's important, but it's not what we're working on here, which is getting some value out of these unique perspectives.

What's important is, who needs to move where? Does the incrementalist need to move closer to the completionist's view or vice versa? In either case, you've got to use the simplest trick in the conflict resolution book: finding common ground. A better way to think about this is, "What do these disparate philosophies need from each other?"

Incrementalists Need Vision

What defines an incrementalist's day is the raw amount of stuff they do. How many meetings? How many bugs do they close? They love the fact that they ran into that engineering manager in the cafeteria who dropped that critical piece of gossip. Motion, motion, motion.

From the outside, it might look like your incrementalist lacks purpose, but look at the name. This person is driven by the goal of constantly—incrementally—making progress, moving forward.

The question is: What is the purpose behind all this movement? What is their goal? What I've noticed with the incrementalists in my life is that for all the motion, it's not always clear in what direction they are headed. It's hard to figure this out because they look so busy, but the question is, what is the nature of the busyness?

Your goal with incrementalists is to get them to define or see the plan from soup to nuts. This is a big deal for them because they normally can't see past the next meeting. Getting them on board with the big picture gives them a sense of foundation they don't usually have.

This is where your completionist comes in.

Completionists Need Action

Completionists spend much of their lives shaking their heads, staring at the floor, muttering, "Boy, could they fuck this up more?" Fact is, for any given technical or product problem, there's a completionist who knows exactly what to do. Problem is, not only can they see the immediate solution; they see the two-year solution and the five-year solution. By the way, the five-year solution drastically changes the immediate solution, which is why everyone else has a problem with it. Everyone else has no insight into the five-year solution.

Feel dumb? I do.

Now put yourself in the completionist's shoes. Sitting there watching these incrementalists with their rapid-fire buzz-speak, pushing a short-sighted corporate agenda that is clearly going to fail. No wonder folks are yelling in the hallways.

With all of their strategic vision, completionists often lack common corporate and people sense. Yes, they have a five-year technical roadmap in their heads, but they have nary a clue how to start pushing that agenda with the 12 different people who need to get on board to make anything happen. This is why completionists often get incorrectly labeled as curmudgeons. Sure, they're cranky, but it's not cranky for crankiness's sake, it's because they don't have the communication and people skills to convince the company of the truth.

Two Different Coffee Addictions

I'm painting a picture of absolutes regarding incrementalists and completionists, but there are dangerous variants that you need to be aware of, and all of these are caffeinated mutations of the core personality.

Incrementalists drink a lot of coffee because of their addiction to motion. Getting lost in this addiction means that incrementalists never finish a thing. They have no concept of "done," because done would mean no more motion and who wants to stop? The warning signs you're looking for here are that when an incrementalist is facing a hard problem, they're constantly coming up with new ways to tackle the problem rather than actually tackling the problem.

Completionists drink a lot of coffee because of their addiction to thought. Unlike incrementalists, these completionists aren't actually saying anything because they're deeply considering the problem. Now, you've got to give completionists time to figure out the plan, but after a significant amount of time, you need to figure out whether they're good at gripping the bat or swinging it.

A quiet completionist doesn't mean they don't have anything to say—they're just unlikely to speak until their plan is fully formed. Your issue is when your completionist has slipped into creative strategic nirvana, where actually finishing something is less important than considering it.

See It Yet?

It's a really simple puzzle. One personality has all the skills necessary to get stuff done but isn't exactly sure what to do. The other personality knows exactly what to do, but doesn't know how to do it. Your job as a manager is to find and marry these personality types in your organization, because when they understand each other's strengths, you've got a complete strategically tactical product team.

Being incremental and being a manager means I'm looking for one thing out of the completionists on my team. I want to be sitting across the table from them seeing the look of understanding in their eyes, and the look says this: "Hey, I know what you're about. I don't trust it, but I understand that I need what you do, so I'm going to sit here, arms folded, and we're going to figure out how to work together."

Both incrementalists and completionists are defined by a common goal. They both thrive on getting stuff done. This makes them essential to any corporate agenda and you want a diverse population of both. Yeah, they're going to argue, but it's the argument you want your teams to have. It's not a fear-based "Should we or shouldn't we?" it's "Let's do this thing, let's make sure it gets done, and let's make sure it gets done right."

Organics and Mechanics

Stop. Grab a pencil and write down the first and last names of your past three managers. Stare at those names for a bit and relive those months or years of reporting to this person. I want your off-the-cuff opinion about each one. My guess is your opinion falls into one of three buckets:

I love this guy. Best manager ever. I still talk to him on a monthly basis because this guy taught me everything I know about what I do. He is my mentor.

Mostly harmless. This guy doesn't really challenge me, but then again, he's not really slowing me down. I'm not learning much, but I don't have to put up with much bullshit. Also, I'm not sure what he actually does, but he leaves me alone . . . so . . . whatever.

Worst. Manager. Ever. This guy makes my life a living hell. I dread our weekly one-on-one. I prepare for an hour and we still end up talking about random useless crap. It's like we're speaking a different language. I don't know what he wants, and even if I did, I wouldn't want to give it to him because I'm so annoyed. I mostly want to give him a poke in the nose.

I want to talk about Worst Manager Ever because, chances are, you're right. . . you are speaking a different language and he's just as frustrated as you.

As an individual contributor or a manager, you interact with two populations: those you work with and those you work for. The conversations with these two populations are distinct. With coworkers, you speak the Truth. You speak it because each of you are slogging it out in your respective trenches, so what good is there to say anything but the Truth?

With managers, you speak the Way. The Way includes the things we shall do to achieve organizational enlightenment. "Verily, I shall scribe a specification and it will be a good thing" or "Yea, it came to pass, I say unto you, I am working weekends." The Way is however you're communicating up to your manager. It's different content and it's different tone, and if you believe you have the worst manager ever, then you're not doing it right.

In order to understand how to speak to your manager, you've gotta figure out how they acquire information, and chances are, they gather it either *organically* or *mechanically*.

The Itch Perspective

Your first job is to figure out whether you're working with an organic or a mechanic. To do that, think of any problem as a very complex itch. Now, this is no normal itch, it's a complex itch and scratching said itch is going to take some work. Here's the inner dialog for a mechanic and then an organic regarding how they're going begin their scratching:

> **Mechanic:** "An itch. Well. This itch seems familiar. In fact, I scratched this type of itch in January 2001. Let me first dig up my notes regarding that itching. Excellent. We're going to need a matrix. The vertical column will be action items I can think of that will assess different scratching scenarios and the vertical axis will measure our progress against these different scenarios. OK, we're going to need a meeting to form a committee . . ."

> **Organic:** "Wow, an itch. Hmmmm . . . well, this sucks. Hey Frank, we've got an itch . . . whaddya think? Yeah, that's what I was thinking. You know, this itch seems familiar . . . I think I'm going to deeply consider this itch while I drive home, but first, where's Mary? She knows all about itches and I bet she'll have some ideas . . . I wonder what happens when I type itch in Google . . . Hey . . . there's an idea . . ."

Mechanics move forward methodically. They carefully gather information in a structured manner and store that information in a manner that makes it easiest to find again. They quietly observe, they stay on message, they are comfortably predictable, and they annoy the hell out of organics.

Organics are all over the place. They tend to be loud and they can tell a joke. They ask seemingly meaningless questions. They lean forward when they talk to you.

When confronted with a horrible situation, you're going to think they're insane because they appear to be still smiling.

A large part of the interpersonal conflict at work can be summed up in the following scenario:

An organic and a mechanic are staring at each other across the desk and are thinking the following:

> **Mechanic:** "This guy is walking chaos."
>
> **Organic:** "This guy is totally uptight."

They are both right because they both violate each other's sense of propriety. Knowing this solves half the problem. The other half is figuring out how the hell to communicate and that's the hard part.

Prior gig, four years ago. I was hired in by the CEO as a director while they continued to search for a VP of engineering. As an aside, let me stress how bad of a career move it is to *not* know who you are going to be working for when you arrive. The 30-minute interview you have with your future manager is a critical piece of information when you decide whether or not to make a move. Here's why.

The VP of engineering showed up a few months later and he seemed like a bright guy. Good technical background . . . a bit quiet for my taste, but I'm loud so we'll balance out, right? Our first one-on-one showed up, so I grabbed my big, black notebook and plopped down in his office and *wham, holy micro-management.*

"What's going on with this? How is person X? What about person Y? Have we done XYZ task? No, why? Why again? No really, why?" Question question question data data my lord does this guy think I'm sitting around surfing the Web? OK, deep breath Rands, it's his first week and he's gathering information so I'm going to cut him slack. He'll chill out once he realizes I've got things under control.

Nope.

One month later and the barrage of questions is nonstop. This guy peppers me with random questions and I consistently leave his office feeling like I've been doing nothing with *my 72-hour work week*. It's a cop out to label this guy a micromanager. Great, he's a micromanager. So what? I'm still going to walk out of his office on a weekly basis thinking I'm useless. He's clearly mechanical, but so what?

Remember, mechanical managers gather information in structured way. They do this because they aren't great at relating to people, so they let the left brain take over as a means of content acquisition. This means that if you have a mechanic for a manager, you need to push the information in a structured, well-known, and consistent manner.

So, I wrote a status template for my mechanical manager. It started with products and listed current relevant bits for each of the products on my team. Following that, I listed personnel issues team by team. Contractor status, requisition status, vacations.

Each week, I'd fill this template out 24 hours before my one-on-one. This was my first pass, which loaded my brain with this week's content. I'd remember things we'd talked about the week before and make sure that I'd have the most recent data on those hot issues. An hour before the one-on-one, I'd review again and fine-tune. When the one-on-one arrived, I pulled out my printout and started. I stayed on message and I never deviated from the template. Every week. The same structure chock-full of dates, data, milestones . . . anything concrete and real.

Consistency. Structure. He loved it. I literally jumped up and down after the one-on-one where he didn't ask a single question because I successfully predicted every single possible question he might ask.

My VP was a mechanic and he wanted to feel the structure that encompassed dealing with every problem. Guess what, I'm an organic. My one-on-ones start with a "Hey how the hell are you?" and then they wander. You're going to walk out of my office thinking we just shot the breeze for a bit, but as we chitchatted, I was carefully gathering content. What was your reaction to question X? What questions did you ask me? Yes, I appear to be collecting trivial crap with my random questions, but I tend to gather more information than mechanics because who the hell knows what I'm going to ask.

That's one situation. There are more and I guarantee yours is unique. My advice follows.

If You Work for an Organic . . .

You've got to trust that they've got a plan even though it may not be immediately apparent. Don't confuse an extremely open mind with cluelessness. Organics often have a more complete picture about what is going down because they are better networked.

If you're an organic yourself, you're going to love your one-on-ones because you'll regularly work each other into a creative frenzy. Topics will vary wildly and the moment they become dull, they'll vanish. It won't feel like work.

If you're a mechanic, you're going to feel a bit lost with your organic manager because you're OK with lightweight forms of micromanagement. It gives you structure. Most organic managers I've worked with can put on a mechanic hat and provide that structure, but you've got to ask because it's not their natural state.

It's true. Organics miss detail as they hurry from place to place.

If You Work for a Mechanic . . .

Like I said above, a mechanic will not believe you're dealing with something until they feel the structure that encompasses a problem you're solving. You must overload your mechanic with data in order to satiate their structured brain. If your mechanic keeps asking you the *exact same question* and none of your responses appear to be the answer, it's time to counter with, "I really don't know what you are asking."

If you're an organic, you will wrongly assume that mechanics don't trust you, and you're right; they don't. You will build trust by acting like a mechanic with them. It takes practice, but since you're already working for one, you've got a great role model. I'm not suggesting you need to transform yourself into a mechanic (which is impossible), you just need to speak mechanic long enough to soothe your mechanical manager. Once he's figured out you've got chops, you can start going organic on him. He'll deal.

It's true. Mechanics rarely inspire organics.

Look Out For …

Like incrementalists and completionists, the most dangerous organic/mechanic type is the switch-hitter. My personal favorites are mechanical organics. These folks have all the slick tricks of organic information gathering, but they've got the astounding organization skills of the mechanic. They know everything and never forget a bit. I mean it.

Organic mechanics are frightening. They have extreme depth of knowledge, but there is no obvious organic thread that ties it all together. Here's the scary part. There is a thread. There is a purpose. They just aren't letting you see it. Organic mechanics will keep you on your heels and just when you think you've figured them out, they'll change everything. I hate that. I mean, I love that.

The Answer Is in the Middle

Organics doing battle with mechanics, or vice versa, is a waste of time. Organizational warfare does one thing. It focuses everyone on their peculiar personality quirks rather on than the business and that means you're wasting cash money. Whether it's my manager or my coworker, when I find myself in an organic/mechanic conflict, I think this:

"A purely mechanical organization lacks inspiration. A purely organic organization is total chaos."

Organics fill mechanical blind spots with their intuition and their passion while mechanics create a healthy, solid home where nutty organics can run into things at speed. It's a team thing.

Inwards, Outwards, and Holistics

There are all sorts of intimidating titles surrounding the management caste. Engineering manager, senior engineering manager, director of engineering, vice president of engineering, chief technology officer. While these names are useful in determining where an individual lies in the organizational chart, the names are merely hints as to what that person actually cares about. And you should care what they care about whether you're a manager or an individual contributor.

Like it or not, your boss has as much effect on your career as you do, and they also effectively sign your paycheck every two weeks, and that means food. Sure, you can leave and go elsewhere, but there's a manager there, too, and he's got his own obscure agenda, as well.

There are three distinct classes of managers, each with their own agenda. The common names for these classes are first line manager, middle manager, and executive or senior manager. Again, these names do a good job of giving you a clue where your manager sits on an organizational chart, but they don't tell you what they actually do and how they are motivated. We need a different set of names for that. We need a set of names that don't confuse us with an implied hierarchy.

The Vision Hierarchy

To understand a manager's agenda, you've got to understand what he wants, and the best way to do that is to figure out what he thinks about all day. What is he paying attention to? Where does he mentally stare all day? It's likely one of three directions.

Inwards: These types of managers are responsible for a small team of folks working on a single product or technology. An inward manager's vision is focused on their team and their product. While they're aware there are other things going on in the organization, they don't tend to be involved cross-functionally unless their team has dependency on an external team.

Inwards are often junior managers, but that isn't always the case. Some very experienced managers have settled into a comfortable groove as inwards because they want to stay near the team and near the code.

Holistics: Traditionally, holistics make up the middle layer of management. Whereas the inward's vision is pointed down at the individual team, the holistic is staring across the organization. They are likely managers of managers; responsible for multiple products and multiple teams.

The holistic's main job is to figure out what the hell is going on *everywhere* in the organization. They're doing this because, as we'll see in a moment, they're actually running your company. This is why they're never in their office; they're running around gathering information. This constant information acquisition gives the impression that they are spread thin and, well, they are. There's a ton of information moving around your average-sized company, and staying tapped into that flood is a full-time job.

Wait, don't these holistics have product to ship? No, they have multiple products, but they've hired rock-star inwards to get the products built to specification and on time so they can focus on figuring out what to build next and who they're going to need to build it.

Outwards: These are the senior managers. VPs, CEOs. The biggest misconception regarding outwards is what they care about. You'd think their number one priority would be the care and feeding of the company. Wrong. The well-being of the company is the responsibility of the holistics. The holistics are the ones who are spending all the time sniffing around the hallways, gathering internal competitive intelligence, and building empires out of talented inwards.

The outward's vision is focused on the outside world. They care about the public perception of the company, the company's relationship with its customers, the financial community, the world. That's why they're never at headquarters, they're off telling other people what a great job all those holistics and inwards are doing. I'm not suggesting that outwards don't care about the daily professional shenanigans within the company; they do, but they've also hired a group of rock-star holistics to run their company. The rub is this: while it's not their job to run the company on a daily basis, they are accountable for it. Tough gig.

Agenda Confusion

These titles get more confusing when you realize that a manager can have two titles. First, there's the title they give themselves and, second, there's the perception of the rest of the organization. In a healthy organization, these roles are the same, but most organizations just aren't healthy

An example: You might be working for a manager who fancies himself a holistic when the organization has him pegged as an inward. This means he's out combing the hallway looking for strategic advantage when he should really be paying attention to you, the senior engineer who has indicated, loudly, "There is no way this product is going to ship on time." My first thought is this is both an opportunity and a problem. The problem is that your manager isn't paying attention to his primary job, but the opportunity is that you are.

A variation of this confusion is when a title has been granted, but is not being used. How about when an inward has been forced into a holistic role via a promotion? How are these guys going to screw you? Well, it's not going to be through action, it's going be through inaction. See, as an inward, they don't care about the political intrigue over in building 27, they want to design and ship product, they want to dive into the details. Problem is, the political intrigue over in building 27 will ultimately determine that your product is irrelevant. Now you're out of a job because your manager's manager didn't attend that cross-functional meeting because what he really wanted to do was code. Sorry about that.

Possibly the worst example of this confusion is also one of the biggest reasons for micromanagement. When you're being micromanaged, it means two things: first, it feels like you're doing unnecessary work, and second, you feel the person asking you to do this work is being unreasonable. You're right on both counts. Micromanagement is often a result of a manager jumping from one management class to another. Maybe it's an outward who is getting panicky at the end of a result cycle, so he starts acting like an inward. Problem is, everyone knows he's an outward. He sounds like an outward and talks like one, too. Sure, everyone is happy to get some face time with the CEO, but everyone is also wondering why he isn't doing his job—running the company.

Watch for Growth

The progression from inward to holistic to outward is a strategic one. A junior manager starts out caring about the quality of one product and, if they continue to grow, they end up caring about the health of an entire company. Watching this growth is essential to your own professional growth.

What you need to know about your manager is how much he cares about this growth and, more importantly whether he sees this as his growth opportunity or the team's. Junior inward managers invariably figure out the responsibility and power held by the holistics and outwards, and when they do, you want to watch them carefully. There is a spectrum here with "advantage for the team" on one side and "advantage for the manager" on the other. Eager young managers who spend all their time looking for advantage for themselves are going to screw the team at some point because of their razor focus on themselves. Are they feeding you the bits of information they find or are they keeping it to themselves? If you're not learning something new in each and every staff meeting, you might have a selfish climber on your hands.

Perhaps your manager doesn't care about growth. Your gut instinct might be that this is a bad situation since working for a manager who isn't interested in growing isn't going to grow his team. Maybe. Maybe your stagnant inward is a seasoned manager who spent time getting beaten up as a holistic or an outward. Maybe they got tired of endless information acquisition or maybe they're just great engineers who love to code. Personally, I think these types of inwards are phenomenal employees and managers because they have a wealth of experience. The question is, are they passing that experience on to you and making sure that you're growing?

My preference is to stock my team with holistic managers and inwards geared to become holistics. While an experienced, steady inward is a reliable manager, I prefer the enthusiasm of employees who are ready for the next thing, especially when the next thing for them is my job.

Free Electrons

Back in my Borland days, we were working hard on Paradox for Windows. I was a QA engineer testing the database creation and modification functionality. Jerry, my counterpart in engineering, was working hard, but getting absolutely nowhere.

We were mid-to-late in a 1.0 product cycle, and most of the engineers were slowly moving from development into bug-fix mode, but not Jerry. He was still implementing . . . over and over again. You are screwed because you've given a critical task to someone who is utterly unable to complete it.

Now, let's first give Jerry a break. He was a fine programmer, but he had two major strikes against him. First, Jerry had never programmed for Windows, so he was learning while he was coding. Second, this was also a 1.0 product. Chapter 19 of this book is titled "1.0," but its actual title should be, "1.0 spelled one point oh my god I'm never going to see my family again." I'll summarize: 1.0 is incredibly hard, and combined with his Windows inexperience, Jerry was in trouble.

Yet, Jerry had pride. Jerry believed that he could pull it off, but being on the receiving end of his code, I observed a disturbing coding practice, which we'll call "moving crap around on your plate." Jerry's approach to fixing his bugs was to move his code around in interesting ways, much the way you used to shove food around on your plate in a feeble attempt to convince your mom that you actually ate your beets. Nothing substantially changes; it just looks different. Another name for this coding practice might be "coding by hope."

The end result with Jerry's code was that each time he'd fix something we'd discover another fundamental problem with the feature. Yes, small, incremental progress was being made with each bug fix, but Jerry was in a losing situation because his basic architecture was crap. When asked for status, his lists of excuses were astonishingly lengthy and believable. They were the excuses of a person who honestly believed he could pull it off and was willing to put in the hours to do it. But all the hours in the world weren't going to help Jerry because he was in over his head.

If you're the manager in this scenario, you've got to make a major change because you cannot release crap. There are companies that do this and end up making a tidy profit. You are not that person, because once you are rewarded for releasing crap, you begin a blind walk down a path of mediocrity that ends up with you working at Computer Associates on a product no one has heard of and that no one cares about.

It's a two-step fix process. We needed to make a Jerry adjustment and then we needed a miracle. I'll start with the easy one.

We needed Jerry. He's the only one who knows what the hell is going on in that pile of spaghetti and he could fix trivial bugs. The engineering manager sat Jerry down and told him we need to focus on quantity. There were scads of trivial little fixes all over the place that had been ignored, and Jerry could handle those. Yes, his ego was bruised, but in a few weeks, Jerry was cranking because people always work better when they're making forward progress on a task they have a chance of completing.

With Jerry on task, we had to face another fact: we were six months from shipping, and we had a major portion of functionality that was cobbled together and barely working. In this scenario, you need a unique talent. You need a *free electron*.

The free electron is the single most productive engineer that you're ever going to meet. I have not even provided a definition and I'm guessing a person that fits the bill has already popped into your mind.

A free electron can do anything when it comes to code. They can write a complete application from scratch, learn a language in a weekend, and, most importantly, they can dive into a tremendous pile of spaghetti code, make sense of it, and actually get it working. You can build an entire business around a free electron. They're that good.

There are two classes of free electrons, *senior electrons* and *junior electrons*. Both have similar productivity yields, but the senior versions have become politically and socially aware. In technology-savvy organizations, many CTOs fall into this category. Think Bill Joy. There's always a risk that senior electrons can spin into a technology high-earth orbit where their ideas simply sound insane, but, whenever they talk, you should listen.

The junior versions have all the ability, they just don't have the experience of dealing with people because they spent a lot of their youths writing their own operating systems as a fun intellectual exercise. These junior electrons represent the single best hire you can make as a hiring manager. If you get two in 20 years, you're doing something right.

Care and Feeding

If you are lucky enough to have a free electron in your organization, you need to be aware you are dealing with a strange breed of engineer and the care of and feeding of this engineer might be different than the rest of the team.

Keep them engaged. First, there are two primary tasks in an engineering organization: research and development. While the free electron is eminently capable of doing development, their value in the organization is research. They define the bleeding edge. If you leave a free electron in the development role too long, they will vanish simply because they're bored. All engineers like to be on the bleeding edge, but free electrons simply must be defining it. A departing free electron will permanently damage the productivity of your group.

Misdirected free electron intensity can yield odd results. On one project, I assigned a couple of slippery memory corruption bugs to a free electron who nodded quietly and promptly vanished for a week. When he returned, the bugs were fixed and the entire database layer had been rewritten. A piece of code that'd taken two engineers roughly six months to design had been totally redone in seven days. Sounds like a great idea until you realize we were working on a small update and did not have the resources or time to test a brand spankin' new database layer. Oops.

Free electrons sometimes will not engage and they won't explain why. Free electrons are high-functioning and have strong opinions about everything . . . but they may never tell you those opinions. If you're asking them to do something that they don't believe in, they aren't going to do it. Ask all you want. The worst case is when you ask a free electron to pull off a diving save and they nod . . . and promptly return to whatever they were doing before you distracted them with your useless request. One week later, you're going to be expecting the miracle, but the free electron is going to say, "Haven't got to that."

One week more, your hair is going to be mostly pulled out, and then you're going to realize you didn't need a miracle in the first place and that inaction was the right move. Your free electron knew that two weeks ago. They just didn't want to take the two hours to draw the picture for you. Annoying, huh? You'll get over it.

It's a team. All of this advice is directed at your free electron, but you need to remember even though they're incredibly productive, they're part of the team. My advice shouldn't be interpreted as giving free electrons special treatment any more than you give each person on your team your focused attention. There's no need to call attention to the fact that you've got a free electron on your team. Trust me, everyone already knows it.

Back to Jerry

Enter Bernard, Borland's resident free electron. Up until he started poking around the code, I had no idea what Bernard actually did. He had an office. It was full of books. He talked a lot and produced little visible work. "Blowhard" is what I thought.

Bernard started tinkering with Jerry's code on a Friday afternoon. The next Monday, I was able to run through my functional test matrix for the first time ever. By the end of that week, Bernard had closed a majority of the high-severity bugs and was beginning to tread in fix areas reserved for Jerry. The following week I was racing to file bugs to keep Bernard engaged.

That is a free electron at work.

Rules for the Reorg

You've been here.

It's after 10 p.m. and you get a random e-mail from your boss saying, "We need to talk." No additional data except for a meeting proposal that shows up 30 seconds later entitled "Re: Needing to Talk." You sit staring at the screen, wondering what could be up. No rumors of layoffs are in the air; the company is doing fine. You can't think of anything you've done, said, or written that merits a managerial follow-up, so what's the deal?

By the time the meeting shows up the next day, you've been stewing for a good 12 hours, which means you've reflected on every single thing you've done for the past six months so you can be prepared for whatever curveball your boss is going to throw. When you walk in his office, he's already facing you and he's got the org chart sitting directly in front of him.

So now you know. You're about to endure a reorganization.

Your boss is pretty good about it. He comes right out and tells you that one of your groups is going to be moved elsewhere. He explains the justification and asks you for your thoughts. You chitchat a bit more, then he totally blows it: "I held off from telling you because things are changing so much and I didn't want to jerk you around. It's all settled down now."

Hah. Right.

Before I explain how your boss just lied to you, let's first understand exactly what a reorganization ("reorg") is, and then I've got some advice for how to weather the chaos. First, a reorg is not a layoff. Layoffs can occur as part of a reorg, but they are a side effect, not a cause. Reorgs are when teams and products are shifted around in order to account for a shift in company strategy. What kind of shift? Who knows. Maybe the market for your product has changed, or maybe the economy is crap. The point is, someone, somewhere in the executive chain decided "We need to make an adjustment to the organization structure," and that means a good solid month of chaos.

Below are some useful rules to pay attention to during the reorg chaos, as well as some tips and tricks for surviving it.

Rule #1: Figure Out Your Role

When you first get wind of the reorg, you have a choice. How are you going to participate? Are you going to sit back and watch the fun or are you going to actively dive into the chaos?

You'll likely need to assess the magnitude of the reorg before you choose. You're especially interested in whatever machinations are in play for your part of the building, but the key to remember is that reorgs represent opportunity. Even if this particular reorg doesn't involve your team, it doesn't mean that you can't pitch your boss on fixing a long-standing organization problem in your group.

The opportunity lies in the fact that a reorg makes an organization very limber. Managers across the organization are thinking the same thing as you: "Well, if we're going to solve problem A right now, we should take a stab at problem B since we're going to be mucking with everything anyway." If you've got an agenda, if you've got a change in mind, it's time to consider pushing it because the chances that you can effect change are vastly higher in the midst of a reorg.

If you're content sitting back and watching everyone else pull the strings, there are still some other things to pay attention to.

Rule #2: People Are Paranoid

There is a painfully long period between when a majority of the organization knows about a reorg and when the actual reorg occurs. It's a painful time because it causes employees to start asking basic questions regarding the company. Who is going where and why? Are there layoffs? Why is this happening and do I have a job when it's all over?

The day before the team learned about the reorg, none of these questions were being asked. The team was working in a state of pleasant ignorance where their biggest worry was the next deadline. Now, they're worrying about what the organization is going to look like tomorrow and the simple fact is, no one knows.

Let's go back to what your boss told you: "I held off from telling you because things are changing so much and I didn't want to jerk you around. It's all settled down now."

Read that again. "Things are changing so much" and "It's all settled down now." He's contradicted himself and you hear this when he says it. Yes, he's trying to communicate, but all he's doing is making you paranoid. You're going to walk out of that meeting thinking, "He doesn't actually know what's going to happen," and you're right. He doesn't.

The fact that no one actually knows what is going to happen tomorrow creates a culture of paranoia and that means you need to start listening carefully.

Rule #3: The Grapevine Gone Mad

A major contributor to the rumor chaos around reorgs is the grapevine. Simply put, information that starts out as fact will slowly become more and more rumor as it moves from person to person. Let's watch . . .

VP of engineering to her staff: "They're building a new hardware group under Ted. It's not clear where they'll be getting all the headcount, but one option would be to sacrifice headcount from other groups."

What'd she say? Pretty clear statement of fact. She's trying to give her staff a heads up. Let's keep moving.

Manager of engineering to his staff: "Ted has a new group. We're liable to lose headcount in our group."

OK, what'd he say? He starts with the facts and then follows up with an opinion—he's losing heads. Why is he saying this? Maybe he's been at the company for years and knows how these things play out or maybe he's just guessing. Who knows? The grapevine is officially in effect. Watch . . .

Senior engineer to his friend: "We're losing heads in our group and they're going to Ted's group. Gosh, I hate Ted."

Welcome to a fully developed rumor ready for consumption by the grapevine.

This is a simple example, but it illustrates basic human nature. We want to know what's going on, and when we don't, we're likely to make stuff up using whatever facts are available to give the impression that we do. When you add opinions and biases to this information-creation process, you end up with a steady flow of compelling fiction crossing your desk.

Outside of the reorg, I put a lot of faith in the grapevine because I find there is less mutation of information as it jumps from person to person, but when jobs are on the line, the grapevine goes insane and some radical crap is going to find its way to you. I advise a patient, journalistic policy, where you confirm tidbits of information with independent sources before you believe anything.

Rule #4: Reorgs Take Forever

The time from when you hear about a reorg to when it's actually done is going to be four times as long as you think. Reorgs take forever. Plans are designed, confirmed with stakeholders, adjusted with feedback, balanced with budgets, run up the flagpole with the big boss, and then taken back to the drawing board. While this official process is going down, there are hallway shenanigans going on, as well as individual political players jockeying for headcount by tweaking the grapevine for their own nefarious purposes. All of this results in more information being inserted into the official process, forcing even more iteration.

My advice here is based on the role that you chose. Clearly if you've got skin in the game and have an agenda to push, you need to stay engaged for the duration. Don't trust when your boss tells you, "We're done," because that means he thinks he's done. He doesn't know about Phil over in platform engineering who still has a couple of moves in him.

If you've chosen the observation role, I recommend sitting back in your chair and enjoying the scurrying. Take comfort in the fact that you're still employed, and hey, if the reorg affects you, maybe a change of scenery is going to do you some good. Don't forget to ask for a window in your new office.

A reorg isn't over until someone important has printed out a new organizational chart and presented it in front of the entire company.

Rule #5: Most Folks Love Reorgs (But Hate to Admit It)

Reorganizations represent opportunity to those who are unhappy with the state of the current organization. As mentioned above, the moment stakeholders hear that there is a reorg brewing, they start working the grapevine to steer the course of the reorg in their favor. When you combine this fact with people's love of gossip, you're guaranteed a big, juicy, drawn-out reorganization.

If you're an observer, you might be annoyed by all the hallway conversation and closed-door meetings, but the fact is, most folks love this shit. Who is getting moved? Really? Wow. No way. He's an idiot! That blows! For some reason, conversations about reorgs sound a lot like conversations about infidelity. People are incapable of shutting up.

The group responsible for generating the most noise around reorgs, ironically, is the group who has the least effect on their eventual outcomes. These are the folks who are lingering in the dark while the management team wades through strategy, political agenda, and fiscal responsibility looking for a plan that gets the company out of wondering who works for whom and starts worrying about building product again.

The Only Rule: Patience

Think of the last contentious decision your team had to make. I'm talking about a big decision where team members were on opposite sides of the fence and you had to spend a good portion of a week sifting through the facts and opinions in order to construct a compromise decision that everyone agreed to, but didn't like.

Now, let's include the entire company in that decision. It doesn't matter what that decision is, what matters is that large groups of people move incredibly slowly. Call it bureaucracy, call it group think, but understand that very large groups of people working together barely looks like working because they move so slowly

Reorgs affect the entire company. Everyone has an opinion and that means group think of a magnitude you're unfamiliar with. I know you're worried about your job, your team, and your career, but take a breath—I'm sure there's other work to do.

An Unexpected Connection

Blue whales.

I couldn't stop researching blue whales. I was 12, and my teacher had just explained to the class that blue whales are the largest mammals on planet Earth.

In hindsight, this reaction was my first confirmed sighting of what in the Nerd Handbook[1] I call the "annoying efficient relevancy engine." Something in the phrase "largest mammal on earth" started the relevancy engine, and once it starts, it's not going to stop until the relevancy is understood.

Two Buckets

The relevancy engine is the nerd's ability to instantly and with little conscious effort parse all incoming information into one of two buckets: Relevant or Irrelevant. It's a defensive information-management strategy built as a reaction to the nerd's innate passion for information—for understanding. See, nerds can and will find out everything about anything, and left to their own devices, they'll do this . . . endlessly.

Items placed in the Irrelevant bucket are aggressively ignored, whereas the items in the Relevant bucket are flagged as compelling and are, if possible, immediately investigated.

---

[1] http://randsinrepose.com/archives/2007/11/11/the_nerd_handbook.html

The reason for this often-unavoidable research compulsion varies by topic. There is something tucked inside of the idea—a puzzle, a game, a system to be discerned—that triggers the nerd's pleasure centers, and, once triggered, the only course of action is understanding. This is why, when you've piqued my interest, I keep asking questions, incessantly, while staring you in the face . . . never blinking.

The Value of Relevance

The real value comes when we've vetted the relevant. The act of obsessively researching yields even more relevant data that allows the nerd to fully index the idea. A mental notepad is created that reads "Blue Whales," and on this notepad is written the three most relevant and interesting facts that make blue whales intriguing. This card is then carefully filed away.

This collection of esoteric indexed data is why a nerd's knowledge feels five miles wide and three inches deep, and why we're randomly great at games like Trivial Pursuit. See, four years ago, someone mentioned to me that the largest organism on the planet was a quaking aspen tree. We heard that one relevant fact and then spent two hours investigating the various methods by which a largest organism might be measured, we read about the largest known fully connected quaking aspen grove in Utah, and we ended up reading about the world's largest single stem tree, a giant sequoia named General Sherman.

It sounds like a lot of work until you understand the payout.

To Wit

Nerds are fucking funny. It's another point from the Nerd Handbook that I suggest is related to the relevancy engine, but I never explained why. Let's try now.

The processing of relevancy has three steps, and it's the third where the magic happens:

- *Collect* the relevant.
- *Research* and *index* if necessary.
- *Connect* the relevant in efficient and entertaining ways.

So, how is the funny created in this flow? It's a big question: what is funny? I'd say there are two big classifications of funny. There are jokes and there's wit. Jokes are memorized comedy retold with moxie. Wit is original comedy created in real time and delivered with precise timing. Nerds are witty because they connect the relevant to the present quickly and in clever ways.

Have you ever sat in a meeting full of engineers? What's the game? The game is, Who can say the funniest and/or snarkiest thing and get the biggest laugh? To play, you need to kick the relevancy engine into high gear. You need to hear everything being said, parse it, compare it to everything you know, and then find the most relevant connection possible. In nanoseconds.

Laughter is often the by-product of these observations, but so too is the hard silence found after the discovery of an uncomfortable truth. It's at that moment you realize the primary goal is not laughter, but the art of the impressive connection.

Connecting the Relevant

The art of the connection is the end result of a nerd's highly obsessive due diligence performed on anything that falls into the Relevant bucket.

Laughter is sometimes the end result of connections—the recognition of the clever between two dissimilar items or the absurd lack of any connection at all—but the result in the nerd's brain is far more satisfying. A successful connection brings efficient order to the two heretofore unrelated objects, and you know what that means: we've discovered structure. *This* is related to *that. I know more than I did a moment ago.*

Discovery of structure in a chaotic world means less chaos, and while we're happy to make you laugh, the idea of a more orderly, structured, and knowable world is what drives us and keeps us warm in bed at night.

Avoiding the Fez

Fez.

Fez is a senior engineer who works for me. He's fictional, but you know Fez. He's the guy who wrote that piece of code 9 million years ago that everyone is dependent on, but no one knows what exactly it does because Fez didn't bother to comment a single line ... oh yeah, and he wrote it in Forth.

Fez has his own office and he nods a lot. It's the nod of a man who believes he's got rock-solid job security because his technology is critical. Fez bugs a lot of people, but when it hits the fan, Fez saves the day because he's carefully cordoned off a critical path that is his and his alone.

Each year, Fez and I sit down, and I present his focal review. I set the stage by asking about his aspirations and he responds with vague nodding.

Sounds good, boss.

OK, boss.

Sure, boss.

Fez is not hearing a word of our discussion because Fez has heard this focal review mumbo jumbo for 12 years straight. He believes he's immune.

The approach of the Fez is a sure-fire way to slowly become irrelevant and, more importantly, become unemployed.

Understanding Where You Stand

Before I explain why there is a little Fez in all of us, let's take a few steps back. The definition of a healthy business is a business that is growing, and by growing I mean it is making more money each year. There's a plethora of different ways that a company can create this growth, but the basic law of business physics that you should never forget is "As a business grows, so shall its employees."

The manner by which a business prunes the employees who aren't assisting in this growth is horrifically efficient. First, we have the employees who have consistently demonstrated an inability or lack of interest in helping with this growth. Their prize is the irrelevant project that no one cares about. Some folks find this banishment to be comforting. "Aaaahh ... no more fire drills ... the execs don't even care about this project, so I can cruise." That's right. They don't care about that particular division because it's not strategic, which means the moment it's time to tighten the budgetary belt that is the first group to be nuked. Poof. Welcome to unemployment. Did you learn your lesson, yet? Probably should have taken the time to figure out what XML stood for.

Then we have Fez. Maybe he's grown complacent with the knowledge that he's the only person who has a particular skill or set of knowledge. It's a powerful position to be in ... for a while.

Maybe the execs won't fire him because of the perception he has essential knowledge, but, I guarantee, those who are dependent on his black box of knowledge are concocting a devious plan to replace him and his knowledge because *they want to grow*. Right this second, three guys down the hall have rewritten Fez's code in C and they're secretly demonstrating their work to interested parties. They are building support, they are building a revolution, and they're not going to stop until the person who is hindering their growth is gone.

Whether it's by organizational evolution or revolution, complacency is a job killer, and if you're following me, you think Fez has blown it.

Wrong.

I did.

I blew it by not convincing Fez that growth is life.

Annual Reviews, Briefly

Let's start with the bad news. There's no silver bullet to solve the Fez issue. Solving Fez is going to involve strategy, effort, inspiration, luck, and, lastly, a bit of time. You won't solve it in a moment and you won't solve it in a single meeting. There is a convenient yearly inflection point where everyone panics about their careers. Annual reviews. I'm going to construct this chapter around annual reviews, but I don't want you to think that performing an annual review will solve the Fez. If you worry about career development once a year, you're screwed. As you'll see, avoiding the Fez is a full-time job, but since you get actual allocated time to stress about employee development, why not stress in a constructive manner?

What's Really on Their Minds

People do care about cash. When that annual review begins, your employee is hanging on every word, carefully listening to your tone, wondering, good review or bad review? If it's sounding good, that must mean cash; and cash rocks. If it's sounding bad, they stop listening and start pre-bittering themselves to hate you for the next month since you clearly have *no idea* where they *added their value* this year.

Compensation adjustments are the reward everyone cares about, but does anyone actually know how they're calculated? What happened over the previous 365 days to result in a *big cash windfall* or an *insignificant pittance?*

If you don't draw a concrete line between a coherent understanding of an employee's performance and their reward or punishment, you are only adding more fuel to the argument that "managers sit around doing nothing all day." Let's begin . . .

First, Gather Your Thoughts, but Don't Think (Yet)

Here's the deal. If I asked you right this second to tell me about your particular local Fez, you've already got a strong opinion, but it's an opinion of the moment. It's the last three interactions you've had with your Fez, and while those are relevant, they hardly represent a complete picture of a year of work.

When you're assessing an employee, you need to assess against their job, not the work they've done over the past two months. This is hard because this is the Silicon Valley and no one knows what happened two months ago. Facebook IPO'd then Summer then the next iPhone, right? *Is Mountain Lion out yet? Did I miss anything important?* You probably did, unless you captured it somehow. Every month, your team produced something and it's your job to document that production. I do this by spending an hour a month jotting down reflections of the team for the past 30 days. What stands out in my mind? What'd we do? Who rocked? Don't get hung up on documenting every single event or talking about every single person . . . just type. Even if you miss massive contributions by a team member, the act of capturing your thoughts at the time they were happening creates a handy mental bookmark. This bookmark captures not only what you wrote, but everything else hiding around it. When you go back and read last summer's terribly small entry— "This month blew. No time to write."—you'll not only remember that you were on a death march, but you'll also remember that Eddie the QA guy was there with you that weekend and, oh hey, he's been here every single weekend and, wow, why aren't we promoting him?

Regular snapshots of your team's work will construct an impression of your team that you are incapable of constructing in the moment because, in the moment, you're cranky about not getting coffee this morning, stressed about your product review next week, and *don't get me started about the 300 mails I have yet to read.* How can you create an objective opinion of someone's performance with all this crap in your head? You gotta step back, take a deep breath, and reflect.

As you sit there staring at the ceiling chewing on a year of thoughts, an overall impression is going to form . . . you can't avoid it, but I'm asking you to ignore it for now. I'm going to distract you by proposing a model that you can use to look at your employees and begin to understand what exactly their career needs. The model is called Skill vs. Will.

Skill vs. Will Plus Epiphanies

It's a simple graph. One axis is skill—how much skill does the employee have to do his job? Is he qualified? Overqualified? How long has he been doing it? When is the last time you know he learned something new? How quickly does he handle tasks compared to his peers?

The other axis is will—this is where we measure the employee's desire. Does she like her job? Really? Has she told you that? Is she viewed as energetic by her team? When is the last time she generated a great idea that blew your mind? Is she talking in meetings or listening? Is she *ever* talking? Is she *always* talking?

This graph is not a precision instrument. It's a tool to better define the impression you're constructing of your employee. Once you've placed someone on the Skill/Will graph, you can begin to consider what your full-time job is—constantly and consistently pushing your employees to the upper-right quadrant. High skill (I'm good at what I do) and high will (I like what I do). This mental map is the first step in constructing a Fez-avoidance insurance policy.

"Rands," you ask, "um, what exactly am I pushing constantly and consistently?"

Great question.

Worst-case scenario: You've ignored everything I've said so far. You're spending 15 days rereading Fez's review from last year. Then, you spend another 15 throwing together this year's review by cutting and pasting the one and only review you wrote for all your employees, making it unique by inserting their full name and project name. Dear lord. You've really blown it.

Yet, you haven't fully blown it. A complete fuck-up is when you take this pathetic excuse for a review and present it. You say, "Employee 629, here is your review. You did this well, you did this poorly. Here's your 2 percent increase and here's your indecipherable objectives for next year. *Back to work.*"

You deserve every single Fez that you get. Please stop reading, pack your things, and quietly exit the Silicon Valley. Thanks.

If you've taken some time to reflect on the full year, if you've mapped your employee against skill and will, you've probably had some epiphany regarding the Fez. You've realized, "Wow, he's bored," or "She really has no clue how to architect software." Great, an epiphany . . . it's a start, but it's not a finish.

You are not the one who needs to have the epiphany. It's your employee who needs it.

I'll explain via the real fictional Fez. Go back and think about where you'd put him on the Skill/Will graph. Your gut might say well, he's worked a lot of years, so he's high skill and he's just bored, so he's low will.

Nice try, but you don't have the 12 months of fictional notes that I have. See, Fez's skill used to be high, but it's fading. It's middle-of-the-road skill now and the slow erosion is also affecting his confidence . . . his will. His diminishing skill is diminishing his will, which, in turn, further diminishes his skill because he has zero confidence to go gather new skills. Yikes. A skill/will negative feedback loop. Didn't see that coming, did you?

Here's the upside. Just as skill and will fade together, they also rise together. If you focus on one, you often fix the other. It's a brilliant management two-for-one.

Back to Fez. Let's say your epiphany is to get Fez some technical training. Send him to a C++ class and *wham*, he's going to be happy. *Hurry*, write that down as an objective because *wow*, you've really nailed that Fez problem.

Easy, eager manager. Slow down.

Assertiveness, Briefly

I've got a task for you and I'm going to ask you in two different ways. You tell me which request you're going to actually do:

- **Request #1:** You—go fix that bug.
- **Request #2:** Hey, can you look into bug #1837?

The difference between these two requests is a management style that shows up in every personality test. You, Mr. Manager, are either *ask assertive,* meaning that you ask in order to get stuff done, or *tell assertive,* which means you tell to make progress.

There are a great many charismatic leaders who've made billions by only telling folks what to do. I am not one of them. It's not that I'm conflict averse or that there are not times that I'm an incessant dictator, it's merely I hate being told what to do, so I treat others like I'd prefer to be treated.

Telling your Fez what the problem is without belief on their part that a problem exists is tantamount to a personal attack. "You, Fez, are doing a poor job and I've decided that objectives x, y, and z are the only way that we're going to save your job."

I exaggerate for example, but I've had fifteen-plus years of reviews and I've had some phenomenal managers turn a review into a speech about me without involving me. Well, I happen to be an expert about me, so can I please be involved in the discussion?

An annual review is a discussion, not a speech. The goal of the discussion is, first, to agree that the review is in the ballpark. Remember, you've been thinking about the review for weeks because you've got a deadline. Fez is seeing it for the first time and he needs time to mentally digest. It's very hard to be mentally nimble when your manager is staring you down asking, "Any questions?" It's doubly hard when he's just told you that you screwed up for the past year

Rule of thumb: If you're delivering big bad news, schedule two meetings. At the first meeting, you're presenting the review, not the objectives. They're going to want to know about compensation and you're going to want to say it, but don't. The moment you say "No increase," the review is over, the employee is pissed, and you're going to be on the defensive. The meeting has become a mental fight and fights only prove who can punch harder.

It's the second meeting where everyone involved has had time to digest the review. You can have a discussion about objectives because Fez drove home the prior night wondering, "My manager is telling me that I'm getting stale and I vehemently disagree with that . . . buuuuuuut maybe there's some truth in what he's saying . . . hmmmmm."

With just a smidgen of agreement that the review is fair combined with you and your Fez agreeing about his place on Skill/Will, you can start talking objectives. What can we do to increase skill or will? New job? New tasks? Training? Maybe move him off that team of pessimists so he can spread his wings with some optimists?

I don't know what is up with your particular Fez, so I can't advise specific objectives, but here are some high-level thoughts about the extremes on the Skill/Will graph:

- **High skill, low will:** Boredom is imminent—needs a change of scenery and responsibility. Stat.

- **High will, low skill:** Needs training, needs mentorship. Needs management. The good news is they really, really want it. Savor this because as soon as the skill kicks in, they're going to start wanting your job. This rules.

- **Low will, low skill:** Boy, did you screw up. It takes a fairly concerted effort to ignore the needs of your employee so long that (a) they no longer have the skills necessary to do their job, and (b) they don't want to do it. Roll those sleeves up, pal. You've got work to do.

- **High skill, high will:** Great job but, ummmmm, guess what? No one can maintain this for very long.

Big Finish

Fez is the personification of career drift.

You've got some Fez in you right now. You may be the rock star of your company right now, but you have no clue that three guys in a garage in San Jose are spending every waking hour working to make you irrelevant . . . they call it the New Whizbang and you're going to hate the New Whizbang when it shows up because you know it replaces your corporate relevancy.

Your manager is not going to hate the New Whizbang because she doesn't feel personally threatened by it. She is going to see you Fezzing out about it and, hopefully, she can figure out to trickle objectivity into your indignation.

I have a simple way of managing against the Fez effect. I tell everyone I hire the same thing: "I hired you because you've got enough skill and enough will to have my job one day . . . whether you want it or not." This statement tells those I work with that I expect them to succeed and reminds me to keep moving because there is nothing like having bright people nipping at your heels to keep you running.

A Glimpse and a Hook

The terrifying reality regarding your résumé is that for all the many hours you put into fine-tuning, you've got 30 seconds to make an impression on me. Maybe less.

It's unfair, it's imprecise, and there's a good chance that I make horrible mistakes, but there's a lot more of you than me, and while hiring a phenomenal team is the most important thing I do, I'm balancing that task with the fact that I need to build product and manage the endless stream of people walking into my office.

But here's a glimpse. I'm going to walk you through the exact mental process I use when I look at a résumé. I don't know if this is right or efficient, but after 20 years and staring at thousands of résumés, this is the process.

The First Pass

Your name. It's simple. Do I know you? Whether I do or not, I'm going to immediately Google you to see if I should. Oh, you a have a weblog. Excellent.

Company names. Do I recognize any companies that you worked at? If I do, I don't look at what you actually do, I assume that if I recognize the company, I'm in the ballpark. If I don't know the company, I scan for keywords in the description to get a rough idea. Hmmm . . . networking words. OK, you're a networking guy.

Job description and history. Here I'm looking for history and trajectory. How many jobs have you had and for how long? How long have you been in your current role? Where'd you come from? QA? Or have you always been an engineer? This is when I start looking for inconsistencies and warning flags.

Other interests and extracurriculars. Yeah, this is part of the first pass. I'm eagerly looking to find something that makes you different from the last 50 résumés I looked at. More on this in a moment.

So, we're done. It's been 10 to 20 seconds and I've already formed an opinion. There's a good chance that I've already made a call whether to move forward on you. If there are other folks checking the résumé out, I can certainly be convinced to take a second look, but a basic opinion has been formed.

Before we move to the second pass, let's talk about the parts of your résumé I didn't look at and never will.

Professional objective. This is likely your lead paragraph and I skipped it. Career center counselors across the planet are slamming their fists on their desks as they read this because they've been telling students, "You need to write a crisp career objective. It defines your résumé."

Yes, it does, but I still don't read it and it's not because there isn't good content there, it's the time issue. See, if your résumé is sitting in my inbox, it means someone has already mapped you to an open job in my group. Reading your objective is going to tell me something I already know. Besides, my job title and description scrub will tell me whether we're in the ballpark or not. If I've got a junior engineering position open and you've got ten years' experience, I'll figure out that mismatch when I look at your history.

This doesn't mean you shouldn't include this objective in your résumé. As you'll see below, there's more to the process than just me reading your résumé, and different folks are looking for different content.

Skills. I skip the skills section not only because this is information I'll derive from your job history, but also because this section is full of misinformation. I'm not going to say that people lie in the skills section, but I know that if a candidate has heard the word Linux in the workplace, there's a good chance they're going to put "Familiarity with Linux" as a skill on their résumé.

Besides, again, I know you've goofed around with Linux because you said so in the description of your last job, right?

Summary of qualifications. Similar to skills, this is another skip section for me. Here's a good example from an imaginary résumé: "Proven success in leading technical problem-solving situations." This line tells me nothing. Yes, I know you're trying to tell me that you're strategic, but there is no way you're going to convince me that you're strategic in a résumé. I'm going to learn that from a phone screen and from an interview.

Unlike skills, which I find to be a total waste of time, I will go back to the summary of qualifications if we end up talking. When you write "Established track record for delivering measurable results under tight schedules," I am going to ask you what the hell you mean on the phone and if your answer isn't instant and insightful, I'll know your qualifications are designed to be buzzword-compliant and don't actually define your qualifications.

The Second Pass

If I can't decide whether to schedule a phone screen after the first pass, I go for another. The goal now is, "OK, I saw something I liked in the first pass, is it real?" This is when I do the following:

In-depth job history. I'm going to actually read the job history for the past couple of jobs. Not all of them, just the last two or three. What I'm doing is fleshing out my mental picture of you. I'm looking for more warning flags. Do your responsibilities match your title? How long were you at your most recent job? If it was a long time, can I get a sense of how you grew? If it was short, can I figure out why you left? Do your last two jobs build on each other? Can I get a sense of where you're headed or are you all over the place?

Your job history—your professional experience—is the heart of your résumé. This is where I spent my time vetting you and this is where you should spend your time making sure I'm going to get the most complete picture of who you are and what you're going to bring to my team.

School. Yeah, this is the first time I'll notice whether you went to college or not. I purposely do this because I've found over years of hiring that a name-brand university biases my opinion too early. There's a lot to be said for a candidate who gets accepted to and graduates from Stanford or MIT, but I've made just as many bad hires from these colleges as great ones.

Seeing a non-computer science degree is not a warning flag. In fact, I'm a huge fan of hiring physics majors as engineers. For whatever reason, the curriculum for physics has a good intersection with computer science. Any technical major for me is perfectly acceptable, and even non-technical majors with a technical job history make for a résumé worth thinking about.

OK, so that second pass took another 15 to 30 seconds and we're done. You've just given me the opportunity to change your life by potentially bringing you in for an interview and that chance is over. Next!

What's unfair about what just happened is this. You spent hours working on your résumé. You sent it to close friends for review and you edited it. You agonized over the different sections and you stressed about the tone, and here I am, the hiring manager, and I read one-tenth of your work in 30 seconds.

Don't despair. There are some easy things you can do to improve your chances.

Differentiate, Don't Annoy

Design your résumé to downgrade. Your résumé needs to withstand some formatting abuse. Go get your résumé right now and convert it to plain text. Can you still see the different sections? Is your job history still cleanly formatted? Can you still see the different jobs as well as the start and stop dates? Screw around with the margins, too. Where are your line breaks? They'd better not be after every line because that means visual chaos if a well-intentioned recruiter starts messing with fonts.

Never include a cover letter. I don't read them. Recruiters don't pass them on. Make sure the key points of your cover letter are living in your career objective and your job history.

Embrace honest buzzword-compliance. Remember, I'm not the only who is going to read your résumé. I'm likely the most qualified to make a call whether you're a fit for my job, but before your résumé gets to me, it's going to be passed through a couple of different recruiters and these folks are just as busy as I am.

The lifeblood of the recruiter is the keyword. Java, C++, Objective-C. The more specific relevant keywords and buzzwords you can shove into your résumé, there more likely you're going to make it past the initial cut.

As I said above, I skip the skills section because most folks already know that recruiters are just searching for specific words when they're sourcing candidates, so they shove every possible buzzword into their résumé. Know this: if you claim "strong Java background" in your résumé, I'm going to be compelled to figure out how strong your skills actually are. Don't include any keyword or buzzword that you aren't comfortable talking about at length.

Differentiate, don't annoy. You're likely going to start developing your résumé from a template. Maybe you'll use a friend's résumé that you like as a starting point. Excellent. How are you going to make it yours?

Remember, I've looked at thousands of résumés, which means I've seen all the standard templates. I know when you're using Microsoft Word and I know when you've developed a format of your own. Right this second, I'm flipping through a dozen college résumés and the ones I'm spending time on are the ones that grab me visually, where there is something different. On this one, the fellow put a subtle gray box around each of his section headings. On this other one, the candidate used a nice combination of serif and sans serif fonts to grab me.

A couple of subtle visual differences to your résumé goes a long way toward keeping me engaged in reading it, but remember, we're engineers here and efficiency matters. Differentiating your résumé to the point that I can't quickly parse it is going to frustrate me. You're not applying to be a visual designer; you're an engineer. Keep to the standard sections and don't make me work to figure out who you are.

Sound like a human. Here's a doozy: This intern says he "planned, designed, and coordinated engineers' efforts for the development of a mission critical system." Zzzzzzzzzzzzz. What did this guy actually do? I honestly don't know. Let's call this type of writing style "résumé mumbo jumbo" and let's agree that usage of this style is tantamount to saying nothing at all.

What was the mission critical system? Why was it critical? How in the world did an intern plan, design, and coordinate the engineering efforts? I'm a fan of giving interns real-world work, but it'd take a world-class intern to plan, design, and manage engineers on whatever this mission critical system is.

Take time to write your résumé for a human. You need to hit all the right buzzwords and keywords to get yourself past the layers of recruiters, but I'm the guy who is really going to take apart your résumé, and if you're saying nothing with résumé mumbo jumbo, I'm learning nothing. Give me specifics and give them to me in a familiar tone. I'm not an automaton; I honestly want to know what you do. Tell me a story.

Include seemingly irrelevant experience. This applies mostly to college types who lack experience in high technology. You're going to stress that your job history doesn't include any engineering and you're thinking your summer working at Barnes & Noble bookstore is irrelevant. It's not. Any job teaches you something. Even though you weren't coding in C++, I want to know what you learned by being a bookseller. Was it your first job? What did you learn about managers? How did you grow from the beginning to the end of the summer? Explain to me how hard work is hard no matter what the job is.

A Glimpse and a Hook

A résumé will never define who you are. It's not the job of your résumé to give me a complete picture, and if you're struggling to include every last detail about who you are, you're wasting your time. Your résumé should be designed to give me a glimpse and a hook.

The glimpse is a view into the most recent years of your professional career. It should convey your three most important accomplishments and it should give me a good idea where your technical skills lie.

The hook is more important. The hook will leave me with a question. Maybe it's something from your "Other Interests" section. How about an objective so outlandish that I can't help but set up a phone screen. I'm not suggesting that you make anything up; I'm asking you to market yourself in a way that I'm going to remember. A résumé is not a statement of facts. It's a declaration of intent.

Nailing the Phone Screen

As we discovered in last chapter, it's almost a miracle when the phone rings and a recruiter wants to set up a phone screen. The fact is, someone, somewhere in the organization has successfully mapped you to an open position. This is a really big deal because, in my experience, the chance that you'll get this job has improved logarithmically. It's not 50/50, but it's vastly better than when you were a random résumé sitting on my desk.

As with last chapter, I'm going to walk you through the precise mental process I go through as part of the phone screen; but before we go there, let's talk motivation.

The Purpose

I've got a requisition, a req. This roughly describes a job I have open in my team, but it's likely not very precise. Job descriptions are notoriously broad and vague because I want to cast the net as wide as possible. It's not just that I want to see as many candidates as possible; I want to see as broad a skill set as possible.

This is important to remember as you're scrubbing job opportunities. I know you're stressing, "The job description says five years of Java required, and, well, I only have two." Don't be absurd. There are usually two buckets of skills in a job description: required and recommended. At the very least, you should be in the ballpark for required, but don't give recommended a second thought. It's recommended. It's nice to have.

Besides, you got a phone screen with me, so I'm already pretty sure that you're close to a fit, but I still have questions, otherwise I would've just brought you in.

The question is, what questions do I have? Guess what—your job is to figure that out.

Your Job Is to Prepare

Before you even talk to me, you're on a fact-finding mission. You've got a job description, and after the phone screen has been set up, you've got my name. You might also have an idea of the product or technology associated with this gig, or you might not, but even without a product name, you've got plenty of information to start with.

Do your research. Google me. Find out anything you can about what I do and what I care about. This isn't stalking—this is your career, and if I happen to be an engineering manager who writes a weblog, well, you can start to learn how I think. Maybe I don't have a weblog but I post to mailing lists. That's data, too. How is this going to help you during the phone screen? Well, I don't know what you're going to find, but anything you can gather is going to start to build context around this job that you know nothing about. This helps with nerves as well. See, I have your résumé and you have nothing. A bit of research is going to level the information playing field.

If you have a product name or technology, repeat the same process. What is the product? Is it selling well? What do other people think about it? I'm not talking about a weekend of research here; I'm talking an hour or so of background research so that you can do one thing when the phone screen shows up: you need to ask great questions.

That's right. In your research, you want to find a couple of compelling questions, because at some point during the phone screen I'm going to ask you, "Do you have any questions for me?" and this is the most important question I'm going to ask.

Back to the Beginning

Before I ask you the most important question, I need to figure out a couple of things. First, in a perfect world, we'd be able to skip the phone screen and just bring you in for a first round interview, but this rarely happens unless I already know you. What I need to know is:

Can we communicate? I'm going to lead off with something simple and disarming. It's either going to be the weather or something I picked up from your extracurricular activities. "Do you really surf? So do I! Where do you surf?" These pleasantries appear trivial, but they're a big deal to me because I want to see if we can communicate. It's nowhere near a deal killer if the pacing of our conversation is awkward, I'll adjust, but how off is it? Are we five minutes in and we still haven't said anything? OK, maybe we have a problem.

A couple of clarification softballs. My follow-up questions will now start to focus on whatever questions your résumé left me with. I've no idea what I'm going to ask because it varies with every single résumé, so my thought is that you should have your résumé sitting in front of you because it's sitting in front of me as well. It's my only source material.

Whatever these follow-up questions are, I'm still figuring out how we communicate. This means you need to focus on answering the questions. It sounds stupid, but if it's not absolutely clear to you what I'm asking, it's better to get early clarification rather than letting me jump in five minutes into your answer to say, "Uh, that's not what I was asking."

See, you and I are still tuning to each other. It's been five minutes, and if we're still not adjusted to each other's different communication styles, I'm going to start mentally waving my internal yellow flag. It doesn't need to be eloquent communication, but we should be making progress.

What's your story? We're past the softball phase of the interview and now I'm going to ask a hard question. This isn't a brainteaser or a technical question, this is a question that is designed to give you the chance to tell me a story. I want to see how you explain a complex idea over the phone to someone you don't know and can't see.

Again, who knows what the actual question will be? But you need to be prepared when I ask that question, which will be clearly, painfully open-ended. I'm not looking for the quick, clean answer; I'm looking for a story that shows me more about how you communicate and how you think. Being an amazing communicator is not a part of most engineering jobs, I know this. I'm not expecting Shakespeare, but I am expecting that you can confidently talk about this question because I found this question in your résumé, which is the only piece of data we currently have in common. If we can't have an intelligent discussion about that, I'm going to start wondering about the other ways we aren't going to be able to communicate.

Your turn: show me what you've got. We're 20 minutes into the phone screen and now I'm going to turn it over to you when I ask, "Do you have any questions for me?"

When I tell friends that this is my favorite question, the usual response is, "So, you're lazy, right? You can't think of anything else to ask, so you go for the path of least resistance." It's true. It an easy question for me to ask, but it is essential because I don't hire people who aren't engaged in what they're doing. And if you don't have a list of questions lined up for me, all I hear is: *You don't want this job.*

A well-thought-out question shows me that you've been thinking about this job. It shows me you're already working for it by thinking about it outside of this 30-minute conversation. Yeah, you can probably wing it and ask something interesting based on the last 20 minutes, but the impression you're going to make with me by asking a question based on research outside of this phone screen will make up for a bevy of yellow flags. It shows initiative and it shows interest.

The Close

And we're done. It went by pretty quick, but the question is, "How'd it go?" Here's a mental checklist to see how you did:

Long, awkward pauses. Were we struggling to keep things moving? Were there long silences? Well, we didn't tune appropriately. Again, not a deal killer, but definitely a negative.

Adversarial interactions. What happened when we had different opinions? Did we talk through it or did we start butting heads? This happens more than I expect on phone screens, and it's not always a bad thing. I'm not interested in you telling me what I want to hear, but if we are on opposite sides of the fence, how do we handle it? If a candidate is willing to pick a fight in a 30-minute phone screen, I'm wondering how often they're going to fight once they're in the building.

How'd it feel? This is the hardest to quantify, but also the most important. Did we click? Did the conversation flow? Did we both learn something? Ideally, I'm a decent representation of the culture of the team I'm hiring for, so if the 30 minutes passed painfully, I'm wondering what kind of pain hiring you might inflict on the team.

Specific next steps. How did I leave it? Did I give you a song and dance about how "we're still interviewing candidates and we'll be in touch within the next week"? Well, that's OK, but what you're really looking for is a specific next step like, "I'm going to bring you in," or "Let's have you talk with more of the team." An immediate and actionable next step is the best sign of success with a phone screen. If I don't give you this as part of the close, ask for it. If I stall, there's a problem.

Like your résumé, the goal with the phone screen is to convince a single person to move forward with hiring you. With your résumé, you send your hope to an anonymous recruiting e-mail address. With a phone screen, you have leverage. It's not the 30-minute window that you need to worry about, you need to worry about how you're going to prepare.

The phone screen is the first time you get to represent yourself as a person, not some résumé sitting on my desk. It's still a glimpse, but it's the first time you can actively participate in the process.

Your Resignation Checklist

Borland was tanking. I'd survived three rounds of layoffs primarily because my project was still generating quite a bit of revenue, but at every meeting I attended, everyone kept using the word *if*.

"Well, if we get funded we'll be able to do this."

"If Paul stays, we can keep this feature."

"I don't know if this is a good idea given what we don't know."

If—everywhere. *If* is uncertainty. *If* is fear. If there were no *if* I'd be able to focus on my job, but I couldn't because no one was sure what was going to happen.

When I finally received an offer from a database company in Redwood City, I was in bliss for a brief moment. The new company had scads of cash, an upside, and a distinct lack of *if*. The bliss quickly faded when I realized I had no idea how I was going to resign. I knew it was customary to give two weeks' notice, so when the beginning of those two weeks showed up, I walked into the boss's office with my terse resignation letter and said it: "I've got another gig; I like it here, but it's time to go."

Boss: "Sorry to hear that. If I could make some changes, would you stay?"

Me: "I have a problem with your *if*."

Boss: "I understand. Well, you're responsible for the import/export engine features. Any chance you could finish that before you go?"

Me: [without pause] *"Absolutely."*

Some data. I had four weeks of work left on the import/export engine, and those were four engineering weeks, which meant I actually had six weeks of work on the inside. While I valiantly worked my ass off for the first week, I started to not care in the second. By the time Thursday arrived, it was clear I didn't have a chance to do a third of the work.

Why did I sign up for an impossible task? I violated the first rule on the resignation checklist.

Rule #1: Don't Promise What You Can't Do

If you're resigning, you'll be tempted to overcommit on deliverables because you're leaving. This is your guilt talking. You feel bad for resigning and you are trying to make up for the fact that you're leaving people you care about in the lurch. You need to remember that, no matter how hard you try, you will become useless in your final days.

It's called short timer's disease, and it begins the moment you resign. In that moment, you leave. You've got two weeks left, but you are not there. You've mentally started imagining your new job, and while you go through the motions of your old job, it's a meaningless blend of unfulfilling repetition.

Your case of short timer's disease, unfortunately, isn't strong enough when your boss asks you to finish that critical feature. Congratulations on having the moral fortitude to have the guilt about leaving, but understand that you are signing up for damaging your reputation when you agree to do work you can't complete.

Rule #2: Respect Your Network

There are, at least, three people you'll need to make sure are aware that you want to stay in touch with them. I don't know who these people are because I don't know who you are or what you do, but I know that if you don't carefully handle this transition, you're going to lose them. If you're looking for a way to identify these people, stare at your lunch crowd. Pick the ones whose meetings you care about. If you've got a folder in your inbox *just for this person,* you're going to want to make sure they know you care.

No matter where you are in your career, you need to continually develop your network of people because it's likely that one of these three people will assist in future employment or opportunity. I've been in high tech for coming up on two decades, and every single job I've had has either been a direct or indirect result of knowing someone from a prior job. You'll hear the phrase, "It's a small valley." It's a small world.

You need to go out of your way to make this happen, but it only need be a small gesture. A brief one-on-one moment where you acknowledge this person is relevant. More than a fly-by "bye" on your last day. Less than a tearful hug in the hallway.

Rule #3: Update "The Crew"

I have a document in my Dropbox titled "The Crew." It's a list of each person that I've worked with in past 20 years that I would hire if I began a startup. There are people on this list that I've failed to talk to in the past decade, but, when the startup happens, I'm going to take the time to find them because they made the list. Each time I quit a job, I take an hour to update the list because there are always people I want to keep.

There's a good chance there is intersection between rules #2 and #3, but they are separate tasks. The people you need to actively stay in touch with are not necessarily the ones you're going to build your future company around.

Still, as with rule #2, a small gesture to your new Crew entries is essential. Remember, you're the one who is leaving, who is changing, so it's your responsibility to create the final impression.

Rule #4: Don't Take Cheap Shots

If you aren't leaving under the best of terms, you'll be tempted to send out the scathing e-mail that sets things right. This is stupid on many levels. It will negate any positive work that you did while you were with the company. You'll also hurt your network because everyone (including those who know that you aren't insane) will remember you as that whack job that freaked out in e-mail and didn't bother to spell check.

Remember, you are leaving and the people you consider to be the problem are staying. It's not your problem anymore, don't waste your energy.

We had a B– QA engineer at a startup who got passed over for a promotion and decided to bail in style. One the last day of his employment, he sent a grammatically painful e-mail that went through his organization, person by person, and hammered them. His incoherent rambling was posted on the cube walls for its comedic value, and no one had a clue that he actually wrote decent test plans.

Rule #5: Do Right by Those Who Work for You and with You

If you're a manager, the previous rules apply to you in triplicate. You're not allowed to fall prey to the dreaded short-timer's disease because you are acting like a leader and you are representing the company until the moment you are out the door. If this doesn't make sense to you, then it's likely you weren't supposed to be a manager in the first place.

My move for this rule is an expensive one. I provide a written review to all my direct reports in my last two weeks. Doesn't matter where we are in the review cycle, I take the time to give everyone who works for me a temperature check. Yes, well-written reviews are painful and time-consuming, and yes, I get short-timer's syndrome like everyone else, but this small gesture is the best way to explain what these coworkers mean to you.

Rule #6: Don't Volunteer to Do Work After You Leave (or, if You Do, Make Sure You Get a Lot of Money for It)

This is a variant of the guilty conscience problem. This is the result of you sitting on your couch two weeks before you resign, tapping your pencil on your teeth, and exploring the hypothetical look on your boss's face when he realizes his go-to person is leaving.

You like him. You're responsible. You don't want to leave anyone in the lurch. Yes, of course, you can finish those last three projects in your spare time.

Stop.

There are some very good reasons to continue to help out at your past job and, if you choose to do so, I highly recommend gouging your prior employer on price because this extracurricular work is coming at the worst time possible—when you're starting a new job. The first few weeks of a job are precious. They present the primal lessons of your new career and you only get to hear them once. And what are you doing? Spending your evenings on work from a prior life when what you should be doing is digesting the lessons of the new job.

You will always regret signing up for work to do after you leave.

Rule #7: Don't Give Too Much Notice

Our last variant of guilty conscience. More tapping of the teeth, fretting about how to support this team that you're leaving. Maybe if you give them more time to adjust to a post-you world, it will be easier on everyone.

Again, wrong.

The basic fact is this: you've chosen to leave and you're going to leave. Giving an excessive amount of notice is professional cruel and unusual punishment both for you and for your team because it extends the organization's stress regarding your departure while also preventing your team from doing something critical: moving on.

Your concern is regarding the gap that is created by your absence. This will be your team's concern as well, but a concern is not a solution. As long as you are sitting there busily being present, your team doesn't believe that you are leaving. They're not going to react to your absence until, come Monday morning, they walk by your empty office and feel your absence. Shit, he's gone.

They Know

I got in early on my final Friday at Borland. I'd convinced myself a 5 a.m. start time would create a dramatic last-ditch effort on my committed work. By the time my going-away lunch arrived, I'd successfully booted my computer, stared at the screen for an hour, and packed my boxes.

As 5 p.m. rolled around, I shut down my computer and dragged my feet into my boss's office. "Yeah, so, I didn't finish much of the import/export work."

His comment: "Yeah, no one thought you could do it."

Glossary

Traditionally, a glossary functions to clarify terms in a book. The fact is I haven't used many of the following terms in this book, but you still need to know them.

Whether you're a manager or working for a manager, there are those out there who will use the words to confuse you. They'll throw them out in the middle of the room sans definition as a power play—as an indication that they control the conversation. There are versions of these people who throw these words out and act like they know what they mean to achieve the same effect.

The only defense against these words is knowledge.

1.0 — The hardest product that you'll ever develop.

360 Review — Feedback gathered from your peers, which is supposed to be included in your focal review. Spending time providing constructive feedback increases the likelihood that you won't be working with idiots.

Action Items — Things you should write down. Failure to follow up on action items results in a gentle erosion of your credibility.

Administrative Assistant — Your best friend as a manager. Admins are heavily tapped into corporate machinations and are often able to work miracles when it comes to getting stuff done. They're also usually tapped into the grapevine. There are executive versions of these folks, too.

Agenda — The things that must occur for any given meeting to be completed. If all participants in said meeting are not aware of the agenda, time will be wasted.

All-Hands — A company-wide meeting, usually run by the CEO. If you're a manager and there are lots of surprises at these meetings, you might be out of touch. People often feel compelled to ask really dumb questions at all-hands meetings.

Android — Google's mobile operating system that uses deserts as version names.

Apple — The house that Steve Jobs built. Based on market cap, the most valuable company on Earth, but they'd prefer if you thought of them not as huge, but scrappy.

Architect — An engineer who knows what he/she is doing. If an architect says something that appears insane, it's worth firing off a couple follow-up questions, as they are often smarter than you.

At-Will Employment — Legal definition that states that both employer and employee are employed "at will," which means they can fire/quit whenever they please. They don't even have to give a reason.

Automation — QA buzzword to describe testing that can be done programmatically. Automation is always pitched as a time saver . . . but it's usually a time sink.

Background Check — A pre-hire check employers use to determine whether or not you are a serial murderer.

Beta — A milestone in the development process that traditionally follows alpha. This used to mean that a product was generally usable by customers—a select group of customers who were willing to put up with things not working quite right. No one is sure what beta means anymore.

Bellwethers — The core set of people you trust to interview candidates.

Board of Directors — The CEO's boss. They can fire the CEO. They tend to set broad corporate policy and have amazing powers of invisibility.

Bonus — Unexpected cash. If you're not seeing a bonus at least every year or so, you're doing something wrong. Your boss should be able to explain what you need to fix.

Bugs — Coding errors by engineers often found by QA. Bugs are a source of significant tension late in a product cycle.

Build — An internal version of a product that is used for testing.

Candidate — A job applicant who has made it into the building.

Cave, The — The place a nerd goes to get in the zone.

CEO (Chief Executive Officer) — The guy/gal in the big office. This is a tough gig. CEOs are usually busier than you can imagine.

CFO (Chief Financial Officer) — The guy/gal who tells you how many PCs or Macs you can buy.

Checked Out — An employee who has already quit inside their head. Whether or not you want this person to actually resign, you should be aware that someone who is checked out brings down the entire team with their incessant uselessness.

CIO (Chief Information Officer) — The guy/gal who tells you whether you can use a Mac or a PC.

Collaboration — A word used to convince you to work with people you'd rather avoid.

Completionist — An individual who absolutely must do the right thing when it comes to designing products. What they lack in practicality they make up for with their phenomenal ideas.

Contractor — A temporary employee who never seems to leave.

COO (Chief Operations Officer) — The guy/gal who makes sure your Mac or a PC arrives.

Credibility — The amount others will believe or trust you. Credibility is as valuable as information, but it's equally hard to measure.

Cross-Pollination — The act of taking an idea generated by one team and vetting it with another. Engineers are full of pride and don't like to do this, but cross-pollination often yields improvements that the original team will never discover.

Crunch Time — A time when there are no weekends.

CTO (Chief Technical Officer) — The guy/gal who tells you which is better, a Mac or a PC.

Culture — An invisible binding force that holds your company together. It's like the Force, except real.

Database — A handy place to stick data if you like your data organized and structured.

Director — Middle management. These are usually the last managers that are in touch with what the products actually do.

Dividend — A share of profits paid to shareholders.

Domain — A sphere of influence. ("That's marketing's domain.")

Doomed — An essential, unscheduled product milestone where the product team realizes they are way behind and choose to kick it into high gear. This term originated with C-3PO in the original *Star Wars*.

Double-Click — Used to have something to do with a mouse; now it's a heavily overused management term used as a segue to say "Let's explore that a bit."

Drug Test — A process used by large companies whereby new hires are scared into not drinking or smoking for about 30 days.

E-mail — The means by which you get spam.

EPS (Earning Per Share) — The portion of a company's profit allocated to each outstanding share of stock. This doesn't happen at most Silicon Valley companies, so don't get your hopes up.

Facebook — The means by which you keep in touch with people you're trying to forget.

Fired — Termination of employment; usually used in extreme circumstances. ("He's stealing from us!") It is not to be used lightly, and never without the heavy involvement of HR.

Geek — See *Nerd*.

Flame Mail — An e-mail you should not send until you've had a chance to calm down.

Focal Review — A yearly meeting with your manager where your performance is evaluated. It's often seen as a vehicle for justifying raises/bonuses, which overshadows the opportunity to convey actual constructive career advice.

General Counsel — The most important lawyer in the company.

Grapevine — A content-rich source of false information.

Google — The means by which you search for things and then receive advertising.

GUI (Graphical User Interface) — An aging term used to describe a user interface that doesn't suck.

Hacker — A label that has acquired an unfair negative connotation. While hackers are capable of being nefarious, they're mostly interested in being clever.

Heinous — Bad. Really bad. Horrible, sky-is-falling bad. Grossly wicked. Handy term when classifying bugs late in the product cycle.

HI (Human Interface) — User interface at Apple.

Holistic — A manager who focuses his attention across the company and not just on his team. Traditionally middle management.

Holy Shit — The moment when a piece of technology totally blows your mind and/or changes your life.

HR (Human Resources) — Happy people who help you do very unhappy things.

Incrementalist — An individual who knows that better is the enemy of done. Incrementalists get stuff done at the cost of quality and completeness.

Individual Contributor — HR term that describes a single employee who has no direct reports.

Instant Messaging — The replacement for e-mail.

Interaction Design — The hard part of user interface design. Interaction designers are responsible for how a user is going to interact with an application, ideally with the least amount of frustration. Interaction designers know what the word *workflow* means.

Intern — A temporary hire, usually from college, who smiles too much.

Interview — The day you wear a tie. Interviews are where you, the hopeful candidate, pitch yourself to a group of folks who have 30 minutes to figure out if they want to spend 5 years listening to your dumb jokes.

Inward — A front-line manager focused on a single product or team. Inwards don't care much about what's going on elsewhere in the company.

iOS — Apple's mobile operating system, which is annoying a lot of nerds by making everything easier to do.

IT (Information Technology) — The most generic term in the world, which describes the folks responsible for that computer on your desk. You probably work in IT and don't even know it.

Job Description — A brief, written description of the responsibilities required for a job.

Layoff — A horrible process whereby employees are terminated because the company either needs to save cash or is otherwise preoccupied with something else.

Lead — A better title than "manager."

Leverage — A word often used in close proximity to *synergy*.

Linux — UNIX with an *L*.

Mac OS 9 — Old version of the Macintosh operating system not based on UNIX.

Mac OS X — New version of the Macintosh operating system, which is based on UNIX.

Malcolm Event — A seemingly insignificant event during the product development processes that screws up your release in an unlikely way.

Manager — The person who signs your review.

Mandate — Order handed down from senior management. Mandates have one of two motivations: they are either used as excuses to dodge explaining rationale (bad) or they are put forth to get people to stop arguing and start moving forward (good).

Market Cap — Simple math. If a company has 1 million shares and those shares are selling for $10, the market cap is $10 million. Often used as a rough means of comparing companies or gauging corporate health. ("Company X's market cap is 40 times revenue!")

Marketing — The folks who gloss over what your product actually does. Essential, as most engineers are unable to successfully communicate with actual customers.

Meeting — Traditionally, a group of individuals getting together to solve a common problem. Often, a tremendous waste of time.

Milestone — Poorly defined, heavily over-communicated date within the software development cycle, where the software development team reflects on how screwed they are.

MRD (Marketing Requirements Document) — A mythical document said to contain "customer requirements."

Multitasking — The ability to do many things at once. Multitasking has heavy interaction with NADD.

NADD (Nerd Attention Deficiency Disorder) — A voracious appetite for consuming information at an impossible rate. Rands gets a quarter every time someone says this.

Nerd — See *Geek*.

NIH (Not Invented Here) — Term to describe behavior in which an engineering team will not consider working with anyone's code except their own. It's not that the external code is good or bad, it's just foreign, which means it must be reviewed, reformatted . . . Oh, what the hell. *Let's rewrite the whole damned thing.* Billions of dollars have been lost to NIH. I mean it. Billions.

Offer Letter — A real document handed to a potential new employee, which describes the terms of their employment. It's important to realize that once a candidate has signed their offer letter, your job as a hiring manager is not done. They are not an employee until their butt is in their seat.

Office — The square box where you live. Some models come with windows and doors.

Office of the CEO — The people who surround the CEO to make sure he/she shows up at meetings on time.

Offsite — A meeting held in a place where the coffee tastes different.

Org Chart — A visual representation of who reports to whom. Org charts are handy in larger organizations for figuring out who you're actually dealing with.

Outward — A manager who focuses his attention outside the company. This person is terribly concerned with how the world views his company. Outwards are traditionally senior management, like CEOs.

P/E (Price/Earnings Ratio) — Determines how much money an investor pays for $1 of a company's earnings. If a company is reporting a profit of $2 per share, and the stock is selling for $20 per share, the P/E is 10—the investor would pay ten times earnings.

Performance Plan — A surprisingly upbeat term that describes a depressing process. Performance plans are written instructions of what an employee needs to do in order to not be fired. Don't even think about doing this without serious HR involvement.

Phone Screen —A brief conversation with a hiring manager or recruiter in which one or two key things are going to determine whether you get an interview.

Process — A seven-letter word that begins with P. Process is not all bad news, especially for large companies where immense groups of people waste a lot of time doing the same thing.

Product Manager — Ideally, the owner of a product. This person is clear on what the product is and where it is going. They often have to deal with pesky engineers who believe they know what the customers want.

Program Manager —The owner of the schedule. Program managers are pretty much useless in small companies, but essential in any large product development group.

QA (Quality Assurance) — Individuals who find bugs.

R&D (Research and Development) — Or software engineering or software development. Really all the same thing. Surprisingly little research is going on these days, what with all the incessant development.

Reorg (Reorganization) — Process whereby employees are shuffled about to accommodate new corporate goals.

Recruiter — Person whose job it is to help you source candidates for your *req* (see below). Recruiters often come off as slimy, but they've got a tough gig balancing good people skills with actually having meaningful conversations with engineers. When you find a good recruiter, stick with them.

Reference Check — Process of calling candidate-supplied references. References are biased, as they are supplied by the candidate, so they are suspect as sources of truth. If you've got any concerns about your new hire, I also recommend digging up back-door references or actually grilling references with real, honest questions.

Release Engineering — Group or individual responsible for building/compiling the product. Release folks live in a confusing limbo where they aren't quite QA, but also aren't quite software engineering.

Req (Requisition) — A virtual document that gives you permission to hire a new employee. Rock on! Acquisition of reqs can be tricky, and once acquired, they are apt to vanish without warning. Use it or lose it. Important fact: From the moment a req is approved, the average number of days to get a butt in a seat is 90 days. Honest.

Resigning — Quitting your job. *Resigning* sounds more professional, but it's the same thing. You can do this whenever you like.

RSU (Restricted Stock Units) — Unlike *stock options* (see below), RSUs are grants of actual stock. Like options, they vest over a period of time to incentivize you to not leave.

Résumé — A very short document that is intended to describe your entire professional life.

Sales — The folks who sell your product. Not a good source of product requirements, as they are biased by the mighty dollar. Often a good source of discontent, though.

Screwed — A professional inflection point where your chosen course of action will allow you to sink or swim.

Short Timer — An employee who has resigned, but still works for the company. Short timers' productivity decreases as a function of the proximity to their last day.

Silicon Valley — A nebulous area south of San Francisco full of money and very bright people.

Slip — A kinder, gentler word for saying that the product is not on schedule. ("We've got a three-week slip.") Frequent slips are often bad career moves, but slips for the right reasons are a good thing.

Software Development Lifecycle — The time between when someone has a clever idea and when that idea is beaten to death and is no longer making money.

Spec (Specification) — A document that tells you how it is. The process of writing a specification tends to be more useful than someone reading it.

Spreadsheet — A poor man's database.

Staff Meeting — A weekly meeting with all your direct reports. Failure to run this type of meeting on a regular basis will result in a breakdown in communication and much wasting of time.

Status Reports — The weekly ritual where you justify your existence to managers; often a sign of corporate bloatification. You should fight the creation of these with all of your might.

Stock — A piece of paper that you'll never see that says you own part of a company. Stocks are easy—you own stocks. Stock options are more confusing.

Stock Options — A piece of paper that you'll never see that says you can buy stock at a certain price. Options often confuse folks, so I'll explain. You are granted an option of 100 shares of your company's stock at $100. Congrats. When you sell your option, you will only receive the delta between your option price and the current price. So, if you sell all your hypothetical options at $110, you are only going to receive $10 per share or $1,000 (minus taxes). People are getting tense about options these days.

Synergy — A word often used in close proximity to *leverage*.

Technical Support — The person you yell at on the phone when something goes wrong with your computer. You really should be yelling at the engineer that designed the thing, but they never answer the phone.

Temp — A coworker who likely will not be sitting in that chair tomorrow; typically assigned work that no one wants or has time to do.

Termination — The politically correct way of saying "You're fired."

Twitter — The means by which you sound like a fortune cookie.

Total Compensation — The sum of everything you are paid by a company. This includes salary, bonuses, and benefits. Total compensation is the dollar amount you should use when comparing multiple job offers.

UI (User Interface) — The sum total of every decision made regarding how a program looks to a user.

Unit Test — Literally the last thing an engineer wants to do.

User Experience Design — A discipline of design responsible for the entire user experience.

UNIX — An interactive time-sharing operating system invented in 1969 so that some guy could play games.

Version Control — A database that keeps track of multiple versions of any given file. Version control is an essential tool for development in groups of engineers.

VP (Vice President) — Usually a direct report of the CEO.

Weblog (Blog) — A representation of a person on the Internet.

Wiki — A web application that allows anyone to edit content. It seems like a recipe for disaster, but it turns out that people like their content tidy.

Windows — The number one desktop operating system on the planet Earth.

Workflow — The manner in which a person uses an application. Designing an application with a particular user's workflow in mind can improve usability.

Zone, The — A magical place where you hit max productivity. The zone is very hard to achieve and even harder to maintain.

I

Index

A

Accessible management metaphor-laced language, 83

Active soaking, 140–141

Agenda detection
definition, 57
meeting type identification, 57–58
organizational ineptitude, 61
participant classification, 58
players identification, 59
pros and cons, 59–61

Allison, 33

Apple, 96, 169–170

Ashton-Tate, 167

B

Bellwethers
core interview team, 179–180
cultural, 180, 182
team consensus, 181, 182
team interviews, 182
technical, 180
vision, 181

Bitter nerd, 194

Blingleforth function, 150

Boondoggle, 88

Boredom
credibility, 177

detection, 173–175
employee motivation
and retention, 173
plan of action, 175–177
software development, 177

Borland's resident free electron, 230

Brainstorm meeting, 135, 136

Bug database, 153

Bug tracking system, 49

C

Chaos theory, 143

Chatty Patty, 209–210

Cliché, 44

Code editor, 149

Coder, 101

Collaborative management style, 64

Communication peace treaty, 54

Completionists
architects, 214
coffee addictions, 216
conflict resolution book, 214
corporate and people sense, 215
degrees of rightness, 214
dreamers, 213
two-year and five-year solution, 215

Computer animation, 143

Context capturing
code capturing, 149
delicious and Flickr, 150
disclosure paragraph, 151
nerd disclosure, 151
New intro down, 150
Removed Wikipedia, 151
status report, 151
version control, 149, 150
Core motivation, 53

Corporate agenda, 216

Corporate machinations, 83

Creative excursion, 129

Credibility-destroying moment, 161

CSS tweak, 131

D

Design 'n' architecture (DNA)
acknowledgment, 96
bet-the-group/division decision, 94
firepower, 94
system DNA, 96
technical leadership, 95
teeth, 95
ticker-tape parade, 94
UX DNA, 96
Dictator, 106–107

Dingfelder, 47–50

Disaster, 43–44

Disinterested/drifting nerd, 194

Distributed ownership, 162

Divergence, 129

E

E-mail, 139

Engineering management, 1

Engineering managers, 10, 49

Engineering mindset
architectural diagram, 100
development environment, 99
owning features, 100
stay flexible, 97

stop coding, 97
unit tests, 100
Exploration, 175

Exuberance, 128

F

Facebook, 168

Fez
annual reviews, 242
assertiveness, 245–246
career drift, 247
code, 242
compensation adjustments, 243
handy mental bookmark, 243
senior engineer, 241
skill vs. will graph, 244–247
unemployment, 242
Fire Phil, 107

Flat organizational mantra, 93

Flubjam, 110

Foreign mandates, 66–67

Free electrons
Borland's resident free electron, 230
care and feeding, 229–230
junior electrons, 228
senior electrons, 228
spaghetti code, 228

G

Github, 98

Gizzy Flibbet project, 110

Google, 98, 138, 179

Grapevine eradication, 163

Guns of the South, 197

H

Hacking
Ashton-Tate, 167
barbarian strategy, 169
chaos, 170
control and communications, 168
dieter, 169–170

disruptors, 168
Facebook, 168
healthy product company, 170
Kahn, Philippe (CEO, Microsoft), 167
predictability, 170
well-documented origin
story, 170
Harold, 52

Healthy business, 39, 241

Holistic manager, 224

Holy shits, 137, 144

Hyper-reactive mode, 160

I

Incrementalists
coffee addictions, 215
conflict resolution book, 214
goal, 214
realists, 213
secrets, 213
Information conduit, 69–70

Information dispersion, 73

Information starvation
aggressive silence, 73
informational gap, 71
information conduit, 69–70
layoffs, 70
prevention, 71–73
Inspiration, 129, 130

Intellectual illumination, 130

Internet Explorer, 9, 47

Inward managers, 224

J

Jedi Master, 105–106

Jerry, 227, 228, 230

Joel Spolsky test, 17

K

Kahn, Philippe (CEO, Microsoft), 167

Kurt, Curveball, 211

L

Laptop Larry, 208–209

Layoffs, 231

LeRoy McManager, 109, 110

M

Malcolm events
accuracy, 147
agreement, 147
artifacts, 145–146
availability, 147
definition, 143
deployment, design and development
phase, 144
documentation, 145
Feature discovery, 144
fuzzy picture, 144
spectrum of cost, 145
stuff-building process, 144
success, 147–148
Management
metaphors, 82
must-do list, 97
pixies, 109, 112–113
skills, 63
Managementese
accessible management metaphor-laced
language, 83
The "Bottom Line," 83
management metaphors, 82
offenses, 81
Managerial fall, 52–53

Managers, 110, 111
action per decision, 13–14
agenda confusion, 225
best manager, 217
blind spots, 10–11
computer science degree, 10
definition, 2
distinct classes, 223
engineering managers, 10
executive/senior manager, 223
growth, 225–226
job, 8–9
language, 11–12

Managers (continued)
　line manager, 223
　middle manager, 223
　mostly harmless, 217
　motivation, 16
　off-the-cuff opinion, 217
　one-on-ones scheduling, 12
　organizational perceptions, 8
　organizational pride and panic, 8, 15–16
　political food chain, 14–15
　solid information-detection skills, 10
　vision hierarchy, 224–225
　worst manager, 217
Mandate dissecting
　Decide phase, 64–65
　Deliver phase, 65
　Deliver (Again) phase, 65–66
　local mandate, 64
　phases, 64
Maslow's Hierarchy of Needs theory, 118
Massive global cross-pollination information
　　cluster-fuck, 101
Maximizing shareholder value, 1
Mechanics, 220–221
　interpersonal conflict, 219
　organics, 221
　scratching, inner dialog, 218
　sense of propriety, 219
　status template, 219
　structured way information gathering,
　　218, 219
Meeting
　active participants, 28
　agenda, 28
　alignment meetings, 28
　basic design, 137
　brainstorm meeting, 135, 136
　components, 28
　vs. conversation, 28
　creation meetings, 28
　creatures
　　anchor, 208
　　Chatty Patty, 209–210
　　Kurt, Curveball, 211
　　Laptop Larry, 208–209

　　Mr. Irrelevant, 209
　　Sally Synthesizer, 210–211
　　The Snake, 211–212
　　Translator Tim, 210
　culture, 31
　decision making, refining and reviewing, 137
　documentation, 136
　fuzzy variables, 29
　hardcore design, 138
　improvisation, 30
　meeting tips, 29
　once-a-week meetings, 135
　players, 135–137
　prototype meeting, 135, 136
　Rands Creativity Plan, 136
　referee, 28, 30–31
　rule, 29
　screw-ups, 29
　sense of accomplishment, 27
　sense of structure, 27
　time, 135
　to-do list, 137
　types, 28
Micromanager, 219
Microsoft's SourceSafe, 122, 151
Microtasks, 177
Monday freakout
　bug tracking system, 49
　caring, job, 49
　IE 9, 49
　stress, 47
　volume and intensity, 48

N

Nerd attention deficiency disorder (NADD)
　context switch, 199, 200
　diagnosis, 198
　downsides, 200
　weblog, 200
Nerd cave
　computer with internet connection,
　　201–202
　drink, 202
　The Place, 204

random collection, 202
risk, 205
snap, 203–204
view, 202
well-defined layout, 202
World-canceling features, 202
The Zone, 203
Nerd management
chaos, 191
collective nerd reaction, 190
consistency, 190
efficiency, 191
inconsistency, 191
logical knowability, 190
Nerd Burden, 189, 195
predictability, 191
problem-solving, 191–195
spot–random policy enforcement, 190
system thinker, 190
worst-case scenario, 189–190
Y2K bug, 189
Ninety-day interview
acronyms, 186
argument, 187–188
drink invite, 187
industry standard, 186
influence testing, 187
inner circle discovery, 188
intricate personalities, 188
knowledge testing, 187
lunch invitation, 186
nascent engagement, 187
people-assessment instincts, 186
Stay Late, Show Up Early, 186
Not-invented-here syndrome, 193

Nudge, 105–106

O

Occasional stints, 176
Off-site
alignment meeting, 87
all-hands, 87
boondoggle, 88
bright-and-shiny inflection point, 90, 92

cross-pollination and communication
activities, 85
deep brainstorming, 87
epiphanies, 91, 92
goal, 87, 88
kickoff meeting, 87
Master of Ceremonies role, 89
outsiders, avoidance, 90
personality tests, avoidance, 90
person recognition, 86
rule of thumb, 88
success, 86
Taker of Notes role, 89
trust falls, avoidance, 90
UI framework, 85
Once-a-week meetings, 135
One-on-ones
basic rules, 39–40
disaster, 43–44
managerial preventative maintenance, 45
Update, 41–42
Vent, 42–43
Organics, 220
interpersonal conflict, 219
mechanics, 221
scratching, inner dialog, 218
sense of propriety, 219
Organizational warfare, 221

Outward manager, 224–225

Overcommunication, 163

P

Passive soaking, 141–142

Phillip, 133

Phil's daily management judgment, 103

Phone screen
clarification softballs, 257
communication styles, 257
fact-finding mission, 256
job descriptions, 255
mental checklist, 258
product name, 256
well-thought-out question, 257

Photoshops, 36
Product roadmap, 112
Pros and cons, 59–61
Prototype meeting, 135, 136

Q

Q&A, 112

R

Rands Creativity Plan, 136
Rands 1.0 Hierarchy, 119, 120
Rands Management Rule Book, 97
Rands Rule of Software Management, 47
Rands test
    business state accuracy, 21–22
    career trajectory, 22–23
    contractual obligation, 20
    explaining company strategy
        to stranger, 21
    Grapevine, 23–24
    handwritten status reports, 19–20
    healthy communication structure, 20
    magnitude and direction, 24–25
    one-on-one, 18
    regular meeting, 22
    team meeting, 19
    well-defined and protected time, 23
Rands web site design
    creativity dial, 129, 130
    exuberance, 128
    footnotes, 130
    happenstance, 130–131
    intellectual illumination, 130
    Scrub group, 129
Reacting vs. thinking, 133–135
Relevancy
    connection, 239
    engine, 237
    jokes, 238
    laughter, 239
    process, 238

relevant and irrelevant buckets, 237–238
    value, 238
Reorg rules
    Figure Out Your Role, 232
    The Grapevine Gone Mad, 233
    Most Folks Love Reorgs, 234
    patience, 235
    People Are Paranoid, 232–233
    Reorgs Take Forever, 234
Resignation checklist
    Cheap Shots, 261
    The Crew, 261
    notice, 262–263
    overcommiting deliverables, 260
    past job helping, 262
    people network, 260–261
    previous rules, 261
    short timer's disease, 260–262
Resume
    buzzword, 252, 253
    cover letter, 252
    The First Pass
        company names, 249
        interests and extracurriculars, 250
        job description and history, 249
        job title and description scrub, 250
        professional objective, 250
        skills, 250
        summary of qualifications, 250
        Your name, 249
    glimpse, 253
    hook, 253
    irrelevant experience, 253
    keywords, 252, 253
    last detail, 253
    The Second Pass, 251
    standard sections, 252
    subtle visual differences, 252
    template, 252
Roland, 122
Rookie engineering managers, 34
Rule of thumb, 64, 138
Rules of engagement, 54

S

Sally Synthesizer, 210–211

Silence, 78–79

Silicon Valley, 2

Sky falling
"Bet Your Car" perspective, 161–163
constant and consistent sky-propping
pressure, 163–164
DEFCON 1 disasters, 159
elusive step, 164–165
process documentation, 159–160
War Room situation, 160–161

Slide reviews, 33

Soaking
active soaking, 140–141
emotion and ignorance, 140
passive soaking, 141–142
protected activity, 140
time, 142

Software development, 99

1.0 software product
communication, 122
culture construction, 124–125
engineering culture, 120
free electrons, 121
Maslow's Hierarchy of Needs
theory, 118
pitch, 119–120, 123
pyramid, 123–124
Rands 1.0 Hierarchy, 119, 120
rules, 121
stagnation warning sign, 122

Stan, 27–29, 52, 54

12 Steps to Better Code, 17

Steve McConnell's Code
Complete, 82

Subterfuge, 77–78

Subtlety, 76–77

Superpowers
Dictator, 106–107
Jedi Master, 105–106
The Machine, 104–105

T

The 48 Laws of Power, 75, 79

Tinderbox, 151

Translation, 53–54

Translator Tim, 210

Triage, 194

Trickle theory
bug scrubbing, 155
confidence, 155
Critic, 154, 155
dull tasks, 155
entropy, 157
hard tasks, 155
iterate, 155–156
mix it up component, 156–157

Turtledove, Harry, 197

Twinge
acquisition, 33–34
catastrophe, 36–37
engineering managers, 37
engineers, 34
Manager's Day, 35
rookie engineering managers, 34
sniffing, 35
task list, 35

U

Update, 41–42

V

Vent, 42–43

Verbal commitment, 54

Version control, 149, 150

Visual and verbal cues, 54

W

Wallace, 51–55

Z

Zeitgeist, 86

CPSIA information can be obtained at www.ICGtesting.com
Printed in the USA
LVOW102125120912

298603LV00010B/61/P